THE
LIFE OF DAVID

the **Smart Guide**
to the **Bible**™ series

BE SMART · BE INSPIRED ™

Angie Peters
Larry Richards, General Editor

THOMAS NELSON
Since 1798

NASHVILLE   DALLAS   MEXICO CITY   RIO DE JANEIRO   BEIJING

General Editor: Larry Richards
Managing Editor: Michael Christopher
Associate Editor: Karen Moore Artl
Scripture Editor: Deborah Wiseman
Assistant Editor: Amy Clark
Design: Diane Whisner

ISBN 10: 1–4185–1011–4
ISBN 13: 978–1–4185–1011–4

Printed in the United States of America
08 09 10 11   9 8 7 6 5 4 3 2 1

Introduction

Introduction

The Bible is full of examples of people whose lives can teach important lessons about how to live, how not to live, and how to have a closer relationship with God. David is one of those people.

In fact, there are more stories in the Bible about David than about anyone else except Jesus Christ Himself. David must have been a pretty special person to rate that kind of coverage in the number one best-selling book of all time!

What's So Special About David?

Most people can name at least a half dozen things they know about David. For example:

- He was a shepherd boy.
- He played music and wrote many of the Psalms.
- He killed the Philistine giant Goliath with a sling.
- He was friends with Jonathan, the son of the man who was trying to kill him.
- He had an affair with Bathsheba and had her husband murdered.
- He wanted to build a temple.

Those are all interesting facts, but the one that makes him really special is that he was called a man after God's own heart.

That raises the question of the day: Just what, exactly, does it take to become a person after God's own heart?

There aren't any neat, one-word answers to that question. After all, the traits that made David dear to God are numerous, but they aren't easily compressed into a tidy outline or fashioned into a clever acrostic. They can only be discovered by getting to know David on a deeply personal level. That means:

- Learning about his background
- Finding out about his family
- Reviewing the history of his people, the Israelites
- Studying the times in which he lived
- Understanding the way he worshipped God

- Reviewing the events in his life

- Considering the way he responded to those events, and

- Examining what motivated him to do the things he did.

That's a long "to-do" list, isn't it?

The good news is that this study guide will give readers a head start on answering the question of the day. It walks readers through the story of David's life that is told mostly in the books of 1 and 2 Samuel, as well as in parts of 1 Kings and 1 Chronicles.

Things to Keep in Mind About David

The story of David often features many levels of rich meaning. To gain the most from a study of his life, here are some things to remember:

1. The majority of David's story is contained in the books of 1 and 2 Samuel, which originally were one book. For the most part, that narrative is chronological and revolves around three key people:

   - Samuel, Israel's last judge and first prophet, who anointed Israel's first two kings and ushered Israel across the threshold from a theocracy into a monarchy

   - Saul, the people's choice for king

   - David, God's choice for king

2. David is a type of Christ. God even placed David in the lineage of His own Son, Christ. There are many similarities between David and Christ, and those parallels can help readers get a better grasp of the character of Christ.

But it's essential to remember that Christ is perfect; David most certainly was not. All people are sinners, and David was no exception. The point of studying David's life isn't simply to gain more knowledge about a man after God's own heart; it's to gain more wisdom about having a relationship with the God of that man's heart.

3. David's story is a nation's story. David is a central figure in God's plan for Israel. To fully understand what God is doing through David, keep a constant eye on what's going on in Israel and the surrounding nations.

4. Many lessons contained in the story of David's life are highlighted by a series of comparisons and contrasts. For example, it's easier to understand why David was a man after God's own heart when you compare his reaction to sin with Saul's reaction to sin. Sin nearly broke David's heart; it merely hardened Saul's. Such similarities and differences between the people in David's life sometimes speak louder than words.

5. The study of David is packed with bonus features. Like the extra celebrity profiles included on modern movie DVDs, a study of David also gives readers an up close, personal look into other leading Bible "stars." It's important not to become too single-minded about studying David to view the wonderful truths about God taught through the lives of people such as:

- Hannah, the infertile woman whose faith in God was rewarded with a son who would spiritually guide the nation of Israel;

- Abigail, the wise and beautiful woman whose willingness to take a risk and speak her mind prevented David from making a fatal blunder; and

- Nathan, the prophet whose courage enabled him to risk his own life to confront the king with his deadly sin.

He Didn't Leap Tall Buildings, Rob the Rich, or Sit at a Round Table

Because David's life seemed to be, well . . . *larger* than life (he did, after all, kill a giant with nothing more than a stone from a riverbed), it's tempting to begin thinking of him as some sort of a legendary superhero—perhaps as some sort of a cross between Superman, Robin Hood, and King Arthur. True enough, when David was at his best, he modeled fantastic traits like faithfulness, humility, honor, and over-the-top passion for God. But David, like the rest of humankind, wasn't always at his best. In fact he was often at his worst. At those times he displayed terribly distasteful qualities, such as dishonesty, pride, doubtfulness, out-of-control anger, and lustfulness. What's interesting is that God in His infinite wisdom didn't see fit to hide any of those far-from-heroic qualities beneath a superhero's cloak. He gives readers an all-access pass to view the slipups as well as the successes.

That seems to be God's way of swiping a fluorescent yellow highlighter over one of the most important lessons taught by David's example: No matter how faithfully a person walks with God, he or she can still fall. And no matter how far down a person falls, he or she is never beyond the reach of God's extended hand.

A Note About the Psalms

Readers can gain fresh insight into what was going on in certain episodes of David's life by reading what was going on in his heart at the time. A behind-the-scenes peek into David's heart is made possible by his personal notes that were preserved in the form of prayers for help and songs of praise. They are recorded in Psalms 3–41. (While the Psalms are certainly one of David's biggest claims to fame, this book doesn't go in-depth into a study of his psalms. That's for another book in this series! It does, however, feature discussions of certain psalms where appropriate.)

Something in David's Story for Everyone

Why would God provide such a "tell-all" on the life of this man who loved Him so much? Possibly because nothing interests people more than other people—but more likely, because David's story has something in it for nearly everyone, and God repeatedly teaches us by allowing us to share the experiences of others. For those who are:

- Feeling overlooked—there's a great episode about a shepherd boy who is almost overlooked by his own father that will give all "invisible" people hope.
- Indignant about something that's wrong but don't think they have the resources or strength to do anything about it—there's the familiar but ever-so-powerful tale of overcoming giant challenges against all odds.
- Married—there's much to learn about marriage relationships, God's way, from people such as Hannah, David, and Abigail.
- Leaders—there are many lessons in leadership to be learned from the number one administrator of Israel. He wrote the book on organization for the temple.
- Parents—the story of all three key characters, Samuel, Saul, and David, repeatedly emphasizes parenting principles and lists of practical parenting "do's" and "don'ts."
- Women who have been victimized by either people or circumstances—there's much to learn about the choice between bitterness and joy from people like Hannah, Michal, and Abigail.

And that's just the short list. The poor and the prosperous, the social elite and the social outcasts, the content and the restless, those who have steady faith in God and those who frequently forget what faith is . . . they're all in David's story, too.

Maybe that's why God offers such an intimate and lengthy look into the life of the man after His own heart: to help *everyone*—no matter their station or situation in life—avoid David's mistakes and emulate his godly traits. The blessings that come from studying a heart like David's just might include becoming a person "after God's own heart," too.

About the Author

Angie Peters has written several books, including *Celebrate Home: Encouragement and Tips for Stay-at-Home Parents* (Concordia Publishing House, 1998, 2005); *Designed to Influence: A Woman and Her Testimony* (Bogard Press, 2004); and *Designed to Build: A*

Woman and Her Home (Bogard Press, 2005). She has also written articles for publications such as *Today's Christian Woman*, *Christian Home & School*, and *ParentLife*. Angie has pursued her passion for teaching and encouraging others by leading women's Bible studies for more than fifteen years. She lives in Benton, Arkansas, with her husband and their three children. It's to them this book is dedicated, with love and thanks for sharing nearly a year of their mom's time, energy, and thoughts with this amazing guy named David.

About the General Editor

Dr. Larry Richards is a native of Michigan who now lives in Raleigh, North Carolina. He was converted to Christianity while in the Navy in the 1950s. Larry has taught and written Sunday school curriculum for every age group, from nursery through adult. He has published more than two hundred books that have been translated into twenty-six languages. His wife, Sue, is also an author. They both enjoy teaching Bible studies as well as fishing and playing golf.

Understanding the Bible Is Easy with These Tools

To understand God's Word you need easy-to-use study tools right where you need them—at your fingertips. The Smart Guide to the Bible™ series puts valuable resources adjacent to the text to save you both time and effort.

Every page features handy sidebars filled with icons and helpful information: cross-references for additional insights, definitions of key words and concepts, brief commentaries from experts on the topic, points to ponder, evidence of God at work, the big picture of how passages fit into the context of the entire Bible, practical tips for applying biblical truths to every area of your life, and plenty of maps, charts, and illustrations. A wrap-up of each passage, combined with study questions, concludes each chapter.

These helpful tools show you what to watch for. Look them over to become familiar with them, and then turn to chapter 1 with complete confidence: You are about to increase your knowledge of God's Word!

Study Helps

The thought-bubble icon alerts you to commentary you might find particularly thought-provoking, challenging, or encouraging. You'll want to take a moment to reflect on it and consider the implications for your life.

Don't miss this point! The exclamation-point icon draws your attention to a key point in the text and emphasizes important biblical truths and facts.

death on the cross
Colossians 1:21–22

Many see Boaz as a type of Jesus Christ. To win back what we human beings lost through sin and spiritual death, Jesus had to become human (i.e., He had to become a true kinsman), and He had to be willing to pay the penalty for our sins. With His <u>death on the cross</u>, Jesus paid the penalty and won freedom and eternal life for us.

The additional Bible verses add scriptural support for the passage you just read and help you better understand the <u>underlined text</u>. (Think of it as an instant reference resource!)

How does what you just read apply to your life? The heart icon indicates that you're about to find out! These practical tips speak to your mind, heart, body, and soul, and offer clear guidelines for living a righteous and joy-filled life, establishing priorities, maintaining healthy relationships, persevering through challenges, and more.

This icon reveals how God is truly all-knowing and all-powerful. The hourglass icon points to a specific example of the prediction of an event or the fulfillment of a prediction. See how some of what God has said would come to pass already has!

What are some of the great things God has done? The traffic-sign icon shows you how God has used miracles, special acts, promises, and covenants throughout history to draw people to him.

Does the story or event you just read about appear elsewhere in the Gospels? The cross icon points you to those instances where the same story appears in other Gospel locations—further proof of the accuracy and truth of Jesus' life, death, and resurrection.

Since God created marriage, there's no better person to turn to for advice. The double-ring icon points out biblical insights and tips for strengthening your marriage.

The Bible is filled with wisdom about raising a godly family and enjoying your spiritual family in Christ. The family icon gives you ideas for building up your home and helping your family grow close and strong.

Isle of Patmos
a small island in the
Mediterranean Sea

something significant had occurred, he wrote down the substance of what he saw. This is the practice John followed when he recorded Revelation on the **Isle of Patmos.**

What does that word really mean, especially as it relates to this passage? Important, misunderstood, or infrequently used words are set in **bold type** in your text so you can immediately glance at the margin for definitions. This valuable feature lets you better understand the meaning of the entire passage without having to stop to check other references.

the big picture

Joshua
Led by Joshua, the Israelites crossed the Jordan River and invaded Canaan (see Illustration #8). In a series of military campaigns the Israelites defeated several coalition armies raised by the inhabitants of Canaan. With organized resistance put down, Joshua divided the land among the twelve Israelite

How does what you read fit in with the greater biblical story? The highlighted big picture summarizes the passage under discussion.

what others say

David Breese
Nothing is clearer in the Word of God than the fact that God wants us to understand himself and his working in the lives of men.[5]

It can be helpful to know what others say on the topic, and the high-lighted quotation introduces another voice into the discussion. This resource enables you to read other opinions and perspectives.

Maps, charts, and illustrations pictorially represent ancient artifacts and show where and how stories and events took place. They enable you to better understand important empires, learn your way around villages and temples, see where major battles occurred, and follow the journeys of God's people. You'll find these graphics let you do more than study God's Word—they let you *experience* it.

Chapters at a Glance

Part 3: In Name Only

Part 4: The Giant Killer

Part 5: Days of Glory

Part 7: Decline and Death

Part One
SETTING THE STAGE

1 Samuel 1–3:
A Woman Cries Out for a Child

Chapter Highlights:
- The High Places
- Hannah's Sorrow
- Hannah's Solution
- Helpful Husband
- A Priest's *Faux Pas*
- Hearing Voices

Let's Get Started

The story of David's life does not open to a snapshot of a light-hearted shepherd boy tending his flocks in the arid heat of the Middle Eastern sun. Instead, the biblical account of the life of the man after God's own heart actually begins with a portrait of a faithful family traveling from the hills of Ephraim to a place called Shiloh, to worship the Lord. This family's circumstances and experiences in the first three chapters of 1 Samuel introduce many important themes that reappear throughout the life of David and the lives of the people of Israel, a nation in transition.

Ramah
1 Samuel 7:17;
19:18–23; 28:3

Elkanah
Hannah's husband, a
Levite

Levites
priests and worship
leaders

Ramah
birthplace, home,
and burial place of
Samuel

Family Road Trip

1 SAMUEL 1:1–7 Now there was a certain man of Ramathaim Zophim, of the mountains of Ephraim, and his name was Elkanah the son of Jeroham, the son of Elihu, the son of Tohu, the son of Zuph, an Ephraimite. And he had two wives: the name of one was Hannah, and the name of the other Peninnah. Peninnah had children, but Hannah had no children. This man went up from his city yearly to worship and sacrifice to the LORD of hosts in Shiloh. Also the two sons of Eli, Hophni and Phinehas, the priests of the LORD, were there. And whenever the time came for Elkanah to make an offering, he would give portions to Peninnah his wife and to all her sons and daughters. But to Hannah he would give a double portion, for he loved Hannah, although the LORD had closed her womb. And her rival also provoked her severely, to make her miserable, because the LORD had closed her womb. So it was, year by year, when she went up to the house of the LORD, that she provoked her; therefore she wept and did not eat. (NKJV)

Elkanah was from a devout family of **Levites**. Each year, he and his family traveled from their home town of **Ramah** to Shiloh, the

go to

Ark of the Covenant
Exodus 25:10–22;
Deuteronomy
10:1–6

placed by Joshua
Joshua 18:1

tabernacle
Exodus 25:22;
29:42–43; 30:6, 36

tent of meeting
Exodus 39:32, 40;
40:2, 6, 29

Garden of Eden
Genesis 2:8–9

Adam and Eve
Genesis 2:7–25

disobey God's rules
Genesis 3

detailed instructions
Exodus 25

place where the **Ark of the Covenant** had been placed by Joshua. In Shiloh, at the tabernacle, they would worship God and make **sacrifices**.

It is important not to take a step further into this study of David's life without fully exploring the word "tabernacle" and all it represents. All by itself, the word "tabernacle" simply means a house or a dwelling place. In the Bible, the term "tabernacle" (and sometimes the phrase "tent of meeting") refers to the place where people can worship God. However, many of the Bible's references to the tabernacle point to a specific example: the tabernacle of the Israelites in the wilderness, which was their center of worship and a symbol of God's presence among them.

In a sense, the Garden of Eden was the first tabernacle. That's where God, **Adam, and Eve** lived in pristine splendor and perfect harmony before the first couple chose to disobey God's rules. When they did, their **sin** separated them from God, because it is impossible for holiness, or perfection, to coexist with unholiness, or imperfection. But because God had created people for His pleasure and fellowship, He wanted to make a way for them to reenter His presence.

He did that by giving His prophet Moses detailed instructions for building a tabernacle, the very one to which Elkanah and his family traveled each year.

A Look Inside

As the pilgrims made their way into Shiloh, their first view of the worship center must have been breathtaking. Just beyond the top of the 7 ½-foot-high linen walls that enclosed the rectangular, 150 foot by 75 foot courtyard, they could glimpse a portion of the roof of the tabernacle itself. And as they stepped through the curtains of blue, purple, and scarlet cascading across a 30-foot-wide entrance on the eastern side of the courtyard, they would have looked straight ahead to see the outside of a flat-topped, 45 by 15 foot structure.

The outer court of the tabernacle was as far as they would have been allowed to go; this was where they could cleanse themselves of sin by making sacrifices, presenting **offerings**, and offering their personal **worship**.

Ark of the Covenant
sacred container symbolizing God's presence on earth

Joshua
spiritual and military leader of Israel

sacrifices
death of a substitute as a covering for sin

Adam and Eve
first man and woman God created

sin
violation of God's will

offerings
gifts

worship
honoring God with praise

If they had been permitted to enter the structure, they would have seen that it was divided into two rooms: an inner court, called "the holy place," and the holy of holies, also called "the most holy place." Heavy curtains separated the inner court from the outer court, and the holy of holies from the inner court. Only the **priests** could go into the sparsely furnished inner court. And only once a year, on **Yom Kippur**, the head priest, who had to be not only a **Levite** but also a son of <u>**Aaron**</u>, was allowed to enter the holy of holies. That was where the **Ark of the Covenant** was kept.

Symbolism in the Tabernacle

God didn't give Moses careful instructions for building the tabernacle without good reason; each detail of the structure's construction and furnishings is laden with symbolism:

- *The Entrance:* There was only one way into the tabernacle, through the gate in the eastern wall; there is only one entrance to fellowship with God, through "the <u>door</u>" called Jesus Christ.
- *The Materials:* The shittim (or acacia) wood used in construction of the tabernacle is slow to decay; this represents Jesus' human body, which has never decayed since it was <u>**resurrected**</u>.
- *Candlestick:* The candlestick on a table in the inner court actually wasn't a candlestick at all; it was a seven-branched oil lamp, known to both ancient and modern Jews as a "menorah." The center stem rose straight up from the oil reservoir; the other stems did likewise but were curved to the outside. The light on the center stem was always kept lit and was known as the *ner tamid*, Hebrew for "eternal light." The other stems were lit from the center stems. Thus, the whole construction can be used as an illustration of a relationship with Christ: He is the source of light, the center stem; His followers are the outer branches. He is the Light of the World; His followers' lights depend entirely on Him. Christians have no light of their own; they are simply conduits for His Word even as the stems were just conduits for the oil.

go to

Aaron
Exodus 4:14–16, 30;
7:2; 17:10; 29:9;
Numbers 26:59;
33:39

door
John 10:9

resurrected
Matthew 28:6–7;
Mark 16:6;
Luke 24:6;
John 2:22;
1 Corinthians 15:20

priests
Levites; those who presided over the nation's religious life

Yom Kippur
Day of Atonement; a solemn day set aside for fasting and sacrifice to make amends for the sins of the past year

Levite
priest and worship leader

Aaron
Moses' older brother; Israel's first high priest

Ark of the Covenant
chest containing the two stone tablets on which God had given Moses the Ten Commandments, a pot of manna, and Aaron's rod that budded

resurrected
brought from death to life

veil was torn
Matthew 27:51

Jesus lives
1 Corinthians 6:19–20

Gilgal
Joshua 4:19–20;
5:9–10

showbread
12 loaves of bread
representing Israel's
12 tribes

Gilgal
first campsite of
Israelites after they
crossed the Jordan

high places
hilltops where
worship took place

- *The Bread:* Also on a table in the inner court was kept the bread of the Presence, or **"showbread,"** which suggests God's provision for and fellowship with His people.

- *The Veil:* The curtain separating the holy place from the most holy place was called the veil and represents the barrier of sin between humans and God. The <u>veil was torn</u> when Jesus died on the cross, illustrating that while His death did not remove the barrier of sin, it did remove the need for individual blood sacrifices. Those who accept Christ's sacrifice for their sins are forgiven and have access to God through Christ.

- *The Tent:* God's presence was in the holy of holies in the tabernacle; <u>Jesus lives</u> in the tent, or tabernacle, of individual human hearts.

what others say

Larry Richards

Why were God's directions so specific? Because each detail of the Tabernacle taught a spiritual truth.[1]

The High Places

Before Joshua had established the tabernacle in Shiloh, it had been located in **Gilgal**, where wars had been raging for fourteen years. During those turbulent times, the people of Israel had begun to make sacrifices at places other than the tabernacle. These places were called **"high places"** because makeshift altars were usually situated on hilltops. Most often, the "high places" in the Bible are associated with pagan worship. After the tabernacle was reestablished at Shiloh, the high places were strictly forbidden and families were instructed to resume worship at the tabernacle only. Not everyone did this, however; that's what made Elkanah and his family stand out as a family of faith. Their annual pilgrimage to worship at Shiloh demonstrated their obedience to God.

what others say

Matthew Henry

God had then tied his people to one place and one altar, and forbidden them, under any pretence whatsoever, to worship elsewhere, and therefore, in pure obedience to that command, he [Elkanah] attended at Shiloh.[2]

Sources of Hannah's Sorrow

polygamy
Deuteronomy
21:15–17

God's blessing
Psalm 127:3, 5

Elkanah's family might have been faithful, but that doesn't mean it was fully functional. In fact, by today's standards, "dysfunctional" would better describe this household. As the family trudged down the arduous mountainous terrain, the lens of the camera recording the journey almost instantly zooms in on one character: Elkanah's wife, Hannah. Her name means "grace," but she clearly was full of heartache.

What were the sources of her sorrow?

1. Three's a crowd. Some of Hannah's sadness sprang from the construction of her marriage: she shared her husband, Elkanah, with another wife, Peninnah.

   While **polygamy** wasn't explicitly forbidden in the Old Testament, a marriage between one woman and one man is God's ideal blueprint, as seen in the following passages:

   • Genesis 2:21–24

   • Matthew 19:4–6

   • Ephesians 5:21–23

   In short, polygamy steps outside the boundaries of the outline God has designed for a strong marriage.

2. Childlessness hurts. Another reason Hannah was upset is evident in the statement that Peninnah had children but Hannah didn't. This woman was battling **infertility**. In the culture of her time, childbearing marked a woman's status among family and peers. From the time God instructed Adam and Eve to "be fruitful and multiply" (Genesis 9:1, 7 NKJV), **fertility** has represented God's blessing. Children were considered gifts from God and actually were measurements of wealth. Infertility, on the other hand, has often represented the worst of all possible misfortunes that could befall a family. Genesis 30:22–23 even indicates that not being able to bear children was a disgrace.

polygamy
marriage to more
than one wife

infertility
the inability to bear
children

fertility
the ability to bear
children

patriarchy
society ruled by
males

   Childlessness was seen not only as a spiritual curse and a social disgrace, but it also presented an Israelite woman with practical problems. Because she lived in a system of **patriarchy**, her legal status was determined by her relationship to

men—her husband, her father, her sons, or her sons-in-law. Therefore, her economic well-being hinged on whether she belonged to a man's household. If her husband died, and she had no sons or sons-in-law, who would care for her in her old age?

3. Hannah's husband's other wife was a real nuisance. Not only did Hannah have to suffer the disgrace and heartbreak of knowing she could not bear a child, but she had to endure the taunts of the woman who had borne Elkanah a tent full of kids. Strife between two women in the same household may not have been what David's son, Solomon, had in mind when he wrote many years later that "the contentions of a wife are a continual dripping" (Proverbs 19:13 NKJV), but no doubt the "drip, drip, drip" of Peninnah's provocations, day after day and year after year, were eroding Hannah's last bit of good temper.

4. The darkness of depression had settled in. Because Hannah had endured the pressures of a less than ideal marriage, the shame and disappointment of infertility, and the persecution of a contentious Peninnah, the stress of her situation eventually manifested in physical ways. She couldn't stop crying and she lost her appetite. Both behaviors are classic symptoms of a depressed woman.

A Helpful Husband

1 SAMUEL 1:8 *Then Elkanah her husband said to her, "Hannah, why do you weep? Why do you not eat? And why is your heart grieved? Am I not better to you than ten sons?"* (NKJV)

Elkanah appears to have tried as hard as he could to fill the void in Hannah's heart and cheer her up. He had offered material gifts as well as kind and encouraging words. Setting aside for a moment Elkanah's unwise decision to marry multiple wives, his care and concern for Hannah are touching. However, well-intended though his efforts to pull her out of her misery might have been, they couldn't fill the void in her heart.

God—not things, not even the love of other people—is the only one who can fulfill the longings of His people!

Eli
judge and high priest whose name means "the Lord is high"

key point

what others say

Robert Alter

The double-edged poignancy of these words is that they at once express Elkanah's deep and solicitous love for Hannah and his inability to understand how inconsolable she feels about her affliction of barrenness.[4]

Hannah's Solution

1 SAMUEL 1:9–11 *So Hannah arose after they had finished eating and drinking in Shiloh. Now **Eli** the priest was sitting on the seat by the doorpost of the tabernacle of the LORD. And she was in bitterness of soul, and prayed to the LORD and wept in anguish. Then she made a vow and said, "O LORD of hosts, if You will indeed look on the affliction of Your maidservant and remember me, and not forget Your maidservant, but will give Your maidservant a male child, then I will give him to the LORD all the days of his life, and no razor shall come upon his head." (NKJV)*

For a reason undisclosed in Scripture, Hannah came to a point at which she could no longer keep hidden the anguish and longings of her heart. She took action by placing her grief in the hands of God through a prayer that must have been like the kind described in Romans 8:26:

Likewise the Spirit also helps in our weaknesses. For we do not know what we should pray for as we ought, but the Spirit Himself makes intercession for us with groanings which cannot be uttered. (NKJV)

Nazirite
set apart for special
service

vow
binding obligation

Hannah released the heavy burden of emotional trauma she was carrying into God's hands as she took a two-step plan of action:

1. **She cried out to God.** It's important to note that Hannah wasn't experiencing a simple bout of the blues. This was deep depression. The Hebrew word used to describe the condition of her soul is *mar*, which means "bitter," "angry," "chafed," "discontented," "great," or "heavy." This woman was crying out in desperation under the heavy weight of her sorrows.

2. **She made a pledge to God.** By saying that no razor would ever be used on her son's head, Hannah was pledging that her coming son would serve the Lord as a **Nazirite**.

This passage, on first reading, might appear to be a mortal bargaining with the Almighty: "You give me what I want and I'll give you something in return." It is tempting to do just that when your personal desire for something overrides your belief that God will always do what's best for His followers. But "let's make a deal" is not what this passage is about at all. Hannah was in fact making a **vow** to God, one that placed her in jeopardy if she did not follow through: "When you make a vow to the LORD your God, you shall not delay to pay it; for the LORD your God will surely require it of you, and it would be sin to you" (Deuteronomy 23:21 NKJV).

key point

Hannah's words showed sweet, and complete, surrender to her Lord. In essence, she was saying, "I love You so much, Lord, that even if You do see fit to give me a son, he will be Yours. I will surrender that which I desire the most to You, knowing that Your favor upon me—plus nothing else, not even a son—is all I truly need."

A Note About Nazirites

something to ponder

Those who wanted to serve the Lord in a special way couldn't simply decide to join the priesthood in the same way people can decide to become ministry leaders today. As mentioned earlier, only men who belonged to the tribe of Levi were given the exclusive privilege of becoming priests. But the Law did make a way for *any* devoted men or women—including those who were not Levites—to demonstrate their dedication to God. They could take a Nazirite vow, based on the Hebrew word *nazir*, which means "to dedicate." The vows were usually taken by adults, but on occasion, as in Hannah's case, a parent could make the vow on behalf of a child.

The guidelines for Nazirites outlined in Numbers 6:1–21 did not set a specific time frame for carrying out the vow. However, it did outline three requirements of the vow-takers:

1. They were not to cut their hair.

2. They were not to drink wine.

3. They were not to touch dead bodies.

If a Nazirite failed to carry out these requirements, he or she had to offer a sacrifice and start over.

Nazirites of the Bible

Name	Scripture	Description
Samson	Judges 13–16	Samson, the last judge before Samuel, was a Nazirite from birth and the first mentioned in Scripture. He was physically strong but morally and spiritually weak.
Samuel	1 Samuel 1–28	Israel's last judge and first prophet, the much-loved man of moral and spiritual integrity who anointed the nation's first and second kings.
John the Baptist	Matthew 3; Luke 1; 3	Prophet born just six months before Jesus; he was sent by God to prepare the people to receive the truth of Jesus.
James the brother of Jesus	Mark 6:2–3; Galatians 1:19	Jesus' brother and author of the book of James is believed by many scholars—based on extrabiblical sources—to be a Nazirite although it's not stated in the Bible.
Paul, the apostle	Acts 18:18; 21:22–26	Paul took the Nazirite vow in an effort to maintain his credibility among the Jews, by demonstrating that he was still one of them even though he had accepted Christ as Messiah.

A Priest's *Faux Pas*

1 SAMUEL 1:12–18 *And it happened, as she continued praying before the LORD, that Eli watched her mouth. Now Hannah spoke in her heart; only her lips moved, but her voice was not heard. Therefore Eli thought she was drunk. So Eli said to her, "How long will you be drunk? Put your wine away from you!" But Hannah answered and said, "No, my lord, I am a woman of sorrowful spirit. I have drunk neither wine nor intoxicating*

drink, but have poured out my soul before the LORD. Do not consider your maidservant a wicked woman, for out of the abundance of my complaint and grief I have spoken until now." Then Eli answered and said, "Go in peace, and the God of Israel grant your petition which you have asked of Him." And she said, "Let your maidservant find favor in your sight." So the woman went her way and ate, and her face was no longer sad. (NKJV)

Hannah's passionate yet silent petition before the Lord had the priest Eli convinced she was drunk. Considering the times, this wasn't as far-fetched an assumption as it might seem.

---

what others say

Adam Clarke

The fact that Eli supposed her to be drunken, and the other of the conduct of Eli's sons already mentioned, prove that religion was at this time at a very low ebb in Shiloh; for it seems drunken women did come to the place, and lewd women were to be found there.[5]

Matthew Henry

Perhaps in this degenerate age it was no strange thing to see drunken women at the door of the tabernacle; for otherwise, one would think, the vile lust of Hophni and Phinehas could not have found so easy a prey there . . . Eli took Hannah for one of these.[6]

A Woman's Wise Response

The priest's accusation must have been very disheartening to Hannah! To be accused of vile behavior could have thrown her a crushing blow. Some people might have responded with a smart retort; others might have cowered in humiliation. Either response would have caused quite a commotion at the temple, and neither one would have accomplished any good results. Hannah, however, calmly defused the situation. She chose her words carefully and infused them with respect and honesty, yielding peace rather than further strife, demonstrating the kind of wisdom described in Proverbs 15:1: "A soft answer turns away wrath, but a harsh word stirs up anger" (NKJV).

Convinced at last that she was sincere, Eli assured Hannah of something she no doubt already knew: God indeed would answer her prayer. At once, her appetite returned to a healthy level, her energy was restored, and the heavy weight of depression fell from her shoulders.

Let It Go!

When people give God their heartaches, their worries, or their fears, they often find it easy to snatch those concerns back and resume fretting over them. They often tell God their needs, then continue to keep rehashing those needs as if they were stones of worry that held great value. Then, with heavy hearts—burdened from all that anxiety—people complain that God "just isn't answering my prayers." Then they wonder why they are not feeling the peace He promises. This scene—Hannah's liberating prayer—offers a perfect example of what happens when a person truly <u>hands all worries over to God</u>.

apply it

Samuel's Birth and Dedication

the big picture

1 Samuel 1:19–2:10

Elkanah and his family returned home, where Hannah soon conceived and delivered a son, naming him **Samuel**, which means "asked of God." Elkanah and the rest of the family continued to make their annual trek to Shiloh to worship, but Hannah—with Elkanah's blessing—stayed home with Samuel, saying she did not want to return to Shiloh until her son was old enough to be left there permanently. True to her word, once Samuel was weaned, probably around age three, she joined the family on the yearly pilgrimage to worship God. Hannah greeted the priest Eli with joy, reminding him that she was the woman who had asked for—and received—a child. She then launched into a praise-filled, prophetic song celebrating her answered prayer.

go to

hands all worries over to God
1 Peter 5:7

Samuel
Israel's last judge and first prophet

It was time for Hannah to fulfill her vow to the Lord. For the first time since she had petitioned God for a son, she traveled with her family to Shiloh. A full range of emotions surely tumbled around in her heart. Undoubtedly, she felt sadness at the prospect of day-today life without her much-loved son underfoot. Yet she must have felt joy too, at every reminder that God had indeed fulfilled her deepest desires. She didn't even pass up the chance to present her testimony to Eli, the temple priest who had initially misjudged her motives during her last visit. Apparently free of any misgivings for his unfair allegation, she told the priest of the Lord's goodness to her in a song detailing how God had helped her, how He works, and who He is.

This passage, often referred to as "Hannah's Song," was probably a mixture of her own words and phrases taken from traditional psalms of praise and thanksgiving. Her song became well-known among the Jews. In fact, Mary, the mother of Jesus, used many similar words and phrases in her own song, recorded in Luke 1:46–55 after the angel Gabriel gave her the announcement of Jesus' birth.

Hannah's Song, often referred to as a psalm of reversals, points to God's ability to lift up the humble and bring down the proud. In the words of Robert Alter it is . . .

what others say

Robert Alter

. . . a fitting introduction to the whole Saul-David history. This psalm (verses 1–10) and David's victory psalm (2 Samuel 22) echo each other and act as formal "bookends" to the extended narrative sequence that includes the stories of Samuel, Saul and David.[7]

Hannah's prayer of need had been silent (her lips moved but her heart had done the talking); however, her prayer of praise was spoken aloud, for others to hear. How many times do we advertise needs and desires through prayers—and public prayer requests—for others to hear! Yet how many times do we grab a microphone to share God's answers to those prayers? May the Lord grant each of us the silence of Hannah as we place our petitions at His feet; and may He give us power-packed words of praise when it's time to proclaim His goodness.

Boys, Boys!

go to

law allowed
Leviticus 7:34

fat had been burned
Leviticus 3:3–5

responsibility
1 Timothy 3:4–5

teach children
Deuteronomy 6:7;
11:19

discipline
Ephesians 6:4

the big picture

1 Samuel 2:11–17

Elkanah and his family went home, leaving Samuel in Eli's care and training while Eli's sons **Hophni and Phinehas** were carrying out their priestly duties at the temple with ever-increasing evil.

Hophni and Phinehas
the prophet Samuel's corrupt sons

Scripture describes Eli's sons as sons of Belial, or "sons of the devil." Their list of evil practices grew longer as each day passed, and their failure to lead worship with integrity led the people astray. Their evil practices included:

1. Taking more of the sacrifices for themselves than the <u>law allowed</u>.

2. Taking the meat before the <u>fat had been burned</u> as a sacrifice to God.

3. Resenting the offerings to the Lord.

Learning from Eli's Example

"But I raised them in the tabernacle!" Surely that thought ran through Eli's mind as he saw his sons defying the God he knew and loved, as they showed nothing but disobedience and disrespect for God's laws.

Today's parents may learn a few "do's" and "don'ts" from Eli's mistakes.

Family Do's and Don'ts

Don't	Become so consumed with "church work" that we neglect our families.
Do	Take <u>responsibility</u> for what goes on inside our homes.
Don't	Assume that taking kids to church will guarantee they will form a personal relationship with God. Free will given to each person, child or not, requires a personal decision to accept all God offers.
Do	<u>Teach children</u> about our faith at every opportunity.
Don't	Be afraid to discipline children.
Do	Administer <u>discipline</u> in a firm and loving way.

strengthen your family

A Boy Behaving Beautifully

ephod
Exodus 39:27–29

ephod
garment worn by
priests

the big picture

1 Samuel 2:18–21

While Eli's sons were busy making a mockery out of their service to the Lord, Samuel was throwing his whole heart into his work for the Lord as Eli's helper in the tabernacle. The young boy was even outfitted with a linen **ephod**, a sleeveless, apron-like garment worn by priests. His mother, Hannah, though far away, continued to love and care for her son, which she demonstrated by making him a new robe each year. Because of their faithfulness, Eli blessed Elkanah and his wife, saying that the Lord would give them even more children. Hannah had three more sons and two daughters. Meanwhile, Samuel was growing up physically, mentally, and spiritually. He was growing closer to the Lord.

God's Little Boy

Even though "God's people"—Eli's sons—were corrupt, their failures did not derail God's work. God was raising up another, Samuel, to fulfill His plans. The child's specific jobs in the tabernacle aren't outlined in Scripture, but most likely he would have taken care of housekeeping chores while absorbing the spiritual training provided by the priest. The old priest was well aware that his charge was an extraordinary boy destined for extraordinary service to God. This is emphasized by the fact that he furnished Samuel with a linen ephod—a small version of the exquisitely crafted sacred garments reserved for priests alone.

A Slight Scolding

the big picture

1 Samuel 2:22–36

Eli might have been getting on in years but he certainly wasn't oblivious to the conduct of his boys. He was hearing scandalous reports about their antics with the harlots who hung around the tabernacle door. So he confronted his sons, urging them to change. They didn't listen. Their refusal to try to please God, their own father, and the people they served was a stark contrast to the conduct of young Samuel. The child not only was growing physically, but his sincere heart and actions were earning the respect of the Lord and those around him.

Eli, as both judge and high priest, could have removed his boys from their positions of power as priests in the house of God. He even could have had them executed for their evil deeds. However, he didn't seem to have the backbone to discipline his own sons. He merely reprimanded them and failed to impose any consequences. This trait would later lead to a major downfall for David!

Adam Clarke

Eli appears to have been a fondly affectionate, easy father, who wished his sons to do well, but did not bring them under proper discipline, and did not use his authority to restrain them. As judge, he had power to cast them immediately out of the vineyard, as wicked and unprofitable servants; this he did not, and his and their ruin was the consequence.[8]

"Just Like Jesus"

The words that describe Samuel—"And the child Samuel grew in stature, and in favor both with the LORD and men" (1 Samuel 2:26 NKJV)—are similar to the words that would later be used to describe Jesus: "And the Child grew and became strong in spirit, filled with wisdom; and the grace of God was upon Him" (Luke 2:40 NKJV).

Tim LaHaye

While Samuel, whose very name means "name of God," is not specifically cited in the New Testament as a **type** of Christ, there are several similarities that tend to forecast the Savior's ministry. Samuel was a prophet, priest, and ruler, as Jesus is. He grew in stature and in favor both with the Lord and men. He was a great intercessor, saying of the rebellious nation, "God forbid that I should sin against the Lord in ceasing to pray for you" (1 Samuel 12:23). Jesus, who cannot sin, "ever liveth to make intercession for [us]" (Hebrews 7:25).[9]

type
person or thing like another in an important way

A Significant Scathing

prophecy

the big picture

1 Samuel 2:27–36

A messenger from God rebuked Eli for allowing the corruption in the tabernacle.

He prophesied a curse on the house of Eli; Hophni and Phinehas in fact would die on the same day. God, through this messenger, then told Eli that in the absence of the priest's ability to raise obedient men to lead in Tabernacle worship, He would raise up His own priest.

something to ponder

For the most part, Eli was a good priest if not a strong father. Even though his first instinct about Hannah had been wrong, he had quickly realized his error in judgment and subsequently blessed her. He also had been accountable to God in nurturing young Samuel and training him in the ways of God. Surely with so many "good" deeds to his credit, he shouldn't be punished for his failure regarding the sins of his sons. Or should he? This theme reappears again and again throughout the story of David's life.

what others say

Matthew Henry

Those who allow and countenance their children in any evil way, and do not use their authority to restrain and punish them, do in effect honour them more than God.[10]

Hearing Voices

the big picture

1 Samuel 3:1–20

In the middle of the night, Samuel, asleep in the tabernacle, twice heard his name being called. Each time he thought the words came from Eli, so he went to the old man—who was nearly blind. Eli, however, sent the child back to bed, saying he hadn't said a word. When this happened a third time the priest realized that the boy was indeed hearing a voice: the voice of God. He instructed Samuel to go back to bed, and to be ready to answer the Lord the next time he heard his name called. Sure enough, the Lord again called Samuel's name and the boy responded just as Eli had told him to. Then God gave Samuel a prophecy that restated the curse He would carry out against Eli's house. When Samuel, at the urging of Eli, told the priest what the Lord had said, Eli accepted the pronouncement. Samuel continued to grow physically, and to grow closer to the Lord. Soon it became widely known that Samuel was the Lord's prophet.

judges
spiritual, political, and military leaders of Israel

prophets
people through whom God speaks

Closing One Door . . .

This passage marks a major transition: through the young boy Samuel, God would usher His nation, Israel, out of the period of the **judges** and into the period of the **prophets**. The judges had been called by God to carry out executive, legislative, and judicial activities of each tribe's government. The end of the period of judges was marked by spiritual and moral decline. The people had failed to listen to God so often He had finally stopped talking to them. They turned more and more to idolatry and other pagan practices.

Eli's sons exemplified the guiding principles of most of the people during this time.

key point

JUDGES 21:25 *In those days there was no king in Israel; everyone did what was right in his own eyes. (NKJV)*

. . . And Opening Another

A prophet is a spokesperson for God, someone who speaks God's Word to the people, influencing their obedience and choices toward a positive outcome. An Old Testament prophet's messages often but not always concerned the future; many messages related God's instructions, judgments, and revelations about the present.

As the first prophet, Samuel launched a period that would be marked by a fresh activity of God after the long period of silence.

Nevi'im, the Hebrew word for "prophets," is also the source of the "N" in the word *Tanakh*, which refers to the entire Old Testament. The Tanakh in turn comprises Torah (Law), Nevi'im (Prophets), and Kesuv'im (Writings), producing the T-N-K acronym, which yields "TaNaKh" (although it's also spelled Tanach but pronounced the same).

History of Israel's Government

Type of Government	Dates	Description
Theocracy	1446 BC (time of the Exodus) to 1367 BC (death of Joshua)	Israel was organized into twelve tribes, each with individual leaders. The tribes were united by their common allegiance to God, who ruled over His people by providing laws, administering justice, and leading in military activities through the representative leadership of Moses, first, and after him, Joshua.
Judges	1367 BC (death of Joshua) to 1044 BC (Samuel's death)	After the death of Joshua, the tribes began to experience spiritual and political turmoil. God sent judges to serve as leaders within local tribes. Some judges were effective; others weren't. The entire period during which Israel was governed by judges was marked by spiritual and moral decline.
Monarchy	1044 BC	A radically different form of government than Israel had ever had; an earthly king would be appointed to rule over Israel.

How Does God Speak to People Today?

Throughout the Bible, God speaks to people in different ways: sometimes through dreams, sometimes through angelic messengers, sometimes through prophets, and sometimes through an audible voice, as with Samuel. God's conversation with humans did not end when the last pages of the Bible were recorded. He still speaks today through a variety of methods, including:

- The Bible—God's written Word
- The Holy Spirit—God's way of living in believers
- Other believers—God uses people to teach and influence one another
- Circumstances

Some good strategies for hearing God's voice involve:

- Obeying God's instructions
- Abiding in God's presence
- Listening
- Praying

Chapter Wrap-Up

- David's story begins with the birth of the prophet Samuel to Elkanah and Hannah, a devout family among the few who still worshipped the Lord in the ways He prescribed.

- When Hannah traveled with her family to worship the Lord at the tabernacle in Shiloh, her heart was heavy with grief because she was infertile.

- Hannah placed her grief in the hands of God through a prayer song dedicating the child God would give her to the Lord's service.

- Eli, the priest at the tabernacle, misjudged Hannah's silent yet impassioned prayer and accused her of being drunk. But then he recognized her sincerity and assured her that God would answer her prayer.

- Hannah returned to the tabernacle with her three-year-old son, Samuel, to fulfill her promise to God by leaving him in the care of Eli, whose sons were corrupt.

- The Lord spoke to Samuel when he was a young boy, marking him as a prophet and transitioning the nation out of the period of judges and into the period of prophets.

Study Questions

1. What was the significance of the tabernacle to the ancient Hebrews?

2. What marked Elkanah and his family as a family of faith?

3. What were the sources of Hannah's sorrow?

4. What steps did Hannah take to remedy her situation?

5. What is a Nazirite vow?

6. How did the priest Eli misjudge Hannah?

7. How did Hannah respond when God blessed her with a son?

8. What were Eli's sons like, and how did their father respond to them?

9. What was Samuel like as a young boy?

10. What was a turning point, both in the life of Samuel and in the history of the people of Israel?

Chapter Highlights:
- It's All About the Ark
- Battle Plan Backfires
- God's Glory—Gone!
- Where to Park the Ark?
- Ebenezer!

1 Samuel 4–7: War with the Philistines

Let's Get Started

God had pronounced a curse against the house of Eli as a consequence for permissive parenting, but that curse had not yet come to pass. And God had broken a long period of silence by speaking to the young boy named Samuel, someone the Lord had set apart as Israel's last judge and first prophet. Both story lines continue to unfold in 1 Samuel, chapters 4–7. Chapter 4 begins a sequence of passages called the Ark narratives, which describe the fulfillment of the death prophecy against Eli and his sons and detail the Israelites' misguided attempts to manipulate God by meddling with the Ark of the Covenant. The next passages chronicle the dismal spiritual decline into which both Eli's household and the nation of Israel itself fell. They then trace the travels of the ark, concluding with a grand finale: Under the leadership of Samuel, the people of Israel turn their hearts back to God, and He willingly returns to His rightful place as Lord of their hearts.

Philistines
fierce warriors and perpetual enemy of Israel who lived mainly in an area just south of today's Tel Aviv

It's All About the Ark

the big picture

1 Samuel 4:1–2

Samuel, probably about seventeen years old now, had come to be recognized as a prophet of God, but the people of Israel didn't give him much respect. Without as much as a prayer to God or a consultation with God's man, they decided to attack their longtime enemies, the **Philistines**. The Israelites subsequently suffered great loss: four thousand men died in the battle.

Why did Israel want to fight the Philistines in the first place? It was all about real estate. The Philistines were fierce people who controlled fertile territory in the coastal area of Canaan from five main

something to ponder

go to

container
Exodus 25:10–22

inscribed
Exodus 32:15–16

Moses
great prophet and
lawgiver who led his
people, the
Israelites, from
Egyptian bondage

**Ten
Commandments**
God's laws for life

cities—Gaza, Ashkelon, Ashdod, Ekron, and Gath—located between the hill country of Judah and the Mediterranean Sea. This land is known today as Palestine. Skilled archers who used iron chariots, the Philistines almost always dominated the Israelites in battles over land. In fact, they had done so for such a long time that the Philistines had come to regard the people of Israel as their slaves.

God in a Box?

the big picture

I Samuel 4:3–4

The people of Israel used the rout as an excuse to do some blame-shifting, bitterly asking why God had allowed them to be defeated by the Philistines. They then decided to retrieve the Ark of the Covenant from Shiloh in a misguided effort to ensure that God would deliver them from their enemies.

The Israelites could have regarded their defeat at the hands of the Philistines as a wake-up call, prompting them to humble themselves before God and renew their commitment to obey, worship, and trust Him for protection and deliverance. Instead, they tried to take matters into their own hands. If God wouldn't voluntarily accompany them to the battle and grant them victory, they reasoned, why couldn't they simply take Him there themselves?

What's so special about the crate the Israelites imported into their camp, thinking it had mystical powers strong enough to guarantee victory against the Philistines? The Hebrew word used for ark, *aron*, is a common name for any kind of a chest. However, this particular Ark wasn't an everyday linen chest. No object was considered more sacred. A focal point for the nation Israel, it was a reminder of God's protection and provision, and was set apart in several ways:

1. *Its Special History:*

   - God had instructed **Moses** to build a special <u>container</u> for holding the tablets upon which the **Ten Commandments** were <u>inscribed</u>.

   - The Ark had accompanied the Israelites as a symbol of God's presence as they wandered in the wilderness.

- The priests had carried the Ark into the bed of the Jordan River, the waters of which God parted so the Israelites could cross into **Canaan** on dry ground.
- The Ark had been carried in the procession around **Jericho** before the <u>walls came tumbling down</u>.

2. *Its Special Names:* Three terms used in Scripture describe the holy vessel:

- <u>ark of God</u>: reflecting the Deity the vessel represents
- <u>ark of the covenant</u>: alluding to the covenant God made with the Israelites when He gave Moses the **Law**
- <u>ark of the Testimony</u>: alluding to the stone tablets containing the Ten Commandments, sometimes called the "Testimony"

3. *Its Special Construction:* Most likely made of acacia wood, the Ark of the Covenant was about four feet long, and a little more than two feet wide and tall. God gave Moses <u>detailed instructions</u> on how to build and embellish the Ark. It was designed for portability, with golden rings through which gold-covered poles could be inserted, for carrying. The solid-gold lid was called the mercy seat because this was where God positioned Himself within the most holy place. The lid also featured two **cherubim** facing each other, with their wings spanning the mercy seat.

4. *Its Special Location:* The Ark was to be kept inside the "holy of holies" section of the tabernacle.

5. *Its <u>Special Contents</u>:*

- The two <u>tablets of stone</u> on which God had inscribed the Ten Commandments.
- The pot of **manna** God had provided the Israelites as sustenance while they wandered in the wilderness.
- **Aaron**'s <u>rod that budded</u> when God appointed him as Israel's first high priest.

go to

walls came tumbling down
Joshua 6:4, 6, 8, 11–12

ark of God
1 Samuel 3:3

ark of the covenant
Joshua 3:6;
Hebrews 9:4

ark of the Testimony
Exodus 25:22

detailed instructions
Exodus 25:10–22

special contents
Hebrews 9:4

tablets of stone
Deuteronomy 31:24–26

rod that budded
Numbers 17:8, 10

Canaan
the land God promised

Jericho
site of Israel's first great victory

Law
the Law of Moses; the Ten Commandments and other laws God gave the Israelites in the Old Testament

cherubim
type of angels that guard the throne of God

manna
nourishing food God miraculously provided each morning

Aaron
Moses' brother and the first high priest

priests carried the Ark
Numbers 4:5–6;
10:33–36;
Psalm 132:8

Levites
priests and worship
leaders

6. *Its Special Handling*: Hands off! No one was allowed to touch the Ark. During the journeys of the Israelites, the <u>priests carried the Ark</u> under a purple canopy in advance of the rest of the travelers. It was always wrapped in a veil, badgers' skins, and blue cloth, and was carefully hidden even from the eyes of the **Levites** who carried it.

what others say

J. Vernon McGee

Knowing the history of the ark—that as it had been carried down into the Jordan River, the water had been cut off so that Israel could cross over—they took the ark of the covenant into battle. The thought was that its presence would bring victory. My friend, this reveals the superstition and paganism of these people who thought there was some merit in the object. The merit was not in that box because God was not in that box. You cannot get God into a box! The merit was in the presence and person of God.[1]

The Bible Almanac

During the wanderings in the wilderness and in the conquest of the Promised Land the ark always went before the enemies of Israel. This was to symbolize God's active presence with His people.[2]

Bibles, crosses, fish, angels, stars . . . Christian symbols adorn bumper stickers and billboards, calendars and greeting cards. How easy it can become to look to the religious symbols themselves for security, protection, or inspiration rather than remembering that these things come only from the One represented by the symbols!

Battle Plan Backfires

the big picture

I Samuel 4:5–11

In a stadium-style cheering frenzy, the Israelites celebrated the arrival of the Ark at their battle camp. Their celebration was so loud that the Philistines heard the commotion. However, their curiosity soon melted into concern as they learned the reason. They believed the God of the Israelites Himself had entered the Israelites' camp—and the Philistines knew enough to be afraid, based on some of the things He had done for His people in the past. However, the war-loving Philistines didn't give up and retreat. Instead, they stormed Israel's camp, killed thirty thousand soldiers, and captured the Ark of God. Both of Eli's sons died.

go to

demons believe
James 2:19

Audacious Opposition

The Philistines acknowledged the power of God, yet they still presumed to oppose Him. Simply believing God exists doesn't mean taking Him at His word and believing that He will do what He promises. As stated in the New Testament, even the <u>demons believe</u> in God—and they tremble in His presence. But that doesn't make them His followers!

Masters of Manipulation

The drive to try to manipulate God is a part of human nature. But for Christians, the worthy goal isn't to try to *control* God—as if we could anyway—it is to *submit* to God. Attempting to manipulate God is to focus on the outcome we desire, while ignoring God's bigger and better plan for our lives. Some ways we try to manipulate God include:

apply it

- Through the way we spend our money
- Through doing good deeds
- Through playing mental or emotional games
- Through making deals and bargaining
- Through performing meaningless rituals
- Through what we pray for

what others say

David Guzik

We often make the same mistake the Israelites did. We believe that if God is with us, we don't need to try so hard. We think if God is on our side, the work will be easy. That may not be true at all! . . . As it turned out, God did *not* feel obligated to bless the Israelites just because they took the ark into battle. He wouldn't allow His arm to be twisted by the superstitions of the Israelites. God is a Person, not a genie to be summoned at the will of man. You can't manipulate God.[3]

Unbearable News

the big picture

1 Samuel 4:12–18

A messenger came to Shiloh and reported the slaughter. Eli, who was sitting on a chair by the road watching for news from the battle front, heard the cries of the people in town and asked what had happened. The messenger hurried over to the ninety-eight-year-old man to tell him that Hophni and Phineas had died, and that the Philistines had captured the Ark. The news was more than the heavy, aged man could endure. He fell off his chair, broke his neck, and died.

Even though his spiritual vision could be as clouded as his physical vision (remember how he mistook Hannah's fervent prayer for drunken behavior), and even though he had a weakness for passive parenting, Eli was a man who truly loved the Lord. He had spent forty years serving God and keeping close to His presence at the tabernacle. Since the soldiers had removed the Ark from its sacred spot and taken it to the war camp in blatant disobedience to God's instructions, Eli must have trembled as he gazed through weak eyes at the blurry horizon, waiting for news from the battlefront. The announcement that his sons had been killed didn't seem to faze him; he knew enough about God to believe that He would do what He said. But news of the Ark's capture was literally heart-stopping. Eli was massively affected, for it could only signal dark days ahead for Israel.

what others say

Kay Arthur

In 1 Samuel 2:35, God says that He will raise up a faithful priest who will do according to what is in His heart and in His soul . . . and that He will build him an enduring house. Eli was not this kind of man . . . and thus his house was judged forever. God put Eli's sons to death not only because of their sin but because their father failed to rebuke them. In essence, Eli compromised his priesthood.[4]

Obedience and Influence Go Hand in Hand

Eli loved the Lord. And he had considerable influence over the lives of many people, including his sons and the people of Israel who looked to him for leadership in worship. While his failures as a father and as a priest didn't cause him to lose his relationship with God, they did restrict his power to influence others in positive ways.

It's no different today; everyone has considerable influence over the lives of many people, including family members, neighbors, and coworkers.

Failures don't sever a person's relationship with God, but if they remain unacknowledged, they can limit his or her effectiveness in accomplishing the Lord's work.

key point

God's Glory—Gone!

the big picture

1 Samuel 4:19–22

When Eli's daughter-in-law, Phinehas's wife, heard the news about the Ark, and about the deaths of her husband and father-in-law, she immediately went into premature labor and delivered a son. As she lay dying, she named him Ichabod, which means "no glory," and then summed up Israel's dismal state of affairs with one sentence: "The glory has departed from Israel, for the ark of God has been captured" (1 Samuel 4:22 NKJV).

What was so significant about the capture of the Ark that it compelled a Jewish woman—whose ultimate joy in life centered on bearing sons—to give her son a dreadful name and then surrender her own will to live?

The capture of the Ark represented the departure of the glory of God. For the Israelites, God's glory had been evident in the cloud that hovered over the Ark of the Covenant by day, and the pillar of fire that accompanied it by night. The removal of the Ark represented the removal of God's continual provision and protection of His people.

something to ponder

Ark on the Move

1 SAMUEL 5:1–5 Then the Philistines took the ark of God and brought it from Ebenezer to Ashdod. When the Philistines took the ark of God, they brought it into the house of Dagon and set it by Dagon. And when the people of Ashdod arose early in the morning, there was Dagon, fallen on its face to the earth before the ark of the LORD. So they took Dagon and set it in its place again. And when they arose early the next morning, there was Dagon, fallen on its face to the ground before the ark of the LORD. The head of Dagon and both the palms of its hands were broken off on the threshold; only Dagon's torso was left of it. Therefore neither the priests of Dagon nor any who come into Dagon's house tread on the threshold of Dagon in Ashdod to this day. (NKJV)

The Philistines took their trophy from Ebenezer to Ashdod, where they placed it in the temple of their pagan agriculture or fertility god, Dagon. They may have been presenting it as an offering to their god or as an insult to the God of Israel. Next morning, the Philistines arose to discover that their god had fallen off its base in front of the Ark, so they set it up again only to find it fallen again the next morning, this time broken into pieces.

what others say

Robert D. Jameison

They were filled with consternation when they found the object of their stupid veneration prostrate before the symbol of the divine presence. Though set up, it fell again and lay in a state of complete mutilation; its head and arms, severed from the trunk, were lying in distant and separate places, as if violently cast off, and only the fishy part remained. The degradation of their idol, though concealed by the priests on the former occasion, was now more manifest and infamous. It lay in the attitude of a vanquished enemy and a suppliant, and this picture of humiliation significantly declared the superiority of the God of Israel.[5]

Matthew Henry

Dagon by falling prostrate before the ark of God, which was a posture of adoration, did as it were direct his worshippers to pay their homage to the God of Israel, as greater than all gods.[6]

Where to Park the Ark?

emerods
Deuteronomy 28:27;
1 Samuel 5:6, 9, 12

five golden mice
1 Samuel 6:5

plague
painful affliction sent
by God

emerods
statues of the
growths or tumors
that appeared in the
rectal area during
the plague

1 SAMUEL 5:6–8 But the hand of the LORD was heavy on the people of Ashdod, and He ravaged them and struck them with tumors, both Ashdod and its territory. And when the men of Ashdod saw how it was, they said, "The ark of the God of Israel must not remain with us, for His hand is harsh toward us and Dagon our god." Therefore they sent and gathered to themselves all the lords of the Philistines, and said, "What shall we do with the ark of the God of Israel?" And they answered, "Let the ark of the God of Israel be carried away to Gath." So they carried the ark of the God of Israel away. (NKJV)

1 SAMUEL 6:11–12 And they set the ark of the LORD on the cart, and the chest with the gold rats and the images of their tumors. Then the cows headed straight for the road to Beth Shemesh, and went along the highway, lowing as they went, and did not turn aside to the right hand or the left. And the lords of the Philistines went after them to the border of Beth Shemesh. (NKJV)

The Lord struck the people of Ashdod with a painful **plague** of large tumors. They quickly decided their city wasn't the best place for the Ark of the Covenant after all. They sent it to two other cities, Gath and Ekron, where the people didn't fare any better. Finally, they decided to return the Ark to the people of Israel—but they weren't sure how to go about it. After extensive deliberations and consultations with priests and seers, the Philistines came up with a plan. They would send gifts along with the Ark in an attempt to appease the God of Israel so that He might heal them and stop punishing them. Their plan was to hitch two cows to a cart on which they placed the Ark, and let the cows take it wherever they would.

Guided by the hand of God, the cows went straight to the Israelite territory of Beth Shemesh. The people there slaughtered the cows to signify the Ark's return.

Their Unusual Taste in Gift-Giving

Along with the Ark, the Philistines sent five golden <u>emerods</u> and <u>five golden mice</u>—one for the leader of each of the five Philistine cities: Gaza, Ashkelon, Ashdod, Ekron, and Gath.

Why such an odd choice of gifts? The gilded objects offered to God acknowledged that the people realized that God was the power

go to

strict guidelines
Numbers 4:5–20

behind the plague. Some scholars say the two images—the tumors and the mice—suggest two separate plagues: (1) the tumors and (2) the mice, or rats, which could have been the cause of the "very great destruction" described in 1 Samuel 5:9. Other commentators say the connection made between the tumors and mice suggests that this was the bubonic plague, a disease spread from rodents to humans with symptoms that include spots, or tumors, on the skin.

"You Shouldn't Have Done That"

the big picture

1 Samuel 6:19–21

Seventy of the men in Beth Shemesh looked inside the Ark of the Covenant, prompting the Lord to put them to death. That made the people who remained turn back to their superstitious ways. They decided the Ark wasn't so welcome after all, so they sent it to Kirjath Jearim, to the house of Abinadab (1 Samuel 7:1).

God had given clear instructions. No one except the priests would be allowed to touch the Ark, much less look inside it: "but they shall not touch any holy thing, lest they die" (Numbers 4:15 NKJV). Even the priests were required to follow strict guidelines concerning its handling. But the men of Beth Shemesh couldn't resist. The consequences were deadly.

What was so special inside that box that God would strike men dead for gazing at it? The answer is simple: God's glory. "Glory" is a word that doesn't carry too much weight in today's culture. But one passage in Scripture helps restore the "glory" to the word "glory" and helps explain why the men had to die for lifting the lid to take a peek inside the ark:

something to ponder

EXODUS 33:18–23 *And [Moses] said, "Please, show me Your glory." Then He said, "I will make all My goodness pass before you, and I will proclaim the name of the LORD before you. I will be gracious to whom I will be gracious, and I will have compassion on whom I will have compassion." But He said, "You cannot see My face; for no man shall see Me, and live." And the LORD said, "Here is a place by Me, and you shall stand on the rock. So it shall be, while My glory passes by, that I will put you in the cleft of the rock, and will cover you with My hand while I pass by. Then I will take away My hand, and you shall see My back; but My face shall not be seen." (NKJV)*

face became radiant
Exodus 34:35

glory faded
2 Corinthians 3:13

lasts
2 Corinthians 3:11

fruit of the Spirit
Galatians 5:22–23

what others say

John MacArthur

So what is the glory of God? It is the embodiment of all of His attributes. God reduced them to a glorious light in order to show them to Moses . . . No one could ever see the full glory of God and live, so God says, "I'm going to let you see a little of My afterglow."[7]

That Special Glow

When Moses had spent time with the Lord, his <u>face became radiant</u> because of its exposure to the light of God's glory. The radiance that Moses experienced after being exposed to God's <u>glory faded</u> with time and was renewed each time he entered God's presence. The apostle Paul stated in the New Testament that the glory available now—following Christ's intervention on our behalf—is the kind of glory that doesn't fade; it <u>lasts</u>. Whenever we spend time with God through Bible study, meditation, and prayer, our faces may not physically glow, but our character, our motivations, and our actions begin to change. We become more like him by "being transformed into the same image from glory to glory, just as by the Spirit of the Lord" (2 Corinthians 3:18 NKJV). Evidence of this transformation is <u>"fruit of the Spirit"</u>—Christlike traits we begin to demonstrate as we grow closer to Him. In a sense, we then become walking billboards for God's love as we live out His joy, peace, patience, kindness, goodness, faithfulness, gentleness, and self-control.

Ebenezer!

the big picture

1 Samuel 7

The Ark remained in Kirjath Jearim for twenty years, and the people finally decided to turn back to God by following Samuel's instructions to:

- Put away foreign gods
- Prepare their hearts for the Lord
- Serve God, and God alone

Samuel said if they did those things, God would deliver them from the Philistines. The Israelites then gathered at Mizpah to fast, worship, and confess their sins.

The next time the Philistines attacked, as Samuel had promised, God threw the Philistines into such disarray that they were routed by the Israelites. To commemorate the occasion, Samuel erected a monument he called Ebenezer, which means "stone of help." Israel then recovered the cities the Philistines had captured, and Samuel continued to be a beloved spiritual leader, circuit judge, and prophet.

Gathering Stones

In erecting the monument to mark God's faithfulness at Ebenezer, Samuel was continuing a rich tradition of making it a priority to remember and acknowledge God's provision and protection. For example, when God had miraculously parted the Jordan River so the Israelites could cross into the Promised Land on dry ground, He gave Joshua clear instructions. He told him to tell the people to gather stones from the dry riverbed as a way of remembering what had happened that day so that they would be able to tell their children, and their children's children. He wanted the stones to:

- Serve as a reminder of what He had done that day; and
- Be used as monuments to bring glory to Himself.

Monuments and Memorials in the Bible

routed by the Israelites
1 Samuel 7:10–11

Ebenezer
1 Samuel 7:12

The Memorial	Scripture	Significance
Bethel "house of God"	Genesis 28:10–22	The stone Jacob used to mark the site where God spoke to him in a dream, and where Jacob vowed to return to worship God in exchange for God's care and protection
Jegar Sahadutha/Galeed "heap of witness"	Genesis 31:44–49	The pillar and heap of stones marking a boundary agreement between Laban and Jacob
Twelve stone pillars at the foot of Mount Sinai	Exodus 24:4	The pillars representing Israel's twelve tribes, erected at the confirmation of the Mosaic Covenant

Monuments and Memorials in the Bible (cont'd)

go to

be still
Psalm 46:10

The Memorial	Scripture	Significance
Twelve stones taken from Jordan River bed	Joshua 4:1–9	The memorial stones to help the Israelites remember how God allowed them to cross the Jordan River, on dry ground, into Canaan
Large stone under an oak tree at Shechem	Joshua 24:25–27	Stone erected by Joshua as a reminder that Israel had renewed its covenant to fear and follow the Lord
Ebenezer "stone of help"	1 Samuel 7:10–13	Stone erected by Samuel to commemorate God's help in defeating the Philistines
Absalom's Monument	2 Samuel 18:18	Pillar erected by Absalom to carry on his name in the absence of a son

patriarchs
godly men who played key roles in the early history of Israel

Stop, Look, and Listen

It's as important for Christians to remember and acknowledge what God does today as it was in the days of the **patriarchs**, or of the judges, or of the kings. However, there's no need to gather stones to remember God's deeds today. To keep track of God's activity:

apply it

- *Stop!* Life moves ahead at breakneck speed. There are meetings to attend, children to raise, calls to make, places to go. Only when you pause and accept God's invitation to be still do you have a chance to notice what He's doing in your life.

- *Look!* Just as a geologist can learn more about the composition of rocks and minerals through close examination, you can learn much about God's character and His work in your life when you search the world for evidence of His design and activity. God promises that when you are looking for Him, He won't hide: "And you will seek Me and find Me, when you search for Me with all your heart" (Jeremiah 29:13 NKJV).

- *Listen!* It's not always enough to stop and search the day's events for evidence of God's handiwork. It's also important to listen to the voice of the Lord Himself as He tells you the things He wants you to know.

- ***Write it down!*** Memories fail over time. That's why it's important to record prayers answered, challenges overcome, strength provided, and security sent in a prayer journal, a computer file, or even a daily calendar.

Charles Spurgeon

Fix your thoughts upon your God in connection with your-selves; and, while we think of Samuel piling the stones and saying, "Hitherto hath the Lord helped us," let us lay the emphasis upon the last word and say, "Hitherto hath the Lord helped US," and if you can put it in the singular, and say, "Hitherto hath the Lord helped ME," so much the better.[8]

Chapter Wrap-Up

- The people of Israel decided to retrieve the Ark of the Covenant from Shiloh in a misguided effort to ensure God would guarantee them victory over the Philistines.

- The Israelites celebrated the arrival of the Ark at their battle camp so loudly that the Philistines heard the commotion, stormed Israel's camp, killed thirty thousand soldiers—including Eli's sons—and captured the Ark.

- The capture of the Ark represented the absence of God's continual provision and protection of His people.

- The Philistines took their trophy from Ebenezer to Ashdod, where they placed it in the temple of their pagan agriculture or fertility god, Dagon, only to discover the first morning that their god had fallen off its base and the second morning that it had broken into pieces.

- The Lord struck the people of Ashdod with a painful plague, prompting them to decide to return the Ark to the people of Israel.

- The Ark remained in Kirjath Jearim for twenty years, and the people finally decided to turn back to God. The next time the Philistines attacked, they were routed by the Israelites; to commemorate the occasion, Samuel erected a monument named Ebenezer.

Study Questions

1. What was the cause of the enmity between Israel and the Philistines?

2. What happened when the Israelites launched an attack on the Philistines without asking for God's guidance?

3. Why was retrieving the Ark of the Covenant from Shiloh a misguided effort?

4. What are some ways people try to manipulate God today?

5. How did the Israelites' plan to bring God's presence to the battlefront by bringing the Ark along backfire?

6. What happened when Eli heard the news of the deaths of his sons and the capture of the Ark?

7. What did the capture of the Ark represent to the people of Israel?

8. What happened to the Ark once it was in the Philistines' hands?

9. When the Ark was returned, what did the men of Beth Shemesh do?

10. What happened when the Israelites finally decided to turn back to God?

Part Two
ISRAEL'S FIRST KING

Chapter Highlights:
• A Distraught Prophet
• Fair Warning!
• The High Cost of a King
• The People's Choice
• A Lesson in Contrasts

1 Samuel 8–9:
A Nation Demands a King

Let's Get Started

Some things—and some people—never change. Chapter 2 of this book opened with the people of Israel attempting to manipulate God by moving the Ark of the Covenant around as if it were a rabbit's foot or four-leaf clover instead of a holy vessel. As this chapter opens, it doesn't seem that too many things are any different. The sons of the aging Samuel, much like the sons of Eli, chose not to follow in the ways of their father, leaving Israel in turmoil once again. And just as the Israelites had thought the Ark of the Covenant could guarantee their victory in battle, they now assumed that having a king "like the rest of the nations" would become their ticket to political security and prosperity. Like an unyielding teen demanding a new privilege simply because everyone else is doing it, the people of Israel stubbornly insisted on having it their way.

go to

turned from idol worship
1 Samuel 7

Beersheba
city at the southern-most point of the Promised Land

"We'll Have What They're Having"

1 SAMUEL 8:1–5 *Now it came to pass when Samuel was old that he made his sons judges over Israel. The name of his firstborn was Joel, and the name of his second, Abijah; they were judges in **Beersheba**. But his sons did not walk in his ways; they turned aside after dishonest gain, took bribes, and perverted justice. Then all the elders of Israel gathered together and came to Samuel at Ramah, and said to him, "Look, you are old, and your sons do not walk in your ways. Now make us a king to judge us like all the nations." (NKJV)*

Samuel had enjoyed much success as judge of Israel. Clearly, God's hand had been on him—as well as on Israel under his leadership. The nation had finally <u>turned from idol worship</u> and had seen peace restored.

However, as Samuel entered his senior years, things began to take a turn for the worse once again. Realizing that his age would soon hinder his ability to serve as Israel's judge, Samuel had appointed his two sons, Joel and Abijah, as judges to follow him. He undoubtedly hoped that they loved the Lord as much as he did, and that they would want to serve the people in a way that would honor God. But the opposite turned out to be true. Samuel's sons went down the wrong path in much the same way as Eli's sons, Hophni and Phinehas, had done. Rather than walking in Samuel's footsteps of integrity, faithfulness, and fairness, Joel and Abijah opted for the get-rich-quick route by taking bribes and dispensing justice to the highest bidders. While the sins of Eli's sons had centered on religious and sexual immorality, the sins of Samuel's sons seemed to spring from materialism and manipulation.

The boys' behavior made Israelites feel uneasy. They had been able to trust Samuel to lead them in the right way, God's way.

The judges did just what their titles implied: administered justice when disputes arose among the people of Israel. The people needed to know that their judges were fair! But with corrupt judges at the helm, how could they be confident of the Lord's blessing on their nation?

Outside of Samuel's family, political troubles were brewing as well.

what others say

Richard D. Phillips

To the west, the Philistines were pressing in once more, and to the east the Ammonites—age-old enemies, though cousins of the Israelites—were on the move. In response to these external threats, the people became uneasy and concern began to spread.[1]

A Loaded Statement

The Israelites' solution seemed simple enough: Solve the twofold dilemma of corrupt leadership and political peril with one act: "Now make us a king to judge us like all the nations" (1 Samuel 8:5 NKJV).

The demand was far more complicated than it seemed.

- Israel was demanding a radical change in its government. God himself had been Israel's king since the **Exodus**, and had provided hands-on leadership of Israel through the system of judges. The Israelites weren't simply asking God for a new man to lead them; they were insisting on an overhaul of the structure of their government. God had in fact planned for Israel to one day be <u>ruled by a king</u>, but that day had not yet come. This demand was far ahead of God's timing.

- Israel was demonstrating disdain for—rather than delight in—its position as <u>God's chosen nation</u>.

ruled by a king
Deuteronomy
17:14–20

God's chosen nation
Leviticus 20:26;
Numbers 23:9

Exodus
Israel's deliverance
from slavery

what others say

Richard D. Phillips

Established through Moses as a theocracy, Israel was to stand apart from the surrounding nations by the fact it had no king but God Himself . . . Samuel's vision for the future arose from his understanding of Israel's distinct identity—its past, its legacy, its particular capabilities and calling. The people's vision, however, was framed by the fears of the present; not by a critical examination of their hearts, but by a desire to conform to whatever seemed to be working well for others. One was motivated by courage and conviction, the others by fear and conformity.[2]

John Wesley

"Be like"—What stupidity! It was their happiness that they were unlike all other nations.[3]

"If the Other Nations Jumped Off a Cliff, Would You Do That Too?"

In the 1950s, a researcher named Solomon Asch tried to measure people's desire to conform, or blend in, with those around them. He designed a test that asked participants to match lines of different lengths on two cards—an easy challenge with an obvious answer. The catch: He required participants to take the test in a room full of people, several of whom he had secretly instructed to give the wrong answer. Amazingly, about three-fourths of the people he tested gave an incorrect answer at least once in order to conform to the group.

key point

That innate desire to be like everyone else was in full force among the population of Israel during Samuel's time. They found it far more comfortable to blend in with the crowd by having a similar government than to stand out by having a unique one. However, throughout the Scriptures, God makes it known that being part of His family means dancing to the beat of a different drum.

God's people, like the nation Israel, are to be set apart as foreigners, strangers, or "aliens" in the world. Forming "friendship with the world," James stated in the book that bears his name, "is enmity with God. Whoever therefore wants to be a friend of the world makes himself an enemy of God" (James 4:4 NKJV).

The People of God Stand Out from the Rest of the World

When it comes to . . .	The world says . . .	The Christian says . . .
Wealth	How much money and how many things we have are what matter most.	Who we are in relationship to Christ is what matters most.
Conformity	Blending in is best.	Standing out is the only way to stand up for Christ.
Knowledge	Knowledge is power.	God's wisdom is power.
Perspective	Here and now are all that matter.	Here and now matter only in their relationship to eternity.
Treatment of others	One's self should come first.	Others should come first.
Dependence	Independence is the only way.	Dependence on God is the only way.
Morality	What's right depends on the time, the people, and the circumstances.	What's right depends on what God says is right.
Hospitality	It's important to impress people.	It's more important to serve people.
Religion	There are many paths to God.	There is only one way to God.

A Distraught Prophet

1 SAMUEL 8:6–9 But the thing displeased Samuel when they said, "Give us a king to judge us." So Samuel prayed to the LORD. And the LORD said to Samuel, "Heed the voice of the people in all that they say to you; for they have not rejected you, but they have rejected Me, that I should not reign over them. According to all the works which they have done since the day that I brought them up out of Egypt, even to this day—with which they have forsaken Me and served other gods—so they are doing to you also. Now therefore, heed their voice. However, you shall solemnly forewarn them, and show them the behavior of the king who will reign over them." (NKJV)

Samuel might have been getting old, but he was still very much a man of God. The people's request to remove God from His place of leadership in their nation, to seat instead a mere mortal on the throne, must have sent chills down the prophet's spine. He immediately voiced his concerns to his Lord, and the Lord, faithful as ever to His beloved servant, answered right away.

Conversation of a Lifetime

The conversation that had started between the Lord and Samuel in the temple when Samuel was a young boy was now as animated and active as ever! This discussion makes it evident that the dialogue between God and man had continued through the years—a sign of the intimacy of their relationship. It also offers a vivid outline of Samuel's order of priorities. When presented with disturbing news, Samuel's first response was not to argue with the demanding people, not to grumble, not to complain to his friends, and not to host a pity party with the theme of "why me?" Instead, he headed straight for a one-on-one with God.

First Things First

Why did the people's request so disturb Samuel? Their dissatisfaction with their current situation might have cast doubts in Samuel's mind about his job performance as a judge. "If I were doing my job well," he may have wondered, "then why are they so unhappy?" Further, he may have felt a sense of guilt over the fact that his sons had not chosen to walk in his ways. Either way, the Lord looked into Samuel's heart as He listened to the man's words, and decided to take care of first things first. He reassured Samuel by setting the record straight about who was *really* getting the boot—God Himself! In other words, he was saying, "Don't take this personally, Samuel. This is not about you, it's about Me."

Fair Warning!

The Lord gave Samuel the go-ahead to let the people have it their way—but not without giving them fair warning about exactly what it was they were asking.

Remember, God wants a close relationship and companionship with people, but He does not force Himself or His will on anyone! He simply offers the invitation and opens the door. It's up to each individual to decide whether to accept the invitation and go through that door. The entire Bible retells the same basic story of God inviting people into relationships with Him. It is filled with promises of what life—and the afterlife—will be like for those who say "yes" to God, as well as with warnings of what life—and the afterlife—will be like for those who say "no."

The High Cost of a King

Many times the world offers tempting delights that ultimately take away from—rather than enhance—a person's freedom, pleasure, or quality of life. This was one of those times. God wanted Samuel to explain to the Israelites exactly what they would be paying in exchange for putting a king on their throne. The price tag turned out to be quite hefty.

The Bottom Line—More Differences Between Life Under Judges or Kings

Concerning the . . .	Under a Judge . . .	Under a King . . .
Military	A volunteer army is assembled; supplies are provided by families of soldiers as needed.	A standing army is drafted and trained; Israelite sons must build and maintain an inventory of military equipment.
Housing	There is no palace to maintain, and no staff is required to serve the king or the administration.	A palace must be established; a staff is required to maintain the palace and serve the king and his administration. Israelite daughters may be taken from Israelite households to serve the king.
Taxes	No taxes are necessary because no funds are needed when there is no palace to operate.	Taxes are required to finance the palace and fill it with furnishings, and his table with food fit for a king.
Personal Life	People enjoy personal freedom.	People become subject to the rule of a king, who may or may not have their best interests in his own mind.

"We're Putting Our Feet Down"

1 SAMUEL 8:19–22 Nevertheless the people refused to obey the voice of Samuel; and they said, "No, but we will have a king over us, that we also may be like all the nations, and that our king may judge us and go out before us and fight our battles." And Samuel heard all the words of the people, and he repeated them in the hearing of the LORD. So the LORD said to Samuel, "Heed their voice, and make them a king." And Samuel said to the men of Israel, "Every man go to his city." (NKJV)

How saddened Samuel must have been that the people stubbornly insisted on having it their way—even after he had spelled out the consequences. Whether or not God approved, they wanted a king with a passion that blinded them to the consequences certain to come.

The people were seeking a physical solution—a new king—to a spiritual problem—their lack of faith in God. He had promised Israel that He would do their fighting for them; if they would simply trust Him, they didn't need to worry about threats from their enemies:

- "The LORD will fight for you, and you shall hold your peace" (Exodus 14:14 NKJV).

Benjamin
the smallest of the
12 tribes of Israel

- "The LORD your God, who goes before you, He will fight for you, according to all He did for you in Egypt before your eyes." (Deuteronomy 1:30 NKJV)

- "Do not be afraid, nor be dismayed; be strong and of good courage, for thus the LORD will do to all your enemies against whom you fight" (Joshua 10:25 NKJV).

It's natural for humans to try to attempt to solve spiritual problems with physical answers. For example, if we're harboring feelings of insecurity, we may turn to food for comfort. If we have feelings of low self-worth, we may seek inappropriate romantic relationships. If we are fearful, we may try to control everything within our power. But the Lord tells us that there is only one solution to our spiritual problems: a relationship with Him. He is our only source of confidence, value, and courage.

The People's Choice

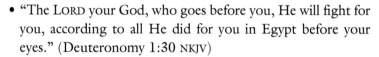

the big picture

1 Samuel 9:1–9

While the people of Israel awaited their new king, Samuel set out on an unusual manhunt. An impressive king was what the Israelites wanted, so an impressive king he would find. But before he had a chance to do so, the prospect whom God would choose to fill the bill was already roaming the countryside—conducting a search of his own. The tall, strong, and handsome Saul, a twenty-something farmer who came from a powerful Benjamite family, was out with his servant looking for his father's donkeys. The pair hiked through mountainous terrain and across the countryside, only to find no donkeys anywhere. Finally, Saul feared the search had gone on so long that his dad might start worrying more about him than the livestock. So he suggested they pack up and head home. But the servant had a better idea. He had heard God's prophet was in town and recommended asking him for directions.

Saul was born in an unnamed city in the land settled by the tribe of **Benjamin**, which was centrally located within Israel. The people of this tribe were known for their ferocity, and for their skill at using slings and arrows. Saul's father, Kish, was a successful farmer whose livestock holdings earned his family respect. For these reasons the people of Israel would most likely think this man worthy to call their king.

Bumbling Fool or Wise Guy?

Saul's errand was noble enough: donkeys were valuable livestock and well worth the time and effort it might take to find them. However, many scholars regard him as a bumbling fool who, from the word "go" was a picture of a misguided man, almost comical in his ignorance. The first episode of Saul's life given in Scripture shows him looking for something he cannot find, and lacking a sense of direction.

something to ponder

what others say

J. Vernon McGee

I know that the Lord has a sense of humor . . . Saul is out looking for the asses of his father, and the asses of Israel are looking for a king. They are bound to get together, friend, and they do. The Lord must smile when a thing like this takes place. What a commentary on the human race![5]

Robert Alter

Saul's entire story, until the night before his death on the battlefield, is a story about the futile quest for knowledge of an inveterately ignorant man.[6]

Appointment with Destiny

1 SAMUEL 9:17–20 *So when Samuel saw Saul, the LORD said to him, "There he is, the man of whom I spoke to you. This one shall reign over My people." Then Saul drew near to Samuel in the gate, and said, "Please tell me, where is the seer's house?"*

Samuel answered Saul and said, "I am the seer. Go up before me to the high place, for you shall eat with me today; and tomorrow I will let you go and will tell you all that is in your heart. But as for your donkeys that were lost three days ago, do not be anxious about them, for they have been found. And on whom is all the desire of Israel? Is it not on you and on all your father's house?" (NKJV)

Noah
Genesis 6:11–7:5

Abraham
Genesis 12:1–5

Moses' mother
Exodus 2:1–10

Many lessons in the far-reaching story of David surface in a series of contrasts. While most of those contrasts will come later, in comparisons between Saul and David, here is an interesting one between Samuel and Saul. Samuel, God's man, knew exactly whom he was speaking to, yet Saul, the people's man, had no clue he was speaking to the very person he was seeking. Further, a "vision" vs. "blindness" thread picked up here seems to continue where it left off after Eli's spiritual blindness caused him to mistake Hannah's despair for drunkenness.

"I Knew You Were Coming So I Baked a . . . Thigh"

Don't miss this! God includes an amazing lesson about what it means to live in faith even as the camera lens begins panning away from Samuel, onto Saul, who now becomes a key player in the story of David.

God had told Samuel the day before that the next day he would show him the man for the job. So, before the prophet even met the king-to-be, Samuel acted upon God's word as truth: He went ahead and set a place for Saul at the table, told the cook to prepare and set aside a special cut of meat, and invited thirty guests. To him, what God said was inevitable rather than "possible"—or even "probable."

God gives this example—and many others—of people who walk by faith, including <u>Noah</u>, who built an ark before a drop of rain fell; <u>Abraham</u>, who packed up his household and started walking to Canaan, the Promised Land, even before he had ever even seen the place; and <u>Moses' mother</u>, who placed her infant son in a tiny basket in the river before she could even comprehend how he might be saved.

Chapter Wrap-Up

- Rather than walking in Samuel's footsteps of integrity, faithfulness, and fairness, his sons, Joel and Abijah, were corrupt, making Israelites feel uneasy.

- The Israelites demanded a king like the other nations, a step that would radically change Israel's form of government. Purposely or not, it also demonstrated a certain amount of disdain for its position as God's chosen nation.

- The request to remove God from His place of leadership in their nation greatly distressed Samuel, who immediately prayed to the Lord for guidance.

- God reassured Samuel and gave him the go-ahead to let the people have their way.

- God warned the people, through Samuel, that their request would require a national draft, taxes, and subjugation to a king who might or might not have their best interests in mind.

- Samuel set out to find an impressive king who would satisfy the Israelites; he discovered tall, handsome Saul—a Benjamite—who had been roaming the countryside looking for his father's donkeys.

Study Questions

1. What were Samuel's sons like?

2. Why did their behavior matter to the Israelites?

3. What did the Israelites propose, and why?

4. What were the implications of their demand?

5. How did the request demonstrate lack of faith on the part of the Israelites?

6. How did Samuel respond to the people's request?

7. What circumstances brought Saul and Samuel together?

1 Samuel 10–12: Saul, First King of Israel

Let's Get Started

As the aging Samuel stepped into a supporting role in the epic of David's life, the young and striking Saul strode—or rather reluctantly shuffled, at first—to center stage. Last night Saul had received strange news from Samuel, whom he didn't know but who obviously knew him quite well. The old prophet had hinted that Saul was to become king of Israel, then had invited him to what turned out to be a most unusual evening. First he'd been seated at the head of the table at a dinner attended by thirty of the town's most prominent citizens. Then he had received the best cut of meat. Indeed—by the time the evening was over, it had seemed to Saul that everyone but he himself had known he would be coming that night!

The next morning, as 1 Samuel chapter 10 opens, circumstances were just as puzzling. Samuel had ushered Saul to the outskirts of town and sent away the servant so the pair could have some privacy.

"But why?" Saul must have wondered. The reality of his situation undoubtedly began to sink in as he felt the **anointing oil** trickle down the sides of his head and into his beard: He was being named Israel's first king. The designation would intimidate him at first, but by the end of the twelfth chapter of 1 Samuel, he would have a taste of success and respect.

anointing oil
substance used to set someone apart for special office

Appointing a King by Anointing a King

> 1 SAMUEL 10:1 *Then Samuel took a flask of oil and poured it on his head, and kissed him and said: "Is it not because the* LORD *has anointed you commander over His inheritance?"* (NKJV)

Anointing someone, which mainly involves pouring or sprinkling oil (usually olive oil) on someone, was a common practice in the Hebrew culture. Throughout the Bible, anointing is mentioned in several types of situations:

- *Everyday courtesy:* A host rubbed oil on a guest's head, bringing comfort to scalps dried by the harsh sun, as a <u>sign of hospitality</u>.
- *Official religious business:* Prophets, priests, and kings were anointed as part of their inauguration into office. The oil was a physical picture of God's spiritual hand of guidance and power "pouring out" on the anointed person's life.
- *Prophetic pointer:* The Messiah, whose name means "anointed one," was the promised <u>deliverer of Israel</u>. <u>Christ was anointed with the Holy Spirit</u> rather than with physical oil.
- *Spiritual significance:* <u>Christians are anointed</u> with the Holy Spirit when they put their faith in God.

Fragile Claim to Power

In the Bible, even the smallest details often carry great significance. For example, the container Samuel used to store the oil he would use to anoint the king was a flask. Most likely made of clay, the flask would have been brittle, or breakable, and not very long-lasting. It also would have been quite small—perhaps five inches or smaller in diameter. In contrast, the container Samuel would use to <u>anoint David</u>, the man after God's own heart, as Saul's successor would be the horn of an animal. That vessel was far more durable, held much more oil, and was a commonly recognized symbol of political power.

sign of hospitality
Luke 7:46

deliverer of Israel
Psalm 2:2;
Daniel 9:25–26

Christ was anointed with the Holy Spirit
Isaiah 61:1;
John 1:41, 32–33
Acts 4:27; 9:22;
10:38; 17:2–3;
18:4, 28

Christians are anointed
2 Corinthians 1:21

anoint David
1 Samuel 16:12–13

what others say

Matthew Henry

It was only a vial of oil that he anointed [Saul] with, the vessel brittle, because his kingdom would soon be cracked and broken, and the quantity small, because he had but little of the Spirit conferred upon him.[1]

A More Powerful Power

1 JOHN 2:27 *But the anointing which you have received from Him abides in you, and you do not need that anyone teach you.* (NKJV)

Just as an oil anointing empowered an ancient king to act in full confidence that he had God's authority and power behind him, the Holy Spirit's anointing empowers twenty-first-century Christians to act with that same kind of confidence. Individuals today don't typically need God's strength and power to establish kingdoms, provide for their people, or protect the borders of their land. But they do need God's supernatural strength and power to raise faithful families, provide love and encouragement to communities full of hurting people, and protect themselves from stumbling off God's good path and onto the more dangerous path the world has to offer.

How to tap into the resources the <u>Holy Spirit</u> offers in limitless quantities? There's no special trick, no effort required in order to try to pry the lid off the vial containing God's presence in order to release His help. The Spirit freely flows into a person's heart—permanently—the moment he or she begins a relationship with Christ.

apply it

<u>Signs, Signs, Signs</u>

the big picture

1 Samuel 10:2-10

As Saul raised his head and wiped the pungent drops of oil off his temple with the sleeve of his robe, Samuel might have sensed Saul's apprehension, disbelief, or confusion about what to do next. So he outlined three events the young man could expect over the next few hours:

1. On the road to **Rachel's tomb**, Saul and his servant would meet two men who would repeat the news that the lost donkeys had been found and that his father had started to worry about his son.
2. Upon reaching a large tree at Tabor, they would meet three men going up to worship God at **Bethel**. One man would be carrying three young goats; a second man, three loaves of bread; and a third, a skin of wine. The men would give Saul and his servant two loaves of bread.
3. They would arrive at a Philistine camp, where they would meet a rather expressive group of prophets. Then the real anointing of the Lord would take place: "Then the Spirit of the LORD will come upon you, and you will **prophesy** with them and be turned into another man" (1 Samuel 10:6 NKJV).

After the third sign had occurred, Saul was to go to Gilgal and wait for the prophet to join him with further instruction. As promised, all the events Samuel prophesied happened that day. Once Saul had been filled by the Holy Spirit, he began to prophesy right along with the rest of the prophets.

go to

Holy Spirit
John 3:34

Rachel's tomb
landmark located at Zelzah on the border between Benjamin and Ephraim

Bethel
city of Canaan about 12 miles north of modern-day Jerusalem

prophesy
speak God's words

Benjamite
from the tribe of
Benjamin, which
occupied the small-
est territory of the
12 tribes of Israel

David Guzik

This reception of the Holy Spirit was the real anointing. The oil
poured out on Saul's head was just a picture of this. A gallon
of oil could have been put on his head, but if the Spirit of the
LORD did not come upon him, it would have meant nothing![2]

The three signs Samuel gave signified three important truths about
God's provision for the man He was placing on Israel's throne:

1. God would take care of Saul's business needs (illustrated by the
   resolution of the donkey issue).

2. God would satisfy Saul's physical needs (illustrated by the gift of
   the loaves of bread).

3. God would fill Saul's spiritual needs (illustrated by the movement of the Holy Spirit into his heart).

apply it

God promises to fill all of our needs too! All we need to do is ask:
"And my God shall supply all your need according to His riches in
glory by Christ Jesus" (Philippians 4:19 NKJV).

Is This the Saul We Know?

1 SAMUEL 10:11–12 *And it happened, when all who knew him
formerly saw that he indeed prophesied among the prophets, that
the people said to one another, "What is this that has come upon
the son of Kish? Is Saul also among the prophets?" Then a man
from there answered and said, "But who is their father?" Therefore it became a proverb: "Is Saul also among the prophets?"*
(NKJV)

Saul was striking in appearance, and had come from a prominent
Benjamite family. Apart from those distinctions, he had led quite an
ordinary life. Apparently spiritual fervor hadn't up to this point been
one of his most notable characteristics. So when the people from his
hometown who had known him since "way back when" saw Saul
hanging out with the local prophets, they were shocked. So shocked,
in fact, that they coined a new phrase—loaded with sarcasm—to add
to the Hebrew lexicon: "Is Saul also among the prophets?"

Mizpah
a city about 7 miles
north of Jerusalem

what others say

Matthew Henry

It became a proverb, commonly used in Israel, when they would express their wonder at a bad man's either becoming good, or at least being found in good company.[3]

He Missed His Chance to Make a Good First Impression

the big picture

1 Samuel 10:13–23

When Saul left the company of the prophets he headed home, where his uncle interrogated him about what he had been doing while traveling. Saul offered only sketchy details and deliberately left out the part about his having been anointed as Israel's king. Then Samuel gathered the people together to worship at **Mizpah**, where he prepared the people to receive their new king. However, after introducing Saul with much pomp and ceremony, the chosen one was nowhere to be found . . . until the Lord suggested the people look for him under the baggage.

If it hadn't been such a serious occasion, the scenario might have been funny: The valiant leader Israel had longed for just couldn't bring himself to face his new subjects! Whether out of shyness or fear, all he could do was run for cover; he dove under the piles of supplies in the wagon train that likely surrounded the encampment rather than rising up and standing before the people he would lead.

what others say

Richard D. Phillips

What had driven him to the place of refuge among the baggage? It is not unlikely that it was the look on the faces of the people as they awaited their save-the-day executive . . . They might have been sheep, but they were not a flock longing to follow their shepherd out into the fields; rather they were sheep who expected to stay snug in their pens while the new king went out to face the wolves alone. It's hard, then, to blame Saul for hiding.[4]

Blessed If You Do, Cursed If You Don't

key point

Fear is often a first response to being called by God to step outside the boundaries of what's comfortable and familiar. Saul isn't alone in Scripture's roster of people who tried to avoid doing what the Lord instructed. Two other well-known God-dodgers would be:

- *Moses*—"B-b-but did You forget that I stutter, Lord?" When <u>God asked Moses</u> to lead the Israelites from slavery, the man tried to appeal to God's "better judgment" concerning his qualifications. He even presumed to suggest an alternative: "I have this brother, Aaron, who's a pretty good speaker."

- *Jonah*—"He'll never find me here!" Like Saul, **Jonah** tried to pull a disappearing act. When God told him to go preach to the people of Ninevah, Jonah went to Tarshish instead.

For a shortcut to finding out the ending of any God-dodger's story, read Deuteronomy 11:26–28, which says that people are blessed when they obey the Lord and cursed when they don't. Moses was blessed after he faced his fears and stepped forward in obedience. And Jonah was blessed after he shook the salt water from his ears and listened to God after all. Will Saul's story play out to be one of blessing or cursing? That's an important question to keep in mind as the study of his life continues.

Having a King 101

go to

God asked Moses
Exodus 3:9–4:13

Jonah
Jonah 1–4

Jonah
prophet of God

the big picture

I Samuel 10:24–27

Samuel, pointing to Saul, reminded the people that this was the man the Lord had given them, then he began to teach the people about their new form of government. He wrote down the regulations on a scroll and most likely placed it in the tabernacle, where it could be preserved for future reference.

Meanwhile, as Saul headed for his home he was accompanied by a small group of excited supporters. Others didn't accept Saul's leadership right away, which they demonstrated by refusing to give him gifts. He good-naturedly "held his peace" (v. 27 NKJV).

They Could Have Heard a Pin Drop

It's easy to imagine the awkward silence that must have hushed the crowd as they stood dumbfounded by the spectacle they had just witnessed. Saul had actually been hiding under the luggage! "What should we do next?" many may have wondered, as they watched a nervous smile spread across the face of the man God had given them in answer to their obstinate demand for a king. No doubt Saul's eyes, as well as the eyes of each Israelite present, gravitated to Samuel for a cue about how to salvage the situation. The prophet might have been tempted to shake his finger and issue a stern "I told you so" to the people standing in front of him looking like sheep without a shepherd. But instead, he resolutely finished the business the people had started by pointing to Saul and reminding them that the Lord had given them exactly what they had asked: "Do you see him whom the LORD has chosen, that there is no one like him among all the people?" (1 Samuel 10:24 NKJV). Then the prophet proceeded with the most pressing matter at hand: teaching a nation how to make the transition from a theocracy to a monarchy.

what others say

The King James Study Bible for Women

As God's judge and prophet, Samuel put in writing the ordinances of the newly established kingdom and deposited the document in the sanctuary of the Lord.[5]

Robert Alter

The reasonable inference is that the content of the speech is a reiteration of the dangers of encroachment of individual rights by the king that Samuel warned of in the assembly at Ramah.[6]

You Can't Please Everybody All the Time

By the time Samuel finished his lecture, some of the people were convinced things were going to be just fine, so they went home for the night. Others were so enthusiastic about their new king they followed at his heels as zealous supporters. Still others either weren't convinced they were ready for the demanding rules and regulations of submission to a king, or they wondered how they could hang their high hopes for a king on this man who had made such a cut-rate first impression.

private anointing
1 Samuel 10:1–8

public presentation
1 Samuel 10:13–23

Israel's acceptance of his kingship
1 Samuel 11:15

Nahash
Ammonite leader

A Graphic Incentive

the big picture

1 Samuel 11

The Ammonite leader, **Nahash**, led an attack against the Israelites at Jabesh Gilead, and made a gruesome proposal. If the Israelites surrendered, he would let them live with only one punishment: he would gouge out the right eye of every man. The Israelite leaders asked for a week to consider their options and told Saul what was going on. Angered by the threat, he butchered two oxen and sent messengers out with the carnage as a warning to those who dared oppose him. The ploy worked and the Ammonites were terrified. Saul rallied his troops, ambushed the enemy's camp, and won victory for his people. Saul gave God the credit for Israel's rescue, and Samuel seized the moment to gather the people to confirm Saul as king.

This victory marked the third and final phase of God's appointment of Saul as Israel's king:

1. The <u>private anointing</u> of Saul

2. The <u>public presentation</u> of Saul as king

3. The victory of Saul over the Ammonites, prompting <u>Israel's acceptance of his kingship</u>

In spite of his shaky start, Saul gained strong footing with this success against the Ammonites. The victory on the battlefield earned him the respect and support of his people. Perhaps even more significant, however, is the picture of good-versus-evil spiritual warfare illustrated by Saul's run-in with Nahash, whose name happens to mean "serpent." Nahash's attack against Israel illustrates Satan's attack against God's people. Just as Nahash wanted to conquer and cripple Israel, Satan wants to stir up conflict among believers and weaken them by distorting God's Word.

Samuel's Speech

1 SAMUEL 12:1–5 Now Samuel said to all Israel: "Indeed I have heeded your voice in all that you said to me, and have made a king over you. And now here is the king, walking before you; and I am old and grayheaded, and look, my sons are with you. I have walked before you from my childhood to this day. Here I am. Witness against me before the LORD and before His anointed: Whose ox have I taken, or whose donkey have I taken, or whom have I cheated? Whom have I oppressed, or from whose hand have I received any bribe with which to blind my eyes? I will restore it to you."

And they said, "You have not cheated us or oppressed us, nor have you taken anything from any man's hand."

Then he said to them, "The LORD is witness against you, and His anointed is witness this day, that you have not found anything in my hand."

And they answered, "He is witness." (NKJV)

Perhaps sensing the need to signal the end of his own season as leader of Israel—and to place Saul firmly at the helm—Samuel gave a long, powerful, touching address to the people of Israel. Then, as if putting His own exclamation mark into Samuel's sermon, God sent thunder and rain. If nothing else up to this point had convinced the people they had sinned by rejecting God and asking for a king, these fireworks seemed to do the trick. Awestruck by the power over nature demonstrated by God through Samuel, they began to beg for mercy. As tenderly as a parent comforts a remorseful child, Samuel then assured the people of Israel that everything would be okay. He reminded them that they knew how to behave, and if they would just do what they knew to be right, the Lord would not reject them because, after all, they were God's chosen people: "The LORD will not forsake His people, for His great name's sake, because it has pleased the LORD to make you His people" (1 Samuel 12:22 NKJV).

Samuel's outline for his speech that day might have looked something like this:

1. **The past:** Remind the people that my own tenure, as a man anointed by the Lord, has been marked by integrity and faithfulness. Recap God's faithfulness and care throughout our nation's history.

death
1 Samuel 25:1

love others
John 13:34

encourage others
1 Thessalonians 5:11

speak the truth
Ephesians 4:15

2. *The present:* Remind the people that their current situation is the result of their own actions. Acknowledge that the Lord is ultimately still in control.

3. *The future:* Explain that, although God has given them the king they wanted, when they wanted him, rather than giving them the one He would have hand-picked in His own timing, Israel could still receive God's blessings if they would only fear, serve, and obey the Lord. If they didn't, they could expect certain judgment!

Samuel's speech didn't mark the end of his public ministry. Just as he promised the Israelites in 1 Samuel 12:23, he continued to serve them as priest and prophet, never ceasing to pray for them and teach them God's Word until his <u>death</u>.

Things to Learn from Samuel

- <u>Love others</u> despite their sins, as he loved the people of Israel in spite of their sins, and as he loved Saul in spite of his.

- <u>Encourage others</u> to grow in their understanding of God's Word, as Samuel did through his ministry of service as priest, prophet and judge.

- <u>Speak the truth</u> regardless of personal feelings, as he did when he foretold the people he loved of God's judgment and condemnation of them.

Chapter Wrap-Up

- Samuel anointed Saul king in a visible symbol of God's power and guidance "pouring out" on the anointed person's life.

- After three signs predicted by Samuel had come to pass, Saul was filled by the Holy Spirit and began to prophesy, along with the rest of the prophets.

- When Samuel gathered the people together to prepare them to receive their new king, after introducing Saul with much pomp and ceremony, the chosen one was nowhere to be found. He was hiding under the baggage.

- Samuel reminded the people that this was the man the Lord had given them; then he began to teach the people about their new form of government. He wrote the regulations down on a scroll and most likely placed it in the tabernacle, where it could be kept safely and preserved for future reference.

- Nahash, the Ammonite leader, led an attack against the Israelites at Jabesh Gilead. Saul rallied his troops, ambushed the enemy's camp, and earned victory for his people, thus marking Israel's acceptance of his kingship.

- As Samuel addressed the people his speech was punctuated by thunder and rain, which convinced the people to repent of their sin in asking for a king.

Study Questions

1. Describe the significance of anointing.

2. What three events did Samuel tell Saul to expect over the next few hours after he was anointed?

3. How—and where—was Saul anointed a second time?

4. What offers a clue that Saul hadn't, until this point in his life, been widely recognized as a man of God?

5. What did Saul do when Samuel prepared the people to meet their new king?

6. What event helped bring about Saul's acceptance by the Israelites?

7. How did God "assist" Samuel when he gave his speech to the Israelites?

8. How did the people respond to Samuel's message?

Part Three
IN NAME ONLY

Chapter Highlights:
- When the Going Gets Tough, Hide?
- Enough Is Enough
- Saul's Kingship Cursed
- Out-of-Control King

1 Samuel 13-15: Saul Stumbles

Let's Get Started

The future was looking pretty bright for the good-looking boy who left his position on the family farm to fill a newly created job atop his nation's government. As king, Saul was in charge of the nation's military, politics, and economics. And he was expected to be a religious leader as well. All this might sound like a tall order for an ordinary man, but Saul wasn't an ordinary man. This man had been commissioned by God and anointed king by the nation's great judge and beloved prophet, Samuel.

As Samuel had suggested to those gathered at <u>Saul's coronation</u>, all Saul would need to do to achieve success was simply to go in "the good and the right way" (1 Samuel 12:23 NKJV). By doing so, and by influencing his people to do the same, he would be inviting the Lord Himself to be the nation's protector, defender, and provider. But failure on that front, Samuel had warned, would spell certain disaster for both the king and the nation. God would withdraw His caring hands and allow the people—king and all—to suffer the consequences. First Samuel chapters 13–15 detail which option Saul chose, and the impact his choice had on himself and his people.

go to

Saul's coronation
1 Samuel 12

Jonathan
Saul's son and David's best friend

When the Going Gets Tough, the Tough . . . Hide?

the big picture

1 Samuel 13:1-7

Two years into his reign, Saul had organized a standing army of 3,000 men, which he divided into two troops: 2,000 were stationed with Saul in Michmash and Bethel, and 1,000 were with his son, **Jonathan**, in Gibeah. Jonathan attacked the military post of the Philistines in Geba. However, as the Philistines turned out to fight, many of Saul's men turned into deserters: they ran to hide in caves and under bushes. They were terrified because they were far outnumbered. Saul and some of his other men stayed put, although they still trembled at what might happen next.

Does something about this passage seem familiar? Check out 1 Samuel 10:21–22: Perhaps Saul had passed on to his people his penchant for hiding from responsibility!

The Philistines: Still Threatening After All These Years

The Philistines and Israel apparently had formed a tenuous relationship that allowed them to live in relative harmony. Most scholars assume the reason behind this peaceful coexistence was Israel's willingness to remain under the Philistines' thumb. They even had allowed a few Philistine military posts to be established in their land. As long as the Israelites subjected themselves to the demands of the stronger and more technologically advanced people, they could live free of conflict and enslavement.

The fragile peace Israel enjoyed, however, wasn't the freedom God had in mind for His chosen people.

key point

Jonathan: "Enough Is Enough"

This is the first time readers meet Saul's son, Jonathan, who certainly makes a grand entry onto the pages of Scripture through this brave military move. Even though his father was king and he wouldn't have been required to perform any military feats to earn his stripes, he felt compelled to use his authority and resources to drive the Philistine bullies from the land.

Jonathan undoubtedly knew the attack would put him and his men in great danger; anyone around would assume the Israelites' bronze weapons couldn't begin to compete with the stronger and harder iron weaponry and equipment of the Philistines.

But even more evident than Jonathan's physical fearlessness was his spiritual fortitude. Whereas his father seemed to be motivated by fear—fear of what people might think of him, fear of failure, fear of responsibility—Jonathan was motivated by faith.

go to

pride
Proverbs 11:2;
13:10; 29:23

Bob Deffinbaugh

From what we know of Jonathan elsewhere, it seems that his actions are prompted by faith. After all, God gave this land to the Israelites and instructed them to drive out the nations dwelling in their land. Subjection to a foreign nation is depicted in Leviticus 26 and Deuteronomy 28–32 as a divine chastening for Israel's unbelief and disobedience. The king is not to facilitate the Israelites' subjection to the surrounding nations but is to be used of God to throw off their shackles (see 14:47–48). This will not happen unless the Israelites act to remove those who occupy their land. Saul seems reluctant and unwilling to "rock the boat." Jonathan seems unwilling to accept things as they are, and thus he leads his men in an attack.[1]

Saul Couldn't Wait Another Minute

1 SAMUEL 13:8–10 *Then he waited seven days, according to the time set by Samuel. But Samuel did not come to Gilgal; and the people were scattered from him. So Saul said, "Bring a burnt offering and peace offerings here to me." And he offered the burnt offering. Now it happened, as soon as he had finished presenting the burnt offering, that Samuel came; and Saul went out to meet him, that he might greet him.* (NKJV)

Saul was making a presumptuous move in presenting a burnt offering because sacrifices and offerings were to be presented by the high priest only. This single act highlighted at least three flaws in Saul's character:

1. *Disobedience*—God's law explicitly stated that only a priest from the tribe of Levi could offer a burnt offering.

2. *Arrogance*—Assuming that, as king, he had the authority to overrule or make an exception to God's law indicates that Saul had an overrated opinion of his position. That's <u>pride</u>, and it's a trait the Lord hates.

3. *Impatience*—Saul wasn't willing to wait for Samuel until the seventh day had ended; sometime in the middle of the seventh day he stopped checking the time, ceased tapping his toes, and said, "That's it! I'm not waiting another minute." To be impatient is to be foolish, in God's book; it demonstrates a lack of faith in God's timing.

Patience Please!

Sarah, Abraham's wife, is another example of impatience in action. God had promised her a child, but rather than wait for His perfect timing, she allowed her biological clock to push her ahead of God's agenda. She arranged for her servant, Hagar, to <u>conceive Abraham's child</u>. The result was tragic.

apply it

> **what others say**
>
> **Elizabeth George**
>
> Whenever we feel impatient, we must look again into the face of God, acknowledge Him, His wisdom, His ways, and His choices for our life, exhale . . . and do nothing, as we resist in patience. This is the kind of faith that makes patience grow.[2]

What's So Special About the System of Sacrifices and Offerings?

It's impossible to sense the full impact of Saul's sin without understanding how important the system of <u>sacrifices and offerings</u> was within God's relationship with His people. Adam and Eve, before **the Fall**, had lived in perfect harmony with God. The pair was sinless; as a result, they enjoyed unhindered fellowship with their holy Creator. But after the Fall, Adam, Eve—and by birthright, their children—were separated from God by that sin. From that point on, the only way for sin-tarnished people to approach a holy God was through the shedding of blood. This was accomplished through the ritual of sacrificing animals. Because God placed so much importance on properly conducting the sacrifices, He named a special line of priests, or holy men, who were to make sure His guidelines were carried out to the letter.

go to

conceive Abraham's child
Genesis 16:2

sacrifices and offerings
Leviticus 1–7

the Fall
disobedience of Adam and Eve

> **what others say**
>
> **Halley's Bible Handbook**
>
> This sacrificial system, of divine origin, was placed of God at the very center and heart of Jewish national life. Whatever its immediate applications and implications may have been to the Jews, the unceasing sacrifice of animals, and the never-ending glow of altar fires, beyond doubt, were designed of God, to burn into the consciousness of men a sense of their deep sinfulness, and to be an age-long picture of the coming

sacrifice of Christ, toward whom they pointed and in whom they were fulfilled.[3]

Saul offered two sacrifices:

1. A burnt offering represented payment for sins.

2. A peace offering represented thanksgiving for an answered prayer, sealed a vow, or expressed thanks for an unexpected blessing.

In presenting the burnt offering, Saul wasn't really paying for sins; he was acting in sin! And, he wasn't really giving thanks or sealing a vow; he was using the ritual as a "good luck charm." This was another example of man trying to manipulate God, much like when the Israelites had taken the <u>Ark of the Covenant into battle</u>.

Saul's Kingship Cursed

Ark of the Covenant into battle
1 Samuel 4:3–6

God's law
Deuteronomy 17:14–20

the big picture

1 Samuel 13:8–10

Later on the seventh day, as promised, Samuel approached the camp. When Samuel discovered what he had done, Saul rattled off a list of excuses:
1. "My people abandoned me."
2. "You weren't here yet."
3. "The Philistines were getting ready to attack."
In other words, "It was an emergency, Samuel! I had to do it!" But the prophet wasn't buying Saul's excuses. The king had known better: <u>God's law</u> called for kings to learn the law and to be submissive to priests as teachers of the law. So Samuel scolded Saul and pointed out his foolishness, pronouncing God's judgment and foretelling of a new king, a better king, to come: "The LORD has sought for Himself a man after His own heart, and the LORD has commanded him to be commander over His people, because you have not kept what the LORD commanded you" (1 Samuel 13:14 NKJV).

Samuel left and Saul stayed behind, a pitiful portrait of a desolate king and diminished army. The number of his soldiers had decreased from 3,000 to 600, and they had only farm tools they could use to fight the Philistines, who were armed with their state-of-the-art weaponry.

The kingdom the Lord would have made everlasting for an obedient servant was to end for Saul because of his refusal to obey the Lord.

obedience
Romans 6:16

righteousness
being sinless in
God's eyes

what others say

Adam Clarke

We see, in this chapter, Israel brought to as low a state as they were under Eli; when they were totally discomfited, their priests slain, their ark taken, and the judge dead. After that, they rose by the strong hand of God; and in this way they are now to rise, principally by means of David, whose history will soon commence.[4]

The Value of the Law

Not only are the laws and guidelines God gives in the Bible designed to protect us and keep us safe, but they are also a means God can use to test our obedience. If He sees that we are obedient, then He will bless us, and if He sees that we aren't, He may withhold blessings, stop using us to do His work, or continue to send additional tests our way until we learn—the hard way—that <u>obedience</u> is the first step toward **righteousness**.

Jonathan: He Just Did It!

1 SAMUEL 14:8–14 *Then Jonathan said, "Very well, let us cross over to these men, and we will show ourselves to them. If they say thus to us, 'Wait until we come to you,' then we will stand still in our place and not go up to them. But if they say thus, 'Come up to us,' then we will go up. For the LORD has delivered them into our hand, and this will be a sign to us."*

So both of them showed themselves to the garrison of the Philistines. And the Philistines said, "Look, the Hebrews are coming out of the holes where they have hidden." Then the men of the garrison called to Jonathan and his armorbearer, and said, "Come up to us, and we will show you something."

Jonathan said to his armorbearer, "Come up after me, for the LORD has delivered them into the hand of Israel." And Jonathan climbed up on his hands and knees with his armorbearer after him; and they fell before Jonathan. And as he came after him, his armorbearer killed them. That first slaughter which Jonathan and his armorbearer made was about twenty men within about half an acre of land. (NKJV)

What a frightened existence Saul was living! The towering, chosen king had become a cowering, rejected one who was still hiding out—this time under a pomegranate tree instead of a baggage pile. Saul seemed oblivious to the responsibility of his high calling and his role in God's plans for Israel. He seemed instead to be interested only in how events would affect him. As a result he was living under a curse. He had been told his days as king were numbered, but he didn't know the timeline. Each time he heard footsteps in the distance, the sound of the snapping twigs surely raised the hair on his neck: "Is that a Philistine coming to kill me? Is Samuel sneaking up on me to dispense God's justice?"

The noblest position in the nation was filled by a fearful man with only his own best interest at heart!

what others say

Matthew Henry

> Those can never think themselves safe that see themselves cast out of God's protection.[5]

In stark contrast to his father, Jonathan lived out the credo: Just do it! He wouldn't be satisfied unless he was doing something—*anything*—to move forward. He was well aware of God's plans for the nation and was determined to take an active part. He seemed unfazed by threats to his personal safety. He was sure of his position—not as a prince of Israel, but as a child of God. Instead of living in fear, he lived on the lookout for opportunities to count on the God he knew and loved—even when those opportunities placed him between the rocks and hard places of the enemy's camp.

Jonathan's "Let's go!" attitude is a spiritually proactive one for Christians to take.

apply it

A Failproof Safety Net

One of the best benefits of following God is the confidence of being in His care. Today's world, with its safety helmets and seat belts, seems far removed from the violent world familiar to the ancient Israelites. But plenty of reasons for fear continue to abound, from seemingly incurable illnesses to things like violent crimes and natural disasters.

go to

meat with blood
Leviticus 3:17;
17:10–14

The safety net God stretches under His people comprises many promises, including:

- Safety (Psalm 4:8; Proverbs 29:25)
- Protection (Psalm 34:7)
- Provision (Psalm 23:1)

An Out-of-Control King

1 SAMUEL 14:28–30 *Then one of the people said, "Your father strictly charged the people with an oath, saying, 'Cursed is the man who eats food this day.'" And the people were faint.*

But Jonathan said, "My father has troubled the land. Look now, how my countenance has brightened because I tasted a little of this honey. How much better if the people had eaten freely today of the spoil of their enemies which they found! For now would there not have been a much greater slaughter among the Philistines?" (NKJV)

God might have rescued the Israelites from obliteration by the Philistines that day, but Saul wouldn't allow the soldiers a victory party—at least not a catered one. On threat of a curse, he had forbidden the soldiers to eat anything, not even to have a taste of food even though they were tired and hungry. And they weren't finished chasing the Philistines out of their land yet. Jonathan didn't get the message, however, and was delighted to lap up some nourishment from a dripping honeycomb. Told of his father's oath, Jonathan dismissed it as nonsense. Later that day, the troops pushed the Philistines even farther away. When the eating taboo was lifted, the famished men began to slaughter and eat the livestock their enemy had left behind, disobeying God's prohibition against eating <u>meat with blood</u>.

what others say

Robert Alter

As we shall have occasion to see later in the David narrative, it was a fairly common practice (though by no means an automatic one) for fighting men to take on themselves a vow of abstinence from food, in order to enter the battle in what amounted to a state of dedicated ritual purity. But Saul in this instance makes a miscalculation, imposing a fast on hungry men, in an effort to force the hand of divinity.[6]

Tripping Others Up

Although the soldiers were accountable for their own sin, Saul, as their leader, had a hand in it too. The Bible is explicit in stating that we are responsible for not only our own spiritual behavior, but for helping keep the people around us away from sin as well:

- Matthew 18:7: "Woe to the world because of offenses! For offenses must come, but woe to that man by whom the offense comes!" (NKJV).
- Romans 14:13: "Therefore let us not judge one another anymore, but rather resolve this, not to put a stumbling block or a cause to fall in our brother's way" (NKJV).
- 1 Corinthians 8:9: "But beware lest somehow this liberty of yours become a stumbling block to those who are weak" (NKJV).

In the remainder of 1 Samuel 14, Saul's sins kept piling up. After he had scolded his men for their sin against God, he ordered a large stone to be rolled in so they could properly kill the animals, thus building an altar for offering sacrifices. The king planned another attack on the Philistines that night, but before that he seemed determined to settle Jonathan's guilt in the honey-tasting crime. Saul was ready to have his son killed, but the people intervened. Even so, Saul continued to expand his kingdom to the south (Edom), east (Ammon and Moab), north (Zobah), and west (Philistia).

Attacking the Amalekites

the big picture

1 Samuel 15

God told Saul through Samuel to attack the **Amalekites**. The instructions were explicit: the king was to show no mercy; he was to kill all the men, women, children, and livestock. Saul gathered his men—now totaling 200,000 foot soldiers plus 10,000 others from Judah—and led the attack. However, instead of leaving total destruction in his wake, as God had instructed, Saul opted to spare Agag, the Amalekite king. He also kept the best livestock.

Amalek massacre
Exodus 17:8–16

Sinai wilderness
Numbers 14:39–45

Amalekites
nomadic tribe of people who were the first to attack Israel after the Exodus

The order for total destruction was in response to the <u>Amalek massacre</u> of the Israelites. The Amalekites had been the first people to attack the Israelites after their exodus. They later attacked Israel again, forcing them back into the <u>Sinai wilderness</u>.

Robert Alter

There is a morally scandalous pairing in the selective massacre Saul and his troops perpetrate: they kill all the defective animals and every man, woman, child and infant, while sparing the good, edible animals and the king (perhaps with the idea that some further profit can be extracted from him).[7]

God Regrets

1 SAMUEL 15:10–11 *Now the word of the LORD came to Samuel, saying, "I greatly regret that I have set up Saul as king, for he has turned back from following Me, and has not performed My commandments." And it grieved Samuel, and he cried out to the LORD all night. (NKJV)*

God's expression of regret didn't mean He had changed His mind and wished He had done things differently.

key point

God's ways are perfect and He makes no mistakes. Rather, it was a cry of sorrow that one of His children—Saul, whom He loved in spite of his disobedience—had continued to rebel against His guidelines. Because Samuel was so close to God, whatever grieved God also grieved him.

The beautiful picture of the relationship between God and Samuel, which sometimes recedes into the background, comes back into view here. Whatever cares Samuel had, he took them directly to the Lord: "Therefore humble yourselves under the mighty hand of God, that He may exalt you in due time, casting all your care upon Him, for He cares for you" (1 Peter 5:6–7 NKJV).

A Scathing Scolding

1 Samuel 15:12–23

Samuel got up early the next morning to visit Saul, who had the audacity to set up a monument to himself. He greeted Samuel by proclaiming that he had carried out God's instructions. But hearing the sheep bleating and the oxen lowing, Samuel asked why the livestock were there. Saul then proceeded to brag on his partial obedience to God's command. When Samuel scolded Saul, he acted like an obstinate child and once again tried to shift the blame. "I did what I was supposed to do; it was the others who took the plunder."

Samuel then launched into a scathing speech:

> Has the LORD as great delight in burnt offerings
> and sacrifices,
>
> As in obeying the voice of the LORD?
> Behold, to obey is better than sacrifice,
> And to heed than the fat of rams.
> For rebellion is as the sin of witchcraft,
> And stubbornness is as iniquity and idolatry.
> Because you have rejected the word of the LORD,
> He also has rejected you from being king.
> (1 Samuel 15:22–23 NKJV)

Saul's Crimes

The words offered by Samuel listed Saul's crimes:

- Saul had failed to obey God—even though the Lord values obedience over ritual.
- Saul had demonstrated rebellion—an attitude the Lord places on par with witchcraft.
- Saul had shown stubbornness—a trait as wicked in the Lord's eyes as sin and idolatry.
- Saul had rejected the word of God—an action that removed him from God's favor.

what others say

Beth Moore

Samuel compares rebellion to the sin of divination or witchcraft. The comparison seems puzzling until we consider that rebellion is a means by which we attempt to set the course of our futures. We try to choose our own futures by our independent actions. Divination attempts to foretell or sway the future. In the same verse, God likens arrogance to the evil of idolatry. When we are arrogant, who becomes God in our lives?[8]

A Confession with a Catch

the big picture

I Samuel 15:24–35

Finally, Saul offered Samuel an insincere admission of guilt, quickly noting that, yes, he had sinned, but with good reason: he had been afraid of the people. With that curt confession, he asked for pardon and invited Samuel to go with him to worship the Lord. Samuel, however, refused to go. As he walked away, Saul grabbed and tore the hem of the prophet's robe. Saul continued to beg, and Samuel finally agreed to stay. The prophet then followed through on Saul's unfinished business by killing Agag. Samuel then left Saul and never came back to see him again.

People-Pleasing Never Pays Off!

The fear of other people or what other people would think drove two of Saul's actions in the above passage:

1. He used his fear of other people as an excuse to disobey God.

2. He used his fear of what other people would think to persuade Samuel to go with him to worship.

what others say

Adam Clarke

This was the best excuse he could make for himself; but had he feared GOD more, he need have feared the PEOPLE less.[9]

Os Hillman

Saul's fear and insecurity made him more afraid of the people and what they thought than of God. At the core of Saul's disobedience was fear of losing control. That fear of losing control led to partial obedience and the loss of his reign as king. How many of us are in danger of losing God's blessing due to partial obedience? How many of us have such a need to control people and circumstances that we fail to fully walk in obedience to God's voice in our lives? Saul provides a great lesson for us as workplace believers. The need to overcontrol things around us can prevent us from receiving all that God has for us.[10]

Samuel: Spineless—or Savvy Spin Doctor?

When Samuel decided to stay and worship with Saul rather than walking away, was he demonstrating weakness or self-control? Up to this point in Samuel's life, he had given no reason for anyone to believe his actions were anything but wise and deliberate. Scholars suggest two possible scenarios supporting his decision to yield to Saul's pleas:

1. He truly loved Saul and accompanied him because of this affection.

2. He wanted to demonstrate unity among the leadership and thus deter any unrest among the Israelites.

Both scenarios most likely are true. Samuel did love Saul, and was terribly disappointed by how the king's behavior had deteriorated. He naturally would want to accompany his friend and counsel him in the hope that he might change his ways.

However, Samuel also knew God's words concerning Saul's kingship would come to pass: Saul's reign was going to end. Samuel just didn't know when, or how. In the meantime, the ingredients for political calamity were easy to spot:

- Israel's current king was on a downward spiral of immorality, unfaithfulness, unpredictability, arrogance, and instability.

- The next king of Israel wasn't even in view yet.

- The Israelites had barely had the chance to adjust to life under a monarchy. The situation was volatile, to say the least. So, as Israel's high priest, prophet, and judge, part of Samuel's responsibility involved becoming what would be called today a "spin doctor." In order to keep circumstances as peaceful as possible, he needed to do some deliberate "damage control." (He should be used to it by now, considering he had been smoothing the wrinkles caused by Saul's destructive decisions since the day the new king had hidden in the baggage!)

While Samuel trusted God to work out the details of removing Saul and replacing him with another king, he stepped in to serve in Israel's best interests—even if it meant giving in to the obstinate king.

key point

Chapter Wrap-Up

- Two years into Saul's reign, Jonathan attacked the military post of the Philistines in Geba, touching off a full-blown battle that scared Saul's men into hiding.

- Samuel instructed Saul to wait for him for seven days, but Saul became impatient and, in direct disobedience to God's instructions, made offerings himself before Samuel arrived at the end of the seventh day.

- When Samuel arrived to discover what the king had done, Saul made excuses for his behavior by saying his people had abandoned him, Samuel hadn't yet arrived, and the Philistines were preparing to attack.

- Samuel scolded Saul, pointed out his foolishness, pronounced God's judgment, and told of a new and better king yet to come.

- Jonathan and his armor bearer surprised the Philistines, causing them to turn against each other. God led Israel to victory that day.

- Saul forbade his soldiers to eat anything while they chased the Philistines out of their land. This edict jeopardized the lives of Jonathan and the famished soldiers who disobeyed the king's order.

- After he had scolded his men for their sin against God, Saul—once more in disobedience to God's instructions—built an altar for sacrifices.

- God told Saul, through Samuel, to attack the Amalekites, showing mercy to no one and leaving no one alive. Saul opted to spare the king's life and keep some of the best livestock. This brought a scathing scolding from Samuel, who informed Saul he had been rejected by God.

Study Questions

1. What motivated Jonathan to drive out the Philistines?

2. Why was it wrong for Samuel to administer the burnt offering at Gilgal?

3. What was Samuel's response to Saul's disobedience concerning the burnt offering?

4. How did Saul's no-food edict show poor judgment on his part?

5. What act nearly cost Jonathan his life?

6. How did Saul sin following the victory over the Philistines?

7. How did Saul sin regarding the victory over the Amalekites?

8. How did Samuel respond to Saul's transgression?

1 Samuel 16:
David in Saul's Court

Chapter Highlights:
- Conversation Starter
- Samuel's King Hunt
- Sizing Up the Sons
- Snapshot of a Shepherd
- Instrument of Relief

Let's Get Started

"Have it your way," God had said to the people of Israel when He had placed Saul on the throne as their first king. But when Saul failed test after test in matters of obedience, integrity, and faith, God withdrew His favor from the king and prepared to bring His own man onto the scene. In 1 Samuel 16, He sent His **prophet** Samuel to the uplands of Judah to seek out a young shepherd named David and **anoint** him as Saul's replacement.

Shaking off his sorrow over Saul's fall from grace, Samuel set off toward Bethlehem. Would Saul have him followed and killed for delivering the Lord's harsh rebuke? The faithful prophet obeyed God's instructions rather than gave in to fear of what the rebellious and temperamental king, in his downward spiral of despair after learning God had taken away his kingdom, might do next.

voice
John 10:4, 27

prophet
person through whom God speaks

anoint
set apart for a task by pouring oil on a person's head

Conversation Starter

> 1 SAMUEL 16:1 *Now the LORD said to Samuel, "How long will you mourn for Saul, seeing I have rejected him from reigning over Israel? Fill your horn with oil, and go; I am sending you to Jesse the Bethlehemite. For I have provided Myself a king among his sons."* (NKJV)

The first passage of this chapter gives us a chance to eavesdrop on a private audience the Lord gave to one of His most faithful servants. While it's not clear whether God spoke to Samuel through a dream or in an audible voice, the opening words of verse 1 reveal an important clue about how God often communicates with His people: He's a conversation starter. That's why His followers need to make sure they are always ready to listen. Samuel may have been consumed by sorrow after seeing his friend Saul fail, but even through the din of his despair his ears were attuned to the Lord's <u>voice</u>. Remember, the Bible states in 1 Samuel 3:19 that listening to God was one of Samuel's strengths, even when he was young.

secluded place
Mark 6:31

anointed Saul
1 Samuel 10:1

How can you be sure you'll hear God's voice when He speaks to you? Here are some suggestions:

- *Study the Bible.* The Bible is, after all, God's Word. All the facts and guidelines for living He provides in the Bible are facts and guidelines for living He wants you to know.

- *Pray.* Prayer is the system God designed so that you can have two-way communication with Him at any time. The Bible tells us to "pray without ceasing" (1 Thessalonians 5:17 NKJV). Doing that keeps the line open for God to speak—and for us to hear Him—at all times.

- *Be quiet.* It's hard to hear anything when people are talking, phones are ringing, computers are humming, car horns are honking, or babies are crying. Jesus consistently urged His followers to retreat to a <u>secluded place</u> so they could distance themselves from the busyness of life and talk—or listen—to Him. He invites you to do the same.

Enough Already!

Samuel surely felt paralyzed with heartache as he mourned Saul's tragic rebellion. After all, he himself had <u>anointed Saul</u> in that history-making, early-morning meeting years earlier. Throughout Saul's reign, a close friendship between the prophet and the king had flourished.

God acknowledged Samuel's grief, but helped him take a step toward healing by asking gently, "How long will you mourn for Saul?" (1 Samuel 16:1 NKJV). His words encouraging Samuel to stop weeping foreshadow some of the words written years later by David's son, Solomon:

> To everything there is a season, a time for every purpose under heaven: a time to be born, and a time to die; a time to plant, and a time to pluck what is planted; a time to kill, and a time to heal; a time to break down, and a time to build up; *a time to weep, and a time to laugh; a time to mourn, and a time to dance;* a time to cast away stones, and a time to gather stones; a time to embrace, and a time to refrain from embracing; a time to gain, and a time to lose; a time to keep, and a time to

throw away; a time to tear, and a time to sew; a time to keep silence, and a time to speak; a time to love, and a time to hate; a time of war, and a time of peace. (Ecclesiastes 3:1–8 NKJV, emphasis added)

For Samuel, it was time for the mourning to end. He must stop crying, dry his tears, and step back into the rhythm and routine of everyday life.

Some scholars say the word "mourn" God used in speaking to Samuel suggests that the prophet also might have been praying for Saul's restoration. Isn't that a typical response when things don't go the way people expect or hope they'll go, or when circumstances take a turn for the worse? Prayers offered in crisis situations often ask God to "undo" what has happened, or beg Him to "fix" the difficult situation.

God states, however, that *all* things—even bad events that don't seem to make sense—are a part of His far-reaching, big-picture plans for caring for and blessing His people: "And we know that all things work together for good to those who love God, to those who are the called according to His purpose" (Romans 8:28 NKJV).

key point

"You Want Me to Do What?"

The tragedy of Saul's failure to serve as a worthy ruler didn't derail God's plans for uniting Israel under one king. God moved forward with His plans to secure the future of His chosen nation by giving Samuel detailed instructions about what to do next:

1. *Fill his horn with oil.* Horns, most commonly those of rams, oxen, and goats, were used as weapons, musical instruments, and vessels for holding oil—an ordinary substance that, on occa-

go to

Jesse's genealogy
Ruth 4:18–22;
1 Chronicles 2

Rahab
Joshua 2; 6:17–25;
Hebrews 11:31;
James 2:25

fear
Psalm 118:6;
Proverbs 1:33;
2 Timothy 1:17

Ruth and Boaz
Ruth 2, 3, 4

genealogy
a list of family
ancestors appears
not once but twice
in the Bible, it is
important not to
overlook this
Bethlehem farmer's
family tree. Jesse's
grandparents were
Ruth and Boaz,

sion, was used for the extraordinary purpose of anointing kings. When Samuel was told to fill his horn with oil, he must have suspected what God hadn't yet said: The prophet would be using the oil-filled vessel to set apart Israel's next ruler.

2. *Go to Bethlehem.* Bethlehem, meaning "house of bread," was a small city in Judah about six miles south of Jerusalem.

3. *Find a man named Jesse, whose son will be the king.* Jesse's **genealogy** showed he was a great grandson of Rahab, the prostitute from Jericho who earned a place on God's roster of faithful heroes in Hebrews 11 for her demonstration of faith.

"Are You Sure About This?"

1 SAMUEL 16:2–3 *And Samuel said, "How can I go? If Saul hears it, he will kill me." But the LORD said, "Take a heifer with you, and say, 'I have come to sacrifice to the LORD.' Then invite Jesse to the sacrifice, and I will show you what you shall do; you shall anoint for Me the one I name to you." (NKJV)*

Certainly Samuel's fears for his life weren't unfounded. If word got back to Saul that the prophet had been seen heading south, anointing supplies tucked under his arm, there might be no limit to the king's rage. He could immediately dispatch any number of soldiers to execute Samuel before the prophet could name his replacement.

Can "fear" be part of a good prophet's vocabulary? Some scholars describe Samuel's protest to God's command as showing a lack of faith. Maybe, they say, he wasn't quite the spiritual giant he was thought to be. Others, however, believe this passage simply highlights the prophet's human nature—fearfulness and all—and helps people know that the best thing to do with their fear is to express it honestly to God, who is able to replace that fear with His power. "The LORD is my light and my salvation; whom shall I fear? The LORD is the strength of my life; of whom shall I be afraid?" (Psalm 27:1 NKJV).

something to ponder

"I'm Just Here on Business"

heifer
a young cow

Samuel had no clue as to how he might secretly enter Bethlehem and anoint a new king while Saul was pacing the palace floor. But God knew exactly what the prophet should do.

what others say

Matthew Henry

Those that go about God's work in God's way shall be directed step by step, wherever they are at a loss, to do it in the best manner.[2]

To ensure that Samuel's appearance wouldn't raise any eyebrows in Bethlehem, God directed Samuel to take a **heifer** along and tell the people that he was in town to make a sacrifice. This would not be an unusual activity for a prophet who, as a servant of God, would often travel to other villages and towns and encourage others to worship God. Sacrifice would have been a key part of that worship and sacrifice.

what others say

Larry Richards

When an Israelite wanted to approach God he or she brought an offering or a sacrifice. Sometimes a person wanted to approach God simply to express thanks. Sometimes a person needed to approach God because he or she had sinned . . . The New Testament teaches that Jesus Christ, God's Son, gave his life on the cross as a sacrifice to pay the penalty for our sins. When we acknowledge our guilt and trust Jesus as Savior, God forgives our sins freely and completely. The repeated Old Testament sacrifices were object lessons, teaching this special language of sacrifice and salvation.[3]

God not only gave Samuel instructions about what to do; He went so far as to tell him, word for word, what to say. Samuel did exactly as God directed and was blessed with safety and protection: "Whoever listens to me will dwell safely, and will be secure, without fear of evil" (Proverbs 1:33 NKJV).

This pattern is repeated often throughout God's Word, particularly throughout the history of the Jews, and continues to appear in the fabric of life today:

sanctify
to make ritually
clean

consecrated
set apart by
cleansing

- God gives instruction.

- People choose whether to obey.

- Their choice—obedience or disobedience—brings either blessing or punishment.

Samuel's King Hunt

1 SAMUEL 16:4–5 So Samuel did what the LORD said, and went to Bethlehem. And the elders of the town trembled at his coming, and said, "Do you come peaceably?" And he said, "Peaceably; I have come to sacrifice to the LORD. **Sanctify** *yourselves, and come with me to the sacrifice." Then he* **consecrated** *Jesse and his sons, and invited them to the sacrifice. (NKJV)*

When Samuel followed the Lord's instructions, he no longer feared for his own life. Instead, he found the town's religious leaders afraid for theirs. Prophets, after all, weren't merely God's mouthpieces; they were agents of God's judgment as well. As the men watched Samuel approach the city, they wondered if perhaps he was coming to Bethlehem to pronounce God's punishment for their own sins. Imagine their anxiety as they greeted him with a nervous, "Er . . . so what, exactly, brings you to our fair city?"

As if on cue, the men's question enabled Samuel to respond with the God-given words he had rehearsed. He gave the reason for his visit, and confidently instructed the leaders—a group that apparently included Jesse—to go through the ritual of making themselves clean so they would be fit to participate in the ceremony of sacrifice.

what others say

Adam Clarke

Change your clothes, and wash your bodies in pure water, and prepare your minds by meditation, reflection, and prayer; that, being in the spirit of sacrifice, ye may offer acceptably to the Lord.[4]

The Smart Guide to the Bible

Sizing Up the Sons

go to

Goliath
1 Samuel 17

Eve
Genesis 3

Rahab
Joshua 2

the big picture

1 Samuel 16:6–12

Samuel evaluated each of Jesse's sons following the sacrifice. Yet he failed to find the one he was seeking and asked if there were any others. Jesse said yes, and then sent for his youngest son, David, who was out in the pasture tending sheep. When the handsome, bright-eyed boy stepped into the room, the Lord told Samuel he was the one.

As Samuel considered Jesse's first son, Eliab, he most likely thought he was looking at king material. (His appearance must have been physically impressive because a later passage refers to Eliab as one of Saul's warriors who fought against the Philistine giant, Goliath.) But because the Lord could see something Samuel couldn't—Eliab's character—He quickly cautioned his prophet: "Do not look at his appearance or at his physical stature, because I have refused him. For the LORD does not see as man sees; for man looks at the outward appearance, but the LORD looks at the heart" (1 Samuel 16:7 NKJV). That was a lesson all the Israelites desperately needed to learn after experiencing life under the rule of Saul, who had been physically striking but morally corrupt. Armed with God's wisdom, Samuel discerned that brothers two through seven weren't cut out of kingly cloth, either. The prophet would keep looking until God showed him the man He had described in 1 Samuel 13:14 as a man "after His own heart."

Learning to Look Inside

The cliché is true: Appearances can be deceiving. Eve learned that lesson well in Eden, where she discovered that treachery and lies rather than care and honesty were at the heart of the beautiful serpent's motives. And the Israeli spies learned it in Jericho, where they discovered hero-sized faith in the heart of a shame-stained harlot, Rahab.

apply it

Scripture states that even "Satan himself transforms himself into an angel of light" (2 Corinthians 11:14 NKJV). That's why it's critical for those who follow Christ to become more and more like Him through Bible study and prayer.

sheep and shepherds
1 Kings 22:17;
2 Chronicles 18:16;
Psalms 95:7; 100:3;
Isaiah 40:11;
John 10:14–16

good shepherd
John 10:7–18

An ability to see past superficial traits and into the hearts of others is one unmistakable mark of a spiritually mature Christian.

Snapshot of a Shepherd

While Samuel was busy searching for God's chosen king, David, whose name means "well loved," was busy caring for his family's flock. It's easy to imagine the youth leaning against the trunk of an olive tree idly savoring the serenity of his pastoral life. Nothing could have been farther from the reality of life as a shepherd, however. He might have kicked back to count clouds once in a while, but most often he would be found diligently carrying out the duties of his not-so-cushy job: hiking across the terrain to lead his sheep to pasture and water; protecting the flock from wild animals; and keeping track of the fluctuating flock numbers as some died and others were born. Good shepherds even went so far as to carry weak sheep from pasture to pasture when necessary.

The bottom line: Shepherding was a demanding job conducted in harsh extremes of climate, so a shepherd worth his salt needed intelligence, courage, self-motivation, observation skills, sensitivity, good health, stamina, and an ability to be content in solitude.

Not coincidentally, all the traits that make for an excellent shepherd also came in handy for a king-in-training. In fact, few vocations of the time would have outfitted Israel's second king with better qualifications for leadership.

Words relating to <u>sheep and shepherds</u> appear more than two hundred times in the Bible, with many of those references used symbolically to represent followers and leaders. One of the most familiar and endearing illustrations of Jesus Himself is as "the <u>good shepherd</u>" who knows His sheep, His followers, and is willing to die for them.

While David was working in the fields, just doing his job the best way he knew how, he had no idea the Lord was grooming him to one day sit upon the throne of Israel.

God often works in the same way today. What He has planned for His followers tomorrow, next month, or even years from now may directly involve the things they're learning or practicing today.

apply it

A Boy Becomes King

1 SAMUEL 16:12–13 So he sent and brought him in. Now he was ruddy, with bright eyes, and good-looking. And the LORD said, "Arise, anoint him; for this is the one!" Then Samuel took the horn of oil and anointed him in the midst of his brothers; and the Spirit of the LORD came upon David from that day forward. So Samuel arose and went to Ramah. (NKJV)

The Bible doesn't give any behind-the-scenes details about what went on in Jesse's home as Samuel sent for and selected David as the next king. Were the brothers elbowing each other in the ribs and whispering among themselves as they speculated on reasons for the prophet's visit? It's easy to imagine the questions that might have popped into their minds as they lined up for Samuel's scrutiny. Surely they suspected the prophet was up to something important; the anointing oil and the horn he had brought along would have been proof of that.

But what? Did they feel a little like the fabled Cinderella's stepsisters would have felt as they wiggled their feet in front of the prince's courtiers, hoping the glass slipper would be a perfect fit?

Human nature would have made David's brothers want to be singled out by Samuel, even though they didn't know the prophet's mission. The birth order suggests that Eliab in particular, as the oldest son, would have expected special treatment—if indeed handing out a special honor was the reason for the prophet's visit. When none of the brothers, not even Eliab, got a thumbs-up from the prophet, family pride might have compelled them to hope their baby brother would be picked as he strode across the threshold. On the other hand, personal pride might have prompted anger, jealousy, and resentment toward David.

Either way, the selection of the youngest and least accomplished of all his brothers breathes added meaning into the New Testament

Samuel anointed Saul
1 Samuel 10:1

passage: "Let no one despise your youth, but be an example to the believers in word, in conduct, in love, in spirit, in faith, in purity" (1 Timothy 4:12 NKJV).

Seized by God's Spirit

The practice of anointing someone with oil—usually olive oil—held great significance in the Hebrew culture because it symbolized God's power. When <u>Samuel anointed Saul</u>, the people's choice, remember, the oil had been dispensed from a fragile clay vial. But when he anointed David, God's choice, the oil was poured from a symbolically and physically strong horn.

When Samuel poured oil on David's head, he was in effect crowning him as king even though David would not take the throne for quite some time. The moment the thick aroma of the oil hit the air inside David's Judean home, the Lord's Spirit took up permanent residence inside David's heart and the foundation stones for God's plans for Israel were set in place.

> **what others say**
>
> **Charles Swindoll**
>
> Before the Holy Spirit came at Pentecost (Acts 2), the Spirit of God never permanently rested on any believer except David and John the Baptizer . . . It was not uncommon for the Spirit of God to come for a temporary period of strengthening or insight or whatever was the need of the moment and then to depart, only to return again for another surge of the need of the moment, then to depart, once again.[5]

After the sacred ceremony at his father's house, David didn't immediately pack away his staff and storm the palace doors demanding the throne from Saul. Instead, he simply carried on with what he knew he should be doing at the moment—tending sheep—while trusting the Lord to open the palace door when the time was right. He continued to spend hour after hour, day after day, in the solitude of the pastures outside Bethlehem.

Saul: A Tormented Soul

1 SAMUEL 16:14–15 *But the Spirit of the LORD departed from Saul, and a distressing spirit from the LORD troubled him. And Saul's servants said to him, "Surely, a distressing spirit from God is troubling you." (NKJV)*

The Lord had found an acceptable home for His Spirit in David's heart, but not so in Saul's. God withdrew His Spirit from the king, creating a void into which evil spirits immediately settled. Saul's duties as king became more and more difficult to handle, because he was operating without the blessing of God's favor and under the increasing influence of evil. Even his servants could see that he needed relief.

Saul threw open the door for the evil spirits' entry into his heart when he closed the door on God through his repeated disobedience. This example vividly illustrates the biblical truth that, in deciding not to follow God, a person automatically chooses to follow Satan.

key point

what others say

Matthew Henry

Those that drive the good Spirit away from them do of course become prey to the evil spirit. If God and his grace do not rule us, sin and Satan will have possession of us.[6]

A High Approval Rating Already

the big picture

1 Samuel 16:16–23

Thinking music might ease his troubled spirit, the servants suggested the name of a gifted musician: David. Saul agreed to give music therapy a try and sent for Jesse's son, who was still out tending sheep. When David entered Saul's court, the king felt instant affection for the boy, appointed him to the honored position as his armorbearer, and sent word asking Jesse to allow David to remain at the palace. Whenever David played his harp for the king, Saul found temporary reprieve from his distress.

The servant's description of David reveals that, although he was young and had spent vast stretches of time outside the village, he already had a stellar reputation: "Then one of the servants answered and said, 'Look, I have seen a son of Jesse the Bethlehemite, who is skillful in playing, a mighty man of valor, a man of war, prudent in speech, and a handsome person; and the LORD is with him'" (1 Samuel 16:18 NKJV). In other words, the talk around town was that Jesse's youngest son was a gifted musician, a strong and courageous man, an experienced warrior, a skilled communicator—and good-looking, too. This guy had been conducting himself like a king long before anyone—including himself—knew he was destined for the throne.

Instrument of Relief

When David played for the king, the music helped Saul in three ways:

1. *Physically*—he felt relieved.

2. *Emotionally*—he was in a better frame of mind.

3. *Spiritually*—he was freed from the evil spirit.

To the Hebrews, music was an integral part of life. It was used:

- *In time of war:* a shophar, a trumpet-like instrument, was used to sound an alarm or send a signal.
- *In time of celebration:* pipes or flutes were played to make the mood festive.
- *In time of distress:* an instrument such as a lyre could refresh a tormented soul—as with Saul.

what others say

Beth Moore

You may rightly imagine that many of your favorite Psalms were first sung by the young voice of David, wavering and cracking somewhere between boyhood and manhood to the accompaniment of a well-worn, deeply loved harp. Surely the very sound of its strings summoned the attentions of many a straying sheep. The words which accompanied it still do.[7]

Chapter Wrap-Up

- The Lord told Samuel to stop mourning for Saul; to go instead to the house of Jesse in Bethlehem, where the prophet would find God's choice for Israel's throne.

- Samuel went to Bethlehem and invited Jesse and his sons to participate in the ritual of sacrifice.

- Samuel evaluated Jesse's older sons but failed to find the one he was seeking, so he sent for Jesse's youngest son, David, who was out in the pasture tending sheep. Samuel knew immediately that David was the one.

- Not by accident, the qualities that made David a good shepherd—including intelligence, courage, self-motivation, and good health—suited David well as a king-in-training.

- Samuel anointed David with oil—poured from a sturdy horn rather than the fragile flask used in Saul's anointing, and the Holy Spirit came into David's life.

- God withdrew His Spirit from Saul, creating a void into which evil spirits immediately settled. Saul experienced visible torment.

- Thinking music might ease Saul's troubled spirit, the servants suggested the name of a gifted musician, David. The young shepherd earned Saul's instant affection because of his ability to alleviate the king's distress.

Study Questions

1. As this chapter opens, why is Samuel grieving?

2. Why did the Lord send Samuel to Bethlehem?

3. Why did Samuel question the Lord about his assignment?

4. How did the Lord alleviate Samuel's fears?

5. Which of Jesse's sons might have seemed the most likely candidate for king? Why?

6. What did Samuel use as a guide for evaluating Jesse's sons?

7. How did David's anointing differ from Saul's?

8. What did David do after he was anointed?

9. How did Saul change after David was anointed?

10. How did David end up in King Saul's court?

Part Four
THE GIANT KILLER

Chapter Highlights:
• The Battleground
• The Challenge
• David Raised His Hand
• Five Smooth Stones
• The Giant Falls

1 Samuel 17: A Giant Challenge

Let's Get Started

Exactly when David's tenure as court musician for King Saul ended—and the events of 1 Samuel 17 began—is not recorded in the Bible. It's likely David had been about twelve years old when summoned by Saul's servants to play his lyre for the tormented king. During the next few years, as the boy's voice deepened and his shoulders broadened, he may have divided his time between the pasture and the palace, leaving the fields only when summoned to play music to soothe Saul's spirit.

Time was on David's side as he watched over his sheep. The long stretches of solitude gave him the opportunity to praise his Creator, meditate on God's words, pray for direction—and, yes, sharpen his marksmanship skills—as he inched his way toward kinghood. Perhaps one of those activities is exactly what he was doing as this chapter opens, which then goes on to describe perhaps the best-known and best-loved episode in David's life: his encounter with the godless giant from the land of Gath.

How to Read This Story

The biblical account of these events contains elements of the unbelievable—after all, a cowardly king, an evil giant, and a young boy usually are the stuff of tall tales. But this chapter is neither fairy tale nor fable.

David's unlikely triumph over the very real giant teaches spiritual lessons of biblical proportions, and the details in the narrative add clarity to the emerging portrait of a young man after God's own heart.

To get the most out of the story, it's helpful to look at it from several angles:

key point

go to

examples
1 Corinthians 10:6,
11

type
symbol of something to come

Valley of Elah
site of confrontation
between David and
Goliath

1. *As history*—By looking at the events themselves, readers can monitor Israel's gradual transformation from a floundering nation under the misguided leadership of its first king toward the stronger, more mature nation it would become under the rule of David.

2. *As a character study*—The Bible gives examples so that each generation may learn from them. This narrative features a unique trio of key characters who colorfully demonstrate what to do—and what *not* to do—when facing conflict, criticism, and danger. There's much to learn from:

   - *David*, a confident believer living in safety and victory within the favor of God;

   - *Saul*, a fearful believer living in danger and defeat outside the favor of God; and

   - *Goliath*, a hardened unbeliever living with a false sense of security and under the mistaken assumption that the favor of God is not necessary when you're big, intimidating, and well-armed.

3. *As a typology*—David serves as a **type** of Jesus, while Goliath serves as a type of devil. That means readers can draw many parallels between David/Jesus and Goliath/Satan that can help enhance understanding of their nature.

4. *As a metaphor*—David can be viewed as any believer, and Goliath can be regarded as any enemy or obstacle that threatens to disrupt the believer's fellowship with God. Looking at the narrative from this angle gives plenty of opportunity for self-examination, and paves the way for spiritual growth.

The Battleground

1 SAMUEL 17:1–3 *Now the Philistines gathered their armies together to battle, and were gathered at Sochoh, which belongs to Judah; they encamped between Sochoh and Azekah, in Ephes Dammim. And Saul and the men of Israel were gathered together, and they encamped in the **Valley of Elah**, and drew up in battle array against the Philistines. The Philistines stood on a mountain on one side, and Israel stood on a mountain on the other side, with a valley between them. (NKJV)*

War with the Philistines raged throughout Saul's entire life, and 1 Samuel 17 opens with yet another face-off between the armies of Israel and those of the fierce people from the coast. The ancient enemies gathered near Gath on opposite sides of a sloping stream bed that cut a gorge through a mile-wide canyon a few miles southwest of Jerusalem. The site of this confrontation has been identified by historians and archaeologists as the modern-day city of Tel es-Safi.

Fighting for Land They Already Owned

DEUTERONOMY 20:1–4 *When you go out to battle against your enemies, and see horses and chariots and people more numerous than you, do not be afraid of them; for the LORD your God is with you, who brought you up from the land of Egypt. So it shall be, when you are on the verge of battle, that the priest shall approach and speak to the people. And he shall say to them, "Hear, O Israel: Today you are on the verge of battle with your enemies. Do not let your heart faint, do not be afraid, and do not tremble or be terrified because of them; for the LORD your God is He who goes with you, to fight for you against your enemies, to save you." (NKJV)*

The land the Israelites were defending had already been given to them by God as part of the <u>Abrahamic Covenant</u>. However, the Israelites had never completely <u>driven out the inhabitants of the land</u>, as God had instructed them to do. The Philistines were some of the people who remained. Because the land was in fact already Israel's, God had instructed His people <u>not to be intimidated</u> by the enemies living in their land. He promised that no matter how formidable they appeared, He would <u>guarantee their victory</u>.

Champion, in the Biggest Sense of the Word

1 SAMUEL 17:4–7 *And a champion went out from the camp of the Philistines, named Goliath, from Gath, whose height was six cubits and a span. He had a bronze helmet on his head, and he was armed with a coat of mail, and the weight of the coat was five thousand shekels of bronze. And he had bronze armor on his legs and a bronze javelin between his shoulders. Now the staff of his spear was like a weaver's beam, and his iron spearhead weighed six hundred shekels; and a shield-bearer went before him. (NKJV)*

go to

war with the Philistines
1 Samuel 14:52

Abrahamic Covenant
Deuteronomy 1:21

driven out the inhabitants of the land
Judges 1; 2:1–3

not to be intimidated
Deuteronomy 31:8

guarantee their victory
Deuteronomy 28:7;
Joshua 10:25

shekels
approximately .4- to .8-ounce units of measure

go to

giants
Genesis 6:4

conquest of northern Canaan
Joshua 11

The Hebrew word for "champion"—*benayim*—used nowhere else in the Old Testament—means "the man between." The Philistines undoubtedly had seen the kind of destruction that could result from all-out war against the Israelites. So to strengthen their military position without risking widespread death and injury, they decided to instigate a representative battle. Their "champion," Goliath, would fight against a "champion" for Israel. The winner of the two-man confrontation would secure victory for the army he represented.

This representative physical conflict staged in the valley of Elah illustrates the representative spiritual conflict waged between Christ and Satan.

Was This Guy for Real?

No wonder Goliath was the Philistines' choice of champion. At more than nine feet tall, he would have towered over his Israelite enemies. Can that be possible? Were there really such things as giants in David's day? What about today? Biblically, scientifically, and historically speaking, the answer is "yes."

- *What the Bible says about giants:* Giants existed both before and after the Flood, and a race of giants called the Anakites still existed throughout Joshua's day. During his conquest of northern Canaan, Joshua led the destruction of the Anakites who were living in Israel, but he did not kill the rest of these unusually large people, who remained in the Philistine cities of Gaza, Ashdod, and Gath—of which the latter was Goliath's hometown.

- *What science says about giants:* "Gigantism" is a rare but well-documented condition caused when the body produces too much of the growth hormone before adolescence ends. The condition can cause people to grow as tall as seven or eight feet.

- *What history says about giants:* Ancient historians referred to the existence of giants, and giants in modern history have included Robert Pershing Wadlow, who measured 8 feet 11 inches when he died in 1940 at the age of twenty-two, and "Andre the Giant," the 7-foot 4-inch, 500-pound professional wrestler who died in 1993.

Giant Armor for a Giant Man

Adding a layer of metal only increased the intimidation factor for the colossal giant, who hardly seemed to need the attendant scurrying ahead of him carrying a large shield. The giant wore:

- Bronze helmet
- Coat of scale armor weighing about 125 pounds
- Bronze shin guards

He carried:

- Bronze javelin
- Long, sturdy spear that could have weighed as much as 17 pounds. The spear featured a 15-pound iron tip.

The Challenge

1 SAMUEL 17:8–11 *Then he stood and cried out to the armies of Israel, and said to them, "Why have you come out to line up for battle? Am I not a Philistine, and you the servants of Saul? Choose a man for yourselves, and let him come down to me. If he is able to fight with me and kill me, then we will be your servants. But if I prevail against him and kill him, then you shall be our servants and serve us." And the Philistine said, "I defy the armies of Israel this day; give me a man, that we may fight together." When Saul and all Israel heard these words of the Philistine, they were dismayed and greatly afraid. (NKJV)*

Goliath's tone was defiant, impatient, and taunting as he issued his challenge and spelled out the terms of the proposed fight: "If your man kills me, the Philistines will be your servants. If I kill your man, then you will be our servants." Living as servants to the Philistines was not something the Israelites would have wanted to do; they had already experienced life under the Philistines and did not want to lose the freedom they had earned. However, if the giant's threats were provoking the Israelites, they weren't provoking them intensely enough, because not one soldier raised a hand to volunteer.

Why Not Saul?

Once again, expectant gazes must have been looking toward King Saul. Politically and militarily, he was the leader of Israel; physically,

go to

head and shoulders above the rest
1 Samuel 9:2; 10:23

baggage cart
1 Samuel 10:22

withdrawn His Spirit
1 Samuel 16:13

Eliab
David's oldest brother

he stood <u>head and shoulders above the rest</u>. Perhaps no other man in the Israelite camp would have been a better candidate for champion. However, once again Saul failed to step forward. This time, instead of hiding under a <u>baggage cart</u>, he was shrinking into the shadows, trying to blend in with the ranks. Scripture says he joined his men in cowering down in fear, "dismayed and greatly afraid" (1 Samuel 17:11 NKJV).

As an Israelite, particularly one whom the priest and prophet Samuel had taken under his wing, Saul would have grown up learning about the many battle victories God had provided His people throughout the generations that had come before him. And in his own lifetime, he had tasted firsthand the sweetness of triumph given by God. But because Saul had sinned against God to the point that God had <u>withdrawn His Spirit</u> from the king, Saul sat defenseless before his enemies. Instead of being mobilized by a faith fostered by remembrance of what God had done for His people in the past, Saul was paralyzed by a fear that had begun festering in his heart when he made the choice to leave God out of the picture.

Dwight D. Eisenhower once defined leadership as "the art of getting someone else to do something you want done because he wants to do it." The fact that Saul not only failed to step forward to fight the giant, but also neglected to motivate any of his men to do so, shows that Saul's leadership abilities were lacking.

> **what others say**
>
> **Richard D. Phillips**
>
> The biggest indicator of Saul's failing leadership was the unwillingness of any of his followers to answer the challenge, day after day, morning and evening, as Goliath wounded their collective pride.[1]

A Directive from Dad

> **the big picture**
>
> **1 Samuel 17:12–19**
>
> David's three oldest brothers—**Eliab**, Abinadab, and Shammah—were soldiers in Saul's army and a part of the company encamped in the Valley of Elah. David was still taking care

of his father's sheep when Jesse, an old man by now, heard how Goliath had been threatening the Israelites. Longing for news from the battlefront, he directed David to take a fresh supply of provisions to his brothers, offer a gift of ten cheeses to their commander, find out about his oldest boys' well-being, and return with a token of their safety.

Why Not Twenty-nine, or Fifteen, or Thirty-one?

Goliath lumbered back and forth along the opposite bank, hurling insults and boasts at the Israelites every morning and evening for forty days.

Numbers often hold great significance in the Bible, and this one is no exception. Forty is used in the Scriptures frequently as a period of judgment or testing.

- Rain fell for forty days during the <u>Flood</u>.
- Moses spent forty years growing up in the <u>court of Pharaoh</u>.
- After their exodus from Egypt, the Israelites spent forty years <u>wandering in the wilderness</u>.
- Jesus spent forty days in the <u>wilderness</u> where He was tempted by the devil before He began His public ministry.

go to

Flood
Genesis 7:5–10

court of Pharaoh
Exodus 2;
Acts 7:20–23

wandering in the wilderness
Exodus;
Nehemiah 9:21

wilderness
Matthew 4:1–11;
Luke 4:1–13

what others say

Charles Swindoll

How applicable to any "giant" we encounter! That's the way with the giants of fear and worry, for example. They don't come just once, they come morning and evening, day after day, relentlessly trying to intimidate.[2]

What Patience!

David did not ask to go to the battlefront. Neither had he asked to be invited to play music for Saul. While David understood that he was destined to be king, he never tried to force his way into the palace. He simply tackled each task set before him and waited for the Lord to work out the details.

key point

"Who Will Fight for Us?"

1 SAMUEL 17:20 *So David rose early in the morning, left the sheep with a keeper, and took the things and went as Jesse had commanded him. (NKJV)*

apply it

This small passage provides much practical insight into what traits are found in a person after God's own heart. David was:

- Energetic (he rose early in the morning)
- Obedient (he did as his father Jesse commanded)
- Responsible (he left the sheep in care of a keeper)

"Hey, Maybe I Can Pay Someone to Do It!"

the big picture

1 Samuel 17:21-25

Since no champion had volunteered to fight for Israel, all-out battle was imminent. The great shouts and battle cries of the soldiers preparing to fight must have pounded against David's eardrums as he made his way into camp. One voice in particular boomed above the din as David heard for the first time the threats the Israelites had been hearing from the giant for the past few weeks. Perhaps David's eyes widened as he took in the bizarre events, even as the men explained what was going on. Their explanation revealed a new twist: Saul was trying to lure a champion from the crowd by offering a generous reward. He would give anyone who could kill the giant a giant payoff—his own daughter, and political favor.

The slow attrition of Saul's power becomes increasingly apparent. First, he had failed to step forward to fight. Second, he had failed to demonstrate the leadership skills it took to convince one of his men to volunteer. And third—now, he was resorting to a bribe to prod someone into action.

Righteous Indignation

1 SAMUEL 17:26 *Then David spoke to the men who stood by him, saying, "What shall be done for the man who kills this Philistine and takes away the reproach from Israel? For who is this uncircumcised Philistine, that he should defy the armies of the living God?" (NKJV)*

This verse—which includes David's first recorded words in the Bible—highlights one of the main reasons David was forever designated as a man after God's own heart: He saw the world through spiritual eyes. Where Saul and the soldiers saw a giant, an intimidating army, and sophisticated weaponry—evidences of the Philistines' physical superiority—David saw nothing more than a man who deserved to die, for defying God.

key point

The Players

David's remarks answered, in spiritual terms, three key questions:

1. *Who is Goliath?* David understood that the giant's true identity had nothing to do with his tunic size or how much weight he could bench-press. Instead, it had everything to do with who he was with respect to God. David summed up Goliath's relationship to God with one word: "uncircumcised." **Circumcision** was assigned by God as the outward sign of the Israelites' unique relationship with Him, and it was a reminder to Abraham and his descendants of His everlasting covenant. Therefore, someone who was uncircumcised clearly was not one of God's people. As an uncircumcised Philistine, Goliath denied God and worshipped idols of wood and stone.

   The rite of circumcision wasn't unique to Israel; it was also used in many other tribes and nations to mark a boy's entry into manhood.

2. *Who are we (that is, David and the Israelites)?* David understood that he and the Israelites were soldiers fighting a spiritual battle for Israel, the land given them by God. To allow the land to slip into the hands of the Philistines would be a reason for "reproach"—*cherpah*—or "shame."

3. *Whom do we serve?* David's remarks also demonstrated that he knew he and the circumcised soldiers served no early commander or physical king, no matter whose insignia was on their banner. Neither did they serve a wood or stone idol, as did their Philistine counterparts. Instead, the recipient of their service was the living God alone.

go to

circumcision
Genesis 17:10–11,
24–27

circumcision
physical sign of
Israel's relationship
with God

go to

Eli had misjudged Hannah's actions
1 Samuel 1:14

what others say

Beth Moore

We must remember we don't stand in victory because of our faith. We stand in victory because of our God. Faith in faith is pointless. Faith in a living, active God moves mountains.[3]

David Raised His Hand

the big picture

1 Samuel 17:27–29

David's oldest brother, Eliab, heard David's assessment of the circumstances and became angry. He accused David of being irresponsible with the "few" sheep that were entrusted to his care, then said that the boy's pride and insolence had drawn him to the battlefront. The exasperation in David's voice must have been audible: "What have I done now?" (1 Samuel 17:29 NKJV), the word "now" suggesting that this wasn't the first time enmity had soured the relationship between David and Eliab.

Eliab couldn't have been more off-base in his assessment of David's motives, much as the priest Eli had misjudged Hannah's actions at the temple years before. David had not been irresponsible in caring for the sheep; on the contrary, he had arranged for their care before leaving home. Further, David had traveled to the Valley of Elah in direct obedience to his father's instructions, not because a proud or insolent attitude had drawn him there. However, there are a few other reasons for Eliab's over-the-top anger that might have come into play here:

- *Jealousy.* As the oldest son, Eliab probably felt entitled to be anointed by Samuel. That his youngest, least significant brother had been singled out for that honor apparently was hard for Eliab to swallow.

- *Ineffectiveness.* Perhaps Eliab, a leader in Saul's army, was feeling like a failure since neither his king nor his troops could produce a champion to fight the Philistine. The fact that his little brother came on the scene with his critical commentary might have stung a little; after all, sometimes the truth does hurt!

- *Fear.* Eliab could have begun to sense some pressure; if his king didn't fight Goliath, and if one of his men wouldn't volunteer for the job, he himself might be pressured into going!

David's brothers rejected him just as <u>Christ's brothers rejected Him</u>. Christ promises that His followers will experience <u>persecution</u>, and coming from family that can hurt worse than anything! Satan seems to enjoy stirring up strife between family members, as well as between members of the body of Christ. Could it be Satan's way of keeping us divided and focused on fighting with each other so that we're not united in our focus on standing against him?

Christ's brothers rejected Him
John 1:11

persecution
John 15:20

"I'm Your Man!"

the big picture

1 Samuel 17:30–37a

When Saul heard what David had said he sent for him, and David immediately volunteered to fight the giant. Saul, still looking at the situation through physical rather then spiritual lenses, objected. He pointed out David's disadvantage of youth and inexperience against Goliath's advantage of age and experience. But David wouldn't be discouraged. He said he had killed lions and bears before, and would kill the Philistine now.

David's argument acknowledged that:

- The Lord had been preparing him all his life for this very moment. Caring for sheep might have seemed like a menial task for someone who had been anointed king. But every moment of David's past—including the time he had spent protecting his flocks from predators with no audience but the animals—had given him the training, skill, and wisdom needed for success against the giant.

- Every battle—whether against animals, humans, or other foes such as illness or family troubles—really is the Lord's: "The LORD, who delivered me from the paw of the lion and from the paw of the bear, He will deliver me from the hand of this Philistine" (1 Samuel 17:37 NKJV).

This is the very reason keeping a journal is a good idea. Reviewing what God has done in the past can strengthen confidence in the fact that His hand on the future.

apply it

A Victorious Circle

Because God had been faithful to David in the past, David fully expected God to be faithful to him in the future. The apostle Paul recognized this victorious cycle in action in his own life in 2 Timothy 4:17–18: "But the Lord stood with me and strengthened me, so that the message might be preached fully through me, and that all the Gentiles might hear. Also I was delivered out of the mouth of the lion. And the Lord will deliver me from every evil work and preserve me for His heavenly kingdom. To Him be glory forever and ever. Amen!" (NKJV). Further, because David had been faithful with a little by protecting his flock of animals, God was about to entrust him with a lot by giving him care over His people, Israel.

> **what others say**
>
> **Charles Spurgeon**
>
> When David was young in years he was old in experience, because he had watched the hand of the Lord in its dealings with him. He had not been an idler among the hills, but a worshipper, a worker, a student, a practical, living man of God . . . thus he gained his experience by the active discharge of his duty as a shepherd. He did what he was called upon to do with holy daring, and in so doing he learned the faithfulness of God. Many men have lions and bears, but no experience.[4]

Ill-Fitting Armor

faithful with a little
Matthew 25:21–22;
Luke 16:10–11;
19:17

> **the big picture**
>
> **I Samuel 17:38–40**
>
> Saul agreed to let David face Goliath, and offered to loan David his armor, which David tried on but quickly removed, because it didn't fit. He opted to fight with his sling instead. Plenty of ammunition for David's slingshot lay in the bed of the stream at his feet. He gathered five stones that had been polished to a smooth finish by the stream's water, then placed them into his pouch. As the giant and his shield-bearer walked toward him, he approached the giant.

The armor Saul loaned David didn't fit in more ways than one:

go to

doubting
Matthew 21:21–22;
Mark 11:22–24;
James 1:6–7

four brothers
1 Samuel 21:18–22

1. David was younger and therefore probably smaller than Saul, who was described as a big guy. The king's armor simply was too large for the teen.

2. David was not yet a soldier, so he was not accustomed to wearing the bulky garb. He would be much more comfortable—as well as confident and capable—in his everyday clothes.

3. David planned to use a sling, which would allow him to attack the giant from a distance. He would not need to get close enough to the giant to need the kind of protection armor would give.

4. David was not fighting a physical battle, so he didn't need physical armor.

what others say

Alan Redpath

[David] knew perfectly well it was no use imitating the enemy by dressing up like him and going out in Saul's armor—he saw the futility of that. Rather, he must put on the whole armor of God that he might stand his ground in that evil day.[5]

No Backup Plan Required

David didn't even hang on to Saul's helmet! It might have been tempting to keep a piece or two of the better-fitting armor "just in case." But David's faith was so great he didn't see the need for a fallback position. Have you ever stepped out in faith, certain of God's leading, only to let doubts creep in so that you eventually start looking for a backup plan? Doubting is risky business! It puts us in danger of losing the benefit of seeing God at work and of seeing Him answer our prayers.

apply it

Five Smooth Stones

Some scholars say David selected five stones because Goliath had four brothers; he might have anticipated the possibility that he

go to

Miriam
Exodus 2:4–8

Josiah
2 Kings 22–23;
2 Chronicles 34–35

Jeremiah
Jeremiah 1:6–8

Mary
Matthew 1:18–2:11;
Luke 1:26–2:7

Timothy
Acts 6–20;
1 Corinthians 4:17;
16:10;
2 Corinthians 1:19;
1 Thessalonians
3:2–6

would need to fight them, too. Others say David gathered five stones simply because that's what any practiced marksman would have done.

The Giant Falls

the big picture

1 Samuel 17:42–45

When Goliath saw David, he looked at the boy with contempt because of his youth. Still hurling insults and swearing by his pagan gods, Goliath said, "Bring it on!" David, focusing on the size of his God rather than the size of the giant, replied, "You come to me with a sword, with a spear, and with a javelin. But I come to you in the name of the LORD of hosts, the God of the armies of Israel, whom you have defied" (1 Samuel 17:45 NKJV).

That the Israelites would send a young person, inexperienced in battle, against him obviously insulted Goliath. Didn't he look and sound frightening enough? Wasn't his armor superior? Why hadn't they sent their biggest guy, their most seasoned warrior? And why didn't this tiny foe carry a sword or a shield?

The fact is, God often uses young people to do some of His most important work:

- Miriam, Moses' sister, was entrusted by God with the care of Moses, the deliverer of Israel.

- Josiah, king of Judah, came to the throne at age eight and purged the kingdom of idolatry when he was just twenty.

- Jeremiah the prophet was still in his teens when God called him to reign in rebellious Judah.

- Mary, mother of Jesus, was possibly in her early teens when she gave birth to Christ.

- Timothy, the apostle Paul's close companion, was not yet twenty when he started working alongside him in ministry.

Bull's-Eye!

go to

become the Israelites' slaves
1 Samuel 17:9

the big picture

1 Samuel 17:46–51

David assured the giant that victory would be his, and explained that his motivation wasn't the bounty promised by his king, nor was it the glory he would receive for the victory. His defeat of Goliath would let everyone know that there was a God in Israel, and that the battle was the Lord's. Then David ran toward the Philistine, loaded his sling, and launched one of his stones, striking a fatal blow to the giant's forehead. The youth then went to the fallen giant and cut off his head.

The din that had been thundering in the valley for forty days must have been abruptly silenced after Goliath's body fell to the ground.

Could David's aim really have been that good? Absolutely. The book of Judges reports that out of 26,000 men from the tribe of Benjamin who were old enough to fight, 700 could "sling a stone at a hair's breadth and not miss" (Judges 20:16 NKJV). Beyond that, a stone thrown from a sling can gain incredible velocity, with absolutely no "give" at all when it lands. By way of comparison, only a few major-league pitchers can consistently throw baseballs at 95 miles per hour or faster. But even so, if another player were hit in the face *even by a slower pitch,* he could easily be injured for life—or killed. But with a sling, a skilled hunter such as David could throw a stone with far more speed and striking power than that!

The Philistines Fled

the big picture

1 Samuel 17:51–54

Seeing that their giant champion had been killed, the Philistines fled in fear, the soldiers of Israel chasing them all the way to the gates of Ekron before returning to plunder the Philistine camp. David took his trophy—Goliath's head—to Jerusalem.

Note, however, that the Philistines didn't do what they had said they would do—they didn't surrender and become the Israelites' slaves. They simply ran off.

David Guzik

We should never expect the devil to live up to his promises. But the soldiers of Israel pursued and defeated the Philistines. David's example had given them great courage and faith in the LORD.[6]

Who Is This Kid?

1 Samuel 17:55–57

One person carefully watching all that had been going on was Saul, who wanted to know more about the young hero.

It seems odd that Saul would be asking questions about his own court musician. He either:

1. Knew David (notice Saul didn't ask for David's name, he asked the name of his father) and recognized him as his musician, but now wanted to know more about the youth's father. Perhaps he wanted to find out whether the boy who had been serving him came from an extraordinary family, or he might have wanted to know which family to reward with the gifts he had promised.

2. Didn't recognize him at all. It could have been quite some time since David had last played music for Saul. David might have grown taller and broader, or grown a beard. Another factor: David had been called to play for Saul during times when the king was tormented by disturbing spirits, so he might not have been clearheaded or attentive.

"Champion" Parallels Between David and Jesus

David	Jesus
Represented his people—Israel	Represents His people—all who believe in Him and accept His offer of salvation
Fought for the Promised Land—the physical real estate—that already had been given to God's people, but that they had lost because of their sins of disobedience	Fought for the Promised Land—the spiritual fellowship with God—that already had been given to God's people, but which they had lost because of their sin of disobedience in the Garden of Eden
Sent to battle by his father, Jesse	Sent to battle by His Father, God

David	Jesus
Rejected by his brothers	Rejected by His brothers
Did not fight with material weapons or earthly strategies	Did not fight with material weapons or earthly strategies

Chapter Wrap-Up

- The account of David and Goliath has much to teach about Israel's history, about the biblical characters involved, about Satan and Christ, and about spiritual growth.

- The Philistines gathered on opposite sides of a streambed in the Valley of Elah to wage a representative battle, one to be fought by a champion from each side.

- No one from the Israelites' army stepped forward to fight the Philistines' champion, Goliath of Gath, who paced back and forth for forty days, taunting and challenging the Israelites.

- David, sent to the battlefront on an errand for his father, was motivated by all this to persuade Saul to let him fight the heavily armed giant.

- David refused Saul's offer of his own armor and weapons, and after picking up five smooth stones from the streambed, he struck down the giant with his first throw.

- Saul demanded to know more about the one who had slain the giant.

Study Questions

1. Describe Goliath.

2. What type of battle were the Philistines and Israelites preparing to wage?

3. Why would none of the Israelites volunteer to serve as Israel's champion?

4. Why did David go to the scene of the confrontation in the first place?

5. How did David persuade Saul to let him fight Goliath?

6. Why did David refuse to take Saul's armor?

7. How did David defeat Goliath?

8. What was Saul's reaction to David's victory?

Chapter Highlights:
- Close-Knit Friends
- Don't Look Back!
- Covenant Friendship
- The Shirt Off His Back
- The King's Man: Moving on Up

1 Samuel 18: A Genuine Friend and a Jealous King

Let's Get Started

David's heroism against Goliath secured him a place in the nation's heart, ended his private preparation for public life, and heralded his more-sudden-than-gradual entry into public service. But while he now enjoyed an elevated position in the army and the beginning of a lifelong friendship (with Saul's son, Jonathan), his promotion from the sheepfold would be no instant "happily ever after" affair. First Samuel 18 outlines how David's career change hurled him into the path of deceit and danger—developments that probably made the giant he had just killed seem like a dwarf.

Yet, in spite of it all, readers are told repeatedly that David "behaved wisely" and that "the Lord was with him." By the close of the chapter, a tremendous reversal has occurred: the lowly shepherd boy is a rising star, enjoying the favor of both God and the people around him, while the reigning king has fallen from God's favor and into the destructive grip of jealousy and rage.

go to

exploit against the Philistines
1 Samuel 14

Close-Knit Friends

1 SAMUEL 18:1 *Now when he had finished speaking to Saul, the soul of Jonathan was knit to the soul of David, and Jonathan loved him as his own soul.* (NKJV)

Saul's son, Jonathan, who hasn't been mentioned since his remarkable <u>exploit against the Philistines</u>, reenters David's story at this point. This time, he didn't instigate a courageous act, he witnessed one. Along with the rest of the Israelites encamped in the Valley of Elah, he had watched as an ordinary-looking shepherd transformed into a celebrated warrior with the launch of one stone from a sling.

Perhaps Jonathan had been moved by the conviction in David's voice as he overheard him ask Saul for permission to fight Goliath. Maybe he had felt the same kind of righteous indignation that

go to

homosexuality
Romans 1:27

flashed in David's eyes as the young man spoke to the giant himself. Possibly he had been touched by the humility David had demonstrated after the fact, when Saul summoned him to find out the identity of his family. Whatever it was that Jonathan sensed in David, it powerfully drew his soul to David's. The word "knit" used to describe the new relationship is taken from the Hebrew word *qashar*, which suggests a strong bond.

The two young men's souls, then, were securely tied together in love.

what others say

Dee Brestin

This Hebrew word translated "knit" is the very same word that is used to describe the intense love that Jacob had for his youngest son, Benjamin. We are told that if any mischief came upon Benjamin, it would send Jacob to the grave in sorrow because his soul was knit with the soul of Benjamin.[1]

An Off-Base Assumption

Some people have used this passage as a biblical basis for homosexuality. Studied in light of the whole Scripture, however, the argument doesn't hold up. First Kings 15:5 states that David "did what was right in the eyes of the LORD, and had not turned aside from anything that He commanded him all the days of his life, except in the matter of Uriah the Hittite" (NKJV). Since what is "right in the eyes of the Lord" does not include practicing <u>homosexuality</u>, it's evident that David's relationship with Jonathan was purely platonic.

what others say

Charles Swindoll

It was a true, deep friendship that transcended the circumstances in which both men found themselves. It was a wholesome, God-honoring relationship that God used in the lives of both men—and even in the future lives of their families.[2]

Three Reasons Any Average Prince Would Not Have Befriended David

executed
1 Samuel 14:44

1. *Arrogance.* As a prince, Jonathan might have displayed the royal superiority of refusing to associate with a man who was, as far as anyone knew, just a peon.

2. *Fear.* As heir apparent to Saul's throne—and with a less-than-ideal relationship with his father—Jonathan could have felt threatened by anyone who caught Saul's attention the way David had. After all, Jonathan's dad had been on the verge of having his son <u>executed</u>, had the army not intervened.

3. *Pride.* As Saul's eldest son, Jonathan could have taken offense that David had made his father, the king, look bad. And as an accomplished warrior, Jonathan could have allowed his ego to be injured by the fact that a man with no military qualifications had succeeded in slaying a giant neither he nor his men had mustered the courage to fight.

Any average prince might have harbored these kinds of poisonous attitudes in his heart and sought ways to use his position and power to trip up the young upstart from the sheepfold. But Jonathan was not your average prince. He was an above-average man who saw the world through spiritual eyes and placed God's high agenda before any of his own earthly ambitions. As a result of Jonathan's relationship with God, no ugly feelings or malicious motives had distorted his vision or taken root in his heart, leaving fertile ground for love to flourish, as expressed in the deep and abiding friendship he developed with David.

Don't Look Back!

> 1 SAMUEL 18:2 *Saul took him that day, and would not let him go home to his father's house anymore.* (NKJV)

This verse makes one thing very clear: David's days of shepherding in quiet solitude came to an abrupt end the day he slew Goliath. Once Saul had seen something he liked in the brave youth, he didn't even give him a chance to run home and pack a few things; he kept him for service in his own army.

follow Jesus
Matthew 8:20–21

David literally dropped what he had been doing to serve Saul, much like Simon Peter, James, and John stopped what they were doing to <u>follow Jesus</u> when He invited them to become His disciples. The comparison only holds up, however, when we remember that, in obeying Saul, David really was obeying the Lord. Often we feel like we're stuck in the sheepfold, doing menial tasks that seem far below what we imagine to be a higher calling in life. Maybe you're in a dead-end job that doesn't maximize your talents or skills. Maybe you're swimming in a seemingly endless cycle of feeding, diapering, and rocking babies. Maybe you're serving on a time-consuming, behind-the-scenes committee at your church. Here are two encouraging tips from this episode of David's life:

1. *Make the most of the time you're spending in the sheepfold.* God is using these hours to equip you for the tasks He has in store for your future role in His plans. You may not realize it, but even if you're sorting mail, singing lullabies, or planning the budget for your church's community service work, you're sharpening the skills and developing the attitudes that God needs you to have for the people you'll meet and the circumstances you'll encounter sometime down the road.

2. *Be ready to leave the sheepfold at a moment's notice.* Often life changes more suddenly than gradually. A letter, a phone call, a new acquaintance . . . any number of catalysts can abruptly change your course. When Saul recruited David for his own service, David was able to step into his new role without missing a beat. He had already provided for the care of his sheep! Will you be ready to drop what you're doing and move into action when you get that call to serve and obey?

Covenant Friendship

1 SAMUEL 18:3–4 *Then Jonathan and David made a covenant, because he loved him as his own soul. And Jonathan took off the robe that was on him and gave it to David, with his armor, even to his sword and his bow and his belt.* (NKJV)

In examining the traits that made David a man after God's own heart, it's easy to see one result of being a God-follower: blessing. God was very good to David in providing him with the friendship of

Jonathan, a like-minded companion. Just what a lifeline that relationship was to become would have been difficult for either young man to imagine at this point. All they knew then was that they had found in each other a kindred spirit. To cement the bond, they made a **covenant**, one that would even extend to their children.

More Than a Contract

"Covenant." The term surfaces most often today in articles and conversations about "Covenant Marriage." The word "covenant" signifies far more than the paper a wedding certificate is printed on. The idea behind covenant marriage is in fact traced back to ancient days, and it mirrors the <u>covenant relationship between God and Israel</u>.

go to

covenant relationship between God and Israel Genesis 17:7–8

covenant
a commitment to an everlasting relationship with one another

what others say

Al Janssen

Today most people don't understand what *covenant* means. Our culture is built on contracts, and everyone knows that a crackerjack lawyer can find a loophole if you really want out. So contracts get longer and longer as the parties try to close all possible loopholes, but litigation increases because people change their minds and want release from their agreements . . . In ancient times, a covenant was a legal agreement, but with two major differences from contracts today. A covenant was made before deity. And the penalty for breaking it was death. People might negotiate out of contracts, but not out of a covenant.[3]

Secrets of a Covenant's Success

Making a covenant seems appropriate for marriage partners or for heads of state who are forging alliances, but it sounds like a pretty official step for a couple of he-men like Jonathan and David. Couldn't they have decided just to meet for breakfast once a week to maintain their male bonding? That might have been enjoyable, but without a covenant the friendship could have lacked two ingredients missing from many relationships today: commitment and permanence. The power of a covenant relationship hinges on:

- *commitment* to the protection, provision, and well-being of the other party; and

- *permanence*, in that there is never an expiration date on a covenant. The mutual affiliation is everlasting.

The Shirt Off His Back

In a touching gesture of humility and devotion to David, Jonathan presented his new friend with his own clothes.

By giving David his robe, his sword, his bow, and his belt, Jonathan was expressing a sense of protection, but his gift of his royal garments acknowledged that he knew what few others around them understood: David was to become the next king.

What a contrast between this scene and the one in which Jonathan's father had made a similar offer to David! David had refused to wear the king's oversized garb, but he gladly accepted his friend's gifts. Why?

For one thing, the gift-givers' motives were different. Saul's motive had been *self-serving*. Most likely he had not offered his armor out of affection for David, or to protect him from harm, but to mark him as one of Saul's men. That way, any victory David enjoyed on the battlefield would be noted as a victory for Saul. Jonathan's motive, on the other hand, was *God-serving*. He offered David his own garments in recognition of the fact that God's plan for Israel's future would be accomplished—even though it meant he himself, the heir apparent, never would sit on the throne.

Another reason David turned down Saul's hand-me-downs but accepted Jonathan's might be because he recognized Jonathan's gifts for what they were, as both tokens of allegiance and symbols of the friendship covenant they shared. The armor Jonathan gave wouldn't have protected David from his enemy any better than the armor Saul had offered. However, the loyalty and support that Jonathan's armor represented guaranteed that David would have an ally against any enemies he had yet to encounter.

The King's Man: Moving on Up

1 SAMUEL 18:5–7 *So David went out wherever Saul sent him, and behaved wisely. And Saul set him over the men of war, and*

he was accepted in the sight of all the people and also in the sight of Saul's servants. Now it had happened as they were coming home, when David was returning from the slaughter of the Philistine, that the women had come out of all the cities of Israel, singing and dancing, to meet King Saul, with tambourines, with joy, and with musical instruments. So the women sang as they danced, and said:

> *"Saul has slain his thousands,*
> *And David his ten thousands." (NKJV)*

If King Saul had been needing a right-hand man, now he had one. David's job performance on the battlefield was going well, so well that he earned a promotion. Saul made him a general, and after David led the Israelites in routing those menacing Philistines the people began singing his praises—literally. (The song of celebration the women of Israel sang wasn't intended, it should be pointed out, to report actual body counts after the war. It was a melodic poem suggesting relative proportions rather than concrete numbers.)

It's easy to imagine the thought behind the song: "Wow! We were very successful under Saul, but now we're even more successful under this new guy David! Isn't life grand!" The song obviously wasn't designed to disparage the king, but he chose to hear it differently, distorted by his insecurity and envy.

Plan A: Kill David

1 SAMUEL 18:8–11 *Then Saul was very angry, and the saying displeased him; and he said, "They have ascribed to David ten thousands, and to me they have ascribed only thousands. Now what more can he have but the kingdom?" So Saul eyed David from that day forward. And it happened on the next day that the distressing spirit from God came upon Saul, and he prophesied inside the house. So David played music with his hand, as at other times; but there was a spear in Saul's hand. And Saul cast the spear, for he said, "I will pin David to the wall!" But David escaped his presence twice. (NKJV)*

Something snapped in Saul's darkened heart that day as he made out the words of the women's victory chants. They were belittling his name to enlarge David's! The anger he felt, described with the

Hebrew word *charis* ("to burn"), lit a fuse of destructive attitudes and invited yet another visit from the tormenting spirits. The king began to rant and rave as his anger exploded into jealousy, suspicion, and finally, murderous hatred.

Saul, with the Spear, in the Music Room

It sounds like a scenario from a murder mystery: two men were sitting in the palace's music room, the younger man playing a tune he had composed to soothe the older man's troubled nerves. Quietly, eyes intent on the musician, the listener pulled a spear from the folds of his robe. He quickly aimed, then launched it even as the younger man, whose ears were trained to detect the faintest audible hint of an attack from a wild animal in the sheepfold, ducked his head. Before the music therapy session ended, two spear tips had lodged in the wall behind the pair. Twice King Saul tried to hurt—yes, kill—David . . . while David had only been trying to help the king.

key point

Bad things can—and do—happen to good people who are doing good things! In fact, it's when people are doing good things for God that Satan often wants to perform his most crippling stunts.

Plan B: Get Someone Else to Kill David

1 SAMUEL 18:12–16 *Now Saul was afraid of David, because the LORD was with him, but had departed from Saul. Therefore Saul removed him from his presence, and made him his captain over a thousand; and he went out and came in before the people. And David behaved wisely in all his ways, and the LORD was with him. Therefore, when Saul saw that he behaved very wisely, he was afraid of him. But all Israel and Judah loved David, because he went out and came in before them. (NKJV)*

Saul wasn't giving up. He decided that if he couldn't carry out Plan A—murdering David himself—he'd move on to Plan B—letting the enemy do it for him. So he gave the young man yet another promotion and sent him off to war, probably expecting to receive news of the young hero's death at any moment. However, because the Lord was continually with David, not even the swords and spears of Israel's foes could stop him.

As the people became even more enamored of David, Saul became more fearful of him. After all, Saul had seen plenty of chances to behave wisely and thus secure God's blessing upon his nation. Yet the king had blown it at almost every turn. The people of Israel had been amazingly patient with him through the years, but now they were seeing in David what a true man of God looked and acted like. Could it be long before they would demand Saul's removal so they could crown David as their king? Yes, Saul apparently had plenty of reasons to be fearful—and they all stemmed from his own choices of evil over good. Saul could have led a whole nation of people and made it better, but now his only goal had become destroying one man's life.

Plan C: If You Can't Beat 'Em, Trick 'Em

> 1 SAMUEL 18:17–19 *Then Saul said to David, "Here is my older daughter Merab; I will give her to you as a wife. Only be valiant for me, and fight the LORD's battles." For Saul thought, "Let my hand not be against him, but let the hand of the Philistines be against him." So David said to Saul, "Who am I, and what is my life or my father's family in Israel, that I should be son-in-law to the king?" But it happened at the time when Merab, Saul's daughter, should have been given to David, that she was given to Adriel the Meholathite as a wife. (NKJV)*

Since his efforts to murder David in the music room and in the combat zone had failed, Saul figured he might stand a better chance of undoing David if he could get the big guys—the Philistines—mad at him. To do so he devised a sneaky scheme. He offered David his daughter, Merab, as an ostensible fulfillment of his promise to the victor over Goliath. The offer placed David in a sticky situation. If he refused, he risked offending the king (as if his presence alone wasn't enough of an offense to the king). If he accepted, he risked stepping into a cunning trap. Here's how the setup might have looked in Saul's devious notes:

- David agrees to marry Merab.
- I, as custom demands, require a dowry high enough to be worthy of a king's daughter.
- There's no way David can afford to pay that kind of money.
- I tell David that, instead of bringing me money as a dowry, he can kill some Philistines.

Michal
Saul's daughter and
David's first wife

- That will trigger the Philistines to fight back and kill David instead.

David, naturally leery of the king's offer, began to protest, asserting that his station in life was too low for him to be paired up with royalty. But Saul immediately came up with another ploy: He gave Merab to another man in a move many scholars believe was designed to stir up David's jealousy and anger, and provoke him to charge at the king—a move that could give Saul legal grounds to execute him.

Plan C, Revisited

the big picture

1 Samuel 18:20–25

Saul heard that his daughter **Michal** was in love with David, so he presented her in a second offer before conniving with his servants to try to convince David to accept the proposal. Again, David reminded Saul through his servants that he was poor and of low social standing. Ready with an answer, Saul gave David a grisly alternative to paying a royal bride price: The king told him to bring him one hundred Philistine foreskins, supposedly as proof of David's merit. In truth, of course, Saul's intent was to get David killed.

what others say

Liz Curtis Higgs

The word "snare"—in Hebrew, *moqesh*—suggests something that would bait or lure David into a net and lead to his destruction. "Snare," as defined in English, means "something deceptively attractive." If King Saul wanted to keep tabs on David's whereabouts, what better way than to marry him to his lovely young daughter?[4]

Sue and Larry Richards

To be married to a king, or to be born into the royal family, brought a few privileges but many duties, and many, many disappointments. Essentially, and with few exceptions, women in the royal families of the ancient world were pawns, moved on the chessboard of geopolitics by men who were far more concerned with policy than with the well-being and happiness of wives or daughters.[5]

How to Deal with a Bad Boss

respect authority
Romans 13:1–5;
1 Thessalonians 5:12

do your job well
Colossians 3:23

remain humble
Proverbs 3:34;
Ephesians 4:2

the big picture

1 Samuel 18:26–30

David agreed to Saul's terms and rose to the challenge, returning with not one hundred but with two hundred trophies. The couple was married, with Saul more afraid of David than ever . . . and with David even more highly regarded by the people than before.

Saul may bring to mind a supervisor who is unfair, cruel, or manipulative. What does David's response to his "bad boss" have to teach twenty-first-century Christians in similar predicaments?

1. *Respect authority.*

2. *Do your job well.*

3. *Remain humble.*

Chapter Wrap-Up

- When David finished speaking to Saul after killing Goliath, Jonathan's soul was drawn to David's and the two became close-knit friends.

- The two men cemented their friendship with a covenant—a commitment to an everlasting relationship with one another. Jonathan gave David a gift of his robe, his sword, his bow, and his belt, expressing a sense of protection and signifying that Jonathan knew David would become the next king.

- Saul, impressed by David's triumph over Goliath, recruited David into service in his army. David's impressive successes earned him fame in Israel and praise from its people, but the attention caused Saul to burn with anger, jealousy, suspicion, and hatred.

- The king tried to kill David two times while the younger man was playing music for Saul.

- When those attempts failed, Saul sent David to war in the hope that he would die in battle. However, because the Lord was continually with David, Israel's foes could not stop him.
- Saul then offered his daughter, Merab, in marriage to David, telling David that instead of paying the usual bride price he could kill some Philistines. Saul hoped this would incite the Philistines to kill David instead.
- To further endanger David, Saul switched daughters on David and told him the bride price would be one hundred grisly trophies from the Philistines. David agreed to the terms and returned with not one hundred but with two hundred trophies. The couple was married, with Saul more afraid of David than ever . . . and with David more highly regarded even than before.

Study Questions

1. Why did the friendship between Jonathan and David defy logic, in many ways?

2. What are the two key ingredients of a covenant?

3. What gift did Jonathan give David?

4. How did David fare on his military assignments for King Saul?

5. What touched off Saul's murderous hatred for David?

6. How did Saul try to do away with David?

7. How did David fare against Saul's murder attempts?

Chapter Highlights:
- Dropping in on an Old Friend
- A Priest's Protection
- David Told a Whopper!
- Run Some More
- A Close Call for Saul

1 Samuel 19–24: Warrior on the Run

Let's Get Started

David was a married man now, but practically nothing about his life seemed to be falling into place. The people of Israel loved him but the king hated him. He was a skilled warrior in the king's army, but he was forced to live as a fugitive. He had a close friend, but the friendship put both lives in jeopardy. He had been anointed by God to serve as king, yet he must have felt anything but regal as he feigned madness to escape his pursuers yet again.

go to

teraphim
Genesis 31:19;
Judges 17:5;
1 Samuel 15:23

teraphim
household idol

Saul—Still Out to Get David

the big picture

1 Samuel 19

After Saul ordered his son and his servants to kill David, Jonathan couldn't bring himself to believe his father really intended such evil. In a stirring defense of his friend, Jonathan convinced Saul to reconsider. But the oath the king made to spare David's life was short-lived. As soon as the next victory over the Philistines brought David even more praise from the people, troubling spirits resettled upon Saul and he began plotting murder again. First he threw another javelin at David, who again dodged it. Then he dispatched a mob of men to ambush David at his own house. However, David's wife, Michal, staged one of the oldest getaway tricks in the book: she helped David escape through a window, then stuffed a **teraphim** under the bedcovers and placed a thatch of goat's hair on the pillow to make it look like her husband was sleeping. By the time Saul's servants caught on, David had made a run for Samuel's hometown, Ramah. The chase came to a surprising end when three sets of Saul's thugs, and finally Saul himself, arrived at the priest's town only to be stopped in their tracks by the Holy Spirit. The pursuers were compelled to join a band of prophets who were in the middle of a worship meeting, and thus they were powerless to do the evil they had originally planned.

go to

unintentionally disobeying
1 Samuel 14:27–28

oath
Numbers 30:2;
Exodus 20:7;
Leviticus 19:12;
Deuteronomy
19:16–19;
James 4:13;
Matthew 5:34;
James 5:12

Jonathan: A Risk-Taking Friend

When Saul issued the murder decree, Jonathan had his first opportunity to live up to the covenant he had forged with David. After warning David to hide, he tried to talk some sense into his father. Both undertakings were risky business for the king's son, for two reasons:

1. Jonathan was deliberately disobeying his father's orders. (Saul had once been ready to put his son to death for a lesser crime: *unintentionally* disobeying his dad's directions.)

2. Jonathan was boldly aligning himself with the person his father saw as his biggest threat. Siding with David against Saul easily could have been a lethal move for the son of such a jealous, hateful, unstable man.

Well-Chosen Words

Understanding that the king was angry and unbalanced, Jonathan remained calm and reasonable in talking with Saul. He appealed to Saul's sense of what was right, and acted as if the king were rational. Jonathan simply listed David's attributes and asserted his innocence. The strategy worked: Saul swore an oath not to have David put to death.

According to God's law, swearing an <u>oath</u> isn't something *anyone* should be doing.

Apart from the Holy Spirit, no one has the power to do what is right in the face of sin! Because Saul lacked the power of the Holy Spirit, he had neither an accurate spiritual compass for determining right from wrong nor the self-control to keep his oath. His resolve—his vow—melted in the heat of the jealous rage he felt when he saw the spotlight shining once again on David's military successes.

Good Fruit, Bad Fruit

In his letter to the people living in Galatia, the apostle Paul said that, without the Holy Spirit, people are controlled by their sinful nature. The outward signs—the "bad fruit"—of a sinful nature are easy to spot: sexual immorality, impurity, debauchery, idolatry, witchcraft, hatred, discord, jealousy, fits of rage, selfish ambition, dissensions, factions, envy, drunkenness, and orgies. Saul is a classic example of a person controlled by his sinful nature. Up to this point in the account of his reign, checkmarks on the list of "bad fruit" could be placed by hatred, jealousy, fits of rage, selfish ambition, and envy. And as Saul's story continues to unfold in the following chapters of 1 Samuel, there will undoubtedly be more checkmarks to add to the list.

trap
1 Samuel 18:21

However, when people allow the Holy Spirit to control their lives they have the power—through the Spirit—to keep from producing "bad fruit" because they have a harvest of "good fruit" coming in. That "good fruit" includes love, joy, peace, patience, kindness, goodness, faithfulness, gentleness, and self-control. David is a classic example of a person who was controlled by the Holy Spirit. Up to this point in the narrative of his life, checkmarks could be placed beside most, if not all, of those characteristics.

When Saul swore the oath he lacked the "good fruit" of goodness and faithfulness necessary to help him keep his word. And when he experienced jealousy over David's accomplishments, Saul lacked the "good" fruit of self-control that would help him refrain from acting on that jealousy.

Michal's Man Trouble

Although she had been used by her father as a <u>trap</u> for David, Michal had no reason to complain: She is the only woman in Scripture expressly said to have loved a man, and that man was David. How her heart must have leaped when her father arranged her marriage to the heroic warrior! Her love for her new husband seemed authentic enough; she helped him stage his escape from Saul's men staked out around their home. But her willingness to betray David to her father (by telling Saul that David would have killed her if she had not helped him get away) makes it difficult to determine whether she was truly David's enemy or his ally. True, she lied to save her own life; but in doing so, she fueled Saul's rage against her husband.

The idol that happened to be handy for Michal to use as a dummy under the bedcovers might be a telling indicator of Michal's spiritual health, and at least a partial explanation of her future behavior.

go to

listening for his cry
Psalm 34:15

iniquity
sin

what others say

Liz Curtis Higgs

Despite her godly name [Michal:"who is like God?"], Michal showed no evidence of being a woman who yearned to please God the way her husband did . . . God had clearly forbidden such graven images, which means the house of Saul had not completely embraced Jehovah God, no matter what sort of public posturing they did. Inside their own walls they had idols. Big ones, if they looked even remotely like a sleeping David.[1]

Inspiration at the Most Awkward Moments

As David climbed out the window and dropped to the ground below to begin running for his life, words of prayer and phrases of praise sprang from his heart. Those thoughts would later be recorded as Psalm 59:

PSALM 59:1–4 *Deliver me from my enemies, O my God; defend me from those who rise up against me. Deliver me from the workers of iniquity, and save me from bloodthirsty men. For look, they lie in wait for my life; the mighty gather against me, not for my transgression nor for my sin, O LORD. They run and prepare themselves through no fault of mine. Awake to help me, and behold!* (NKJV)

The words of this psalm outline a helpful plan of action for facing adversaries:

Step 1: Talk to God. David understood that God was always <u>listening for his cry</u>, and he acted on that knowledge by passionately praying for what he wanted most: deliverance and protection.

Step 2: Identify the enemy. Often, prayers offered during a crisis make God out as the enemy: "Why are You allowing this?" is a question posed in desperation or even anger. That wasn't what David did. He acknowledged his enemies for who they were: "workers of **iniquity**." He knew firsthand the identity of the true enemy, and he also knew beyond the shadow of a doubt whose camp he was in: God's.

Step 3: Launch an intense self-examination. David was a proponent of self-examination; after all, he was credited with Psalm 139:23–24: "Search me, O God, and know my heart; try me, and know my anxieties; and see if there is any wicked way in me, and lead me in the way everlasting" (NKJV). In this instance, David seems to have examined his own heart to see whether he was guilty of any behavior that might have been offensive to God. An examination like this can yield two possible results: First, it might unearth some type of sin, which might come in the form of things like a destructive attitude, a stagnant heart, a shaky faith, or impure motives. (Whatever our sins, if we confess them, God promises to remove them, forget about them, and restore our relationship with Him!) Second, a self-examination might reveal nothing more than a pure heart, as David found in this case.

anoint David
1 Samuel 16:12–13

company of prophets
1 Samuel 10:5–18;
1 Kings 18:4

what others say

Burton Coffman

> These urgent repeated cries for God's help emphasize the dramatic nature of the crisis David faced. He was one man, alone, hated, pursued, proscribed by the king, condemned to death without a trial, and an entire army at the disposal of his chief enemy had been commissioned to kill him. Hopeless? No indeed; God was with David![2]

Dropping in on an Old Friend

Possibly no one on earth understood David's peril better than the prophet Samuel. The aged priest, after all, had once been Saul's closest friend and adviser, and he knew firsthand the king's mental and spiritual condition. He also had been the one to anoint David as Saul's successor, so he knew the potential for a clash between the king and his replacement, and he fully recognized what role David was to play in Israel's history. That may have been why David fled to Samuel. If ever he needed protection and direction from someone older and wiser than he, it was then! And what better place to seek refuge from an evil man than in the company of a holy one.

Nothing Could Stop That Prayer Meeting!

Samuel and his company of prophets, meaning the prophet's students, were heart-deep in praise and worship when Saul's servants burst onto the scene looking for David. But the pursuers didn't stop the worship; instead, the worship stopped the pursuers.

They were paralyzed by the power of the Holy Spirit and compelled to join the prophets' chorus of praise. When Saul decided to do for himself what three sets of his servants had failed to do, he met the same outcome. In an episode much like the one that kicked off his reign as king, he began to prophesy along with the rest of the people present. As chapter 19 closes, he strips off his robes. The gesture was highly symbolic because the clothing he wore was what had identified him as king.

Just How Mad Was Jonathan's Dad?

the big picture

I Samuel 20

David knew by now not to trust Saul from one moment to the next. Saul might have been overcome by the Spirit, but judging by the king's past mood swings, David knew Saul's bout of holiness could only be temporary. So he fled from Samuel and the company of prophets to meet his closest ally, Jonathan.

Exhausted and exasperated, David's first recorded words to his friend are heart-wrenching: "What have I done? What is my iniquity, and what is my sin before your father, that he seeks my life?" (1 Samuel 20:1 NKJV). David simply could not make any sense of Saul's behavior and was looking to his best friend, Saul's son, for answers. The pair then devised a plan to determine Saul's true motives toward David. When Jonathan found out that Saul still intended to kill David, he relayed the news to David and the two parted with a tender farewell.

As they talked both before and after confirming Saul's murderous intentions toward David, the two friends renewed their commitment to one another through a series of solemn oaths that restated:

- *Jonathan's willingness to help David:* "So Jonathan said to David, 'Whatever you yourself desire, I will do it for you'" (1 Samuel 20:4 NKJV).

- *Jonathan's faithfulness to David:* "But Jonathan said, 'Far be it from you! For if I knew certainly that evil was determined by my father to come upon you, then would I not tell you?'" (1 Samuel 20:9 NKJV).

- *The endurance of the covenant:* "And you shall not only show me the kindness of the LORD while I still live, that I

134 ——————————— **The Smart Guide to the Bible** ———————————

may not die; but you shall not cut off your kindness from my house forever, no, not when the LORD has cut off every one of the enemies of David from the face of the earth" (1 Samuel 20:14–15 NKJV).

- *The love of the two friends for each other:* "Now Jonathan again caused David to vow, because he loved him; for he loved him as he loved his own soul . . . As soon as the lad had gone, David arose from a place toward the south, fell on his face to the ground, and bowed down three times. And they kissed one another; and they wept together, but David more so" (1 Samuel 20:17, 41 NKJV).

- *The presence of the Lord in the friendship:* "And as for the matter which you and I have spoken of, indeed the LORD be between you and me forever" (1 Samuel 20:23 NKJV).

There never would be any getting back to normal for David. His departure from Jonathan severed his last tie to his wife and everything else associated with his new home. He was now a fugitive facing a future of life on the run.

David would not be able to rest at the palace again until his coronation upon <u>Saul's death</u> about twenty years later.

go to

Saul's death
1 Samuel 31:3–6

meeting
1 Samuel 23:16–18

key point

what others say

Ronald Youngblood

Apart from one other brief <u>meeting</u>, this was the last time the two men would see one another. Friendship is a scarce commodity, and there can hardly be a more wrenching feeling than the sensation that a close and long-standing companionship may, for whatever reason, have come to an end.[3]

A Priest's Protection

1 SAMUEL 21:1–2 Now David came to Nob, to Ahimelech the priest. And Ahimelech was afraid when he met David, and said to him, "Why are you alone, and no one is with you?"

So David said to Ahimelech the priest, "The king has ordered me on some business, and said to me, 'Do not let anyone know anything about the business on which I send you, or what I have commanded you.' And I have directed my young men to such and such a place." (NKJV)

David might have been a fugitive, but he was a fugitive after God's own heart. That's why he headed three miles down the road to Nob. Nob was a town inhabited by priests, one of whom was **Ahimelech**, who served as high priest at the tabernacle. Seeing a man as prominent and powerful as David traveling alone puzzled Ahimelech, so he asked David why he didn't have any traveling companions. David lied and said that he was on a secret mission for the king.

Up to this point in David's life, the biblical narrative has highlighted David's humility, his pure heart, his musical talent, his valor, his skill, his courage, his obedience, and his faith. It has almost seemed as if a big red "S"—for "Superman" or even for "Saint"—was stitched to the front of his tunic! But now David gives reason for that "S" to stand for a far less flattering word: "Sinner."

As tempting as it is to make David out to be a fearless, faithful, and, yes, flawless superhero, in truth he at times did give in to fear, falter in faith, and fail to follow God's commands.

key point

The Truth About Lying

David's reason for lying is plain enough: he was trying to save his skin, and Ahimelech's too. But does having a good excuse ever justify telling a lie? Does God ever condone lying, or let liars slide? Consider what the Bible says about the subject:

- Truth is one of the <u>characteristics of God</u>.
- <u>Truthfulness</u> is a fundamental part of the Bible's teaching.
- Lying, like all sin, <u>originates with the devil</u>.
- The Bible uses strong words such as "abhors," "hates," "detests," and "despises" to describe God's reaction to dishonesty.
- Lying, like any sin, can destroy a person's **witness** and damage his or her relationship with God.

Lying, then, clearly is not what God wants people do. He knows its source—Satan—and sees its cost. He doesn't want His followers to have anything to do with the former and wants to help them avoid having to pay the latter.

go to

characteristics of God
Numbers 23:19;
1 Samuel 15:29;
Romans 3:4;
Titus 1:2;
Hebrews 6:18

truthfulness
Exodus 20:16;
23:1–2, 7;
Deuteronomy 5:20;
19:18–19; 22:13–21;
Proverbs 6:16–19;
12:22;
Matthew 5:37

originates with the devil
John 8:44

Ahimelech
Eli's grandson

witness
ability to introduce others to a relationship with God

Good Guys, Bad Lies

When <u>Ananias and Sapphira</u> told a lie, they dropped dead. But such a dramatic judgment isn't the fate of all liars in the Bible. In fact, some of Scripture's most illustrious saints, including <u>Abraham</u>, <u>Jacob</u>, the Egyptian <u>midwives</u>, <u>Rahab</u>, and <u>Peter</u> told tall tales or crafted deception.

It's important to realize that when people in the Bible—even those who, like David, are considered heroes of the faith—tell lies, it's not an endorsement of sin, it's simply a record of what sinful people have done. Sometimes God reveals in His Word the price they paid for their sin; other times, He doesn't mention the consequences at all.

If folks like these could tell lies and still be called people of God, why isn't lying okay all the time? The answer is simple: Because lying is wrong; it is never part of God's good plan for His people. However, because God is sovereign, He can accomplish His plan in spite of men's and women's lies and deceptions.

apply it

Show Me Your Showbread

the big picture

1 Samuel 21:3–6

Getting back to the business at hand, David then asked Ahimelech for food. Further embellishing the tale he had already begun, he said he hadn't had time to pack provisions when he left, and that he would be meeting his traveling companions soon. All the priest had on hand, however, was the holy bread meant only for priests and **ceremonially clean** people to eat. David assured him that he—and the men he would supposedly be meeting—were qualified, so the priest complied.

go to

Ananias and Sapphira
Acts 5:1–11

Abraham
Genesis 20:2

Jacob
Genesis 25:23;
27:35

midwives
Exodus 1:17–21

Rahab
Joshua 2:4–6

Peter
Matthew 26:72

ceremonially clean
following the rules
the Israelites were to
live by

frankincense
aromatic oil

Like all other aspects of the tabernacle, the showbread was presented and handled according to a set of detailed rules.

1. The table of showbread—which stood 3 feet long, 1' 6" wide and 2' 3" high—was located on the right-hand side of the entrance to the tabernacle, opposite the golden lampstand. It was made of gold and acacia wood.

2. There were twelve loaves of showbread—one for each tribe of Israel—made of fine flour and sprinkled with **frankincense**.

go to

eat the old bread
Leviticus 24:5–9

couldn't be eaten
Leviticus 15

Doeg
Saul's Edomite spy

Gath
Philistine city and
Goliath's hometown

3. The bread was always to be fresh, so it was replaced once a week.

4. The priests were permitted to <u>eat the old bread</u>.

5. The showbread was holy, so it <u>couldn't be eaten</u> by anyone who wasn't ceremonially clean.

A Spy "Doeg" in the Room

1 SAMUEL 21:7–10 Now a certain man of the servants of Saul was there that day, detained before the LORD. And his name was Doeg, an Edomite, the chief of the herdsmen who belonged to Saul. And David said to Ahimelech, "Is there not here on hand a spear or a sword? For I have brought neither my sword nor my weapons with me, because the king's business required haste."

So the priest said, "The sword of Goliath the Philistine, whom you killed in the Valley of Elah, there it is, wrapped in a cloth behind the ephod. If you will take that, take it. For there is no other except that one here." And David said, "There is none like it; give it to me." Then David arose and fled that day from before Saul, and went to Achish the king of Gath. (NKJV)

One of Saul's men, **Doeg** of Edom, was at the tabernacle eavesdropping on the exchange between David and Ahimelech. He had heard the discussion about the showbread, and next he listened as David requested weapons from the priest. The only sword available, Ahimelech said, was the sword of Goliath. "I'll take it," David said, and so with the bread tucked under one arm and Goliath's sword under the other, he headed straight for Gath.

Why would David seek refuge from Saul in **Gath**, Goliath's hometown, in the enemy territory of the Philistines? Considering Saul's rage against David, his determination to have David killed, and the number of men at Saul's disposal, his homeland wasn't looking to be a very safe place. David must have figured he'd be just as safe—maybe even safer—in a place where Saul and his men were not welcome. It probably seemed like a good idea at the time.

Abimelech
title similar to pharaoh

acrostic psalms
poetry in which each verse begins with a consecutive letter of the Hebrew alphabet

the big picture

1 Samuel 21:11-15

> The servants of Achish, the king of Gath, couldn't believe their eyes when they saw who was approaching. Incredulous, they asked, "Is this not David the king of the land? Did they not sing of him to one another in dances, saying: 'Saul has slain his thousands, and David his ten thousands'?" (1 Samuel 21:11 NKJV). David became fearful when he stopped listening to his internal navigational system—the Holy Spirit—and heard the words of Achish's servants. "What on earth have I done?" he must have thought as he realized his predicament. He might as well have been wearing a bull's-eye, standing there in Goliath's hometown holding Goliath's spear in front of Goliath's former friends and fans. Desperation often makes people do crazy things, and this is a case in point: David began scratching and drooling so he would appear insane. The deception worked (add "good actor" to the list of David's strengths!) and the king, sarcastically claiming he had enough madmen of his own to contend with, sent David on his way.

Even the men of this ungodly city understood David's true identity as "King of the land"!

David's Ebenezer: Psalm 34

Just as Samuel erected a stone monument at Ebenezer to commemorate the Lord's deliverance of the Israelites from the Philistines; David wrote many psalms to commemorate the Lord's rescue of him. Psalm 34 is one such song of praise. The introductory caption to the psalm states it was written to describe God's deliverance of David's life when he feigned madness to escape from Achich, the **Abimelech** of Gath.

This is the second of the **acrostic psalms**, in which each verse begins with a consecutive letter of the Hebrew alphabet. (The first one is Psalm 25.) Translation issues alter the alphabetical feature of the psalm, however, when it's read in English. The words and phrases David used in this psalm more fully describe the reasons the Lord favored David, gave a clearer picture of the God he served, and listed things the readers should do to experience a closer relationship with Him.

What Psalm 34 Says About David

- He made God front and center of everything he did.
- He made praise a priority.
- He based his value on his identity with the Lord.
- He invited others to join him in praising God.
- His first response when he was fearful was to seek God.
- He freely shared his personal experience with God.
- He understood with his heart things that could not be seen with the eyes.
- He passionately enjoyed the Lord's fellowship.
- He counted on God's provision.

What Psalm 34 Says About God

- He is a deliverer.
- He is holy.
- He is attentive.
- He is omnipresent.
- He is trustworthy.
- He is tenderhearted.
- He is the Redeemer.

What Psalm 34 Teaches Us

- The "fear of the Lord" is a discipline to be learned.
- People should refrain from using words in an evil or deceitful way.
- People should turn away from doing bad things.
- People should make good choices.
- People should strive to live peacefully.
- People should leave revenge for wrongdoings up to God.

Into Hiding

Ruth
Ruth 1:4; 4:21–22

Adullam
hilly area at the western edge of Judah about 10 miles southeast of Gath

the big picture

1 Samuel 22:1–5; 1 Chronicles 12:16–18

David fled to the cave of **Adullam**, where he was joined by his family and a band of about four hundred followers. From there, David took his family to find refuge in Mizpah of Moab, where he had family ties: his great-grandmother <u>Ruth</u> had lived there. Then, on the advice of the prophet Gad, David and his followers went into the forest of Hereth in Judah, a few miles east of Adullam.

The refugees couldn't have found a better hiding place than the caves of Adullam. Carved into the soft limestone ridges of what is now called Deir-Dubban, six miles southwest of Bethlehem, the caves' most unique feature was a number of fifteen- to twenty-foot-deep pits or underground vaults, some of which were nearly square and ideal for concealing a number of people.

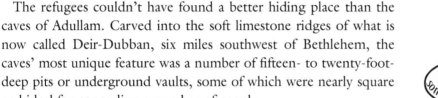

A Close-Up of the Motley Crew

It would be tempting to think of David's group of followers as a glamorous and elite assembly of soldiers who had been hand-picked for their valor, honesty, and integrity, much like King Arthur's dazzling Knights of the Round Table. But there were no Sir Galahads in this bunch. David's followers are described as being:

1. ***In distress***—"Distress," from the Hebrew word *maw-tsoke'*, suggests some of the men were in a "narrow" place, figuratively speaking, and that they were in confinement or had a disability. In other words, something about their lives wasn't right, and they felt as if the walls were closing in.

2. ***In debt***—Some of these guys hadn't paid their bills, and the collectors were starting to come around. The pressure was building and they had nowhere else to turn. Neither Saul nor his henchmen were likely to help them formulate a debt reconsolidation plan.

go to

receives sinners
Luke 15:2

distressed
Matthew 11:28

in debt
Luke 7:41–43

Satan was rejected by God
Isaiah 14:12–23

Satan still rules this world
John 12:31; 16:11

3. *Discontent*—Sometimes people allow their troubles to make them *marah*, or "bitter," and that's what had happened to these men. The reasons aren't disclosed, but it's easy to imagine becoming embittered while raising a family under the reign of a king as volatile and misguided as Saul.

Considering that Saul's army consisted of the most accomplished warriors, it may appear as if David got the short end of the stick when it came to supporters! But as David's story illustrates again and again, appearances aren't what really matter:

what others say

John Gill

In this [David] was a type of Christ, who <u>receives sinners</u> <u>distressed</u> with a sense of sin, discontented in their present state, and <u>in debt</u>, and, unable to pay their debts.[5]

A Limited Reign

Saul, the man rejected by God because he proudly presumed to be wiser than God, was still reigning over Israel while David, the man chosen by God, was hiding out in caves and forests with the few loyal followers who knew he was the true king of Israel.

Sound familiar?

It should, because it's a good illustration of what's going on today between Satan and Jesus Christ. <u>Satan was rejected by God</u> when, under his former name of Lucifer, he proudly presumed to be wiser than God. Yet <u>Satan still rules this world</u> while Jesus Christ waits with His followers who recognize Him for who He is—the true King of all creation.

what others say

Alan Redpath

Just as in David's day, there is a King in exile who is gathering around Him a company of people who are in distress, in debt, and discontented. He is training and preparing them for the day when He shall come to reign.[6]

The Spy Doeg Speaks

go to

curse
1 Samuel 2:27–36

1 SAMUEL 22:6–10 When Saul heard that David and the men who were with him had been discovered—now Saul was staying in Gibeah under a tamarisk tree in Ramah, with his spear in his hand, and all his servants standing about him—then Saul said to his servants who stood about him, "Hear now, you Benjamites! Will the son of Jesse give every one of you fields and vineyards, and make you all captains of thousands and captains of hundreds? All of you have conspired against me, and there is no one who reveals to me that my son has made a covenant with the son of Jesse; and there is not one of you who is sorry for me or reveals to me that my son has stirred up my servant against me, to lie in wait, as it is this day."

Then answered Doeg the Edomite, who was set over the servants of Saul, and said, "I saw the son of Jesse going to Nob, to Ahimelech the son of Ahitub. And he inquired of the LORD for him, gave him provisions, and gave him the sword of Goliath the Philistine." (NKJV)

When Saul, who was staying in Gibeah, heard that David and the men who were with him had returned to Judah, he scolded his servants and, demonstrating his increasing paranoia, accused them of conspiring against him. Suddenly Doeg the Edomite remembered a tidbit of information that just might get himself out of hot water with the king. He told Saul about seeing David in Nob, and about Ahimelech giving the fugitive the food and the sword. Saul immediately went to the priest, confronted him, and ordered him and all the other priests—eighty-six in all, along with their families and all the livestock—to be slain as punishment for what he mistakenly believed, in his paranoia, to be their part in the conspiracy against him. None of the king's servants wanted to obey the order, so Saul ordered Doeg to do it. Abiathar, Ahimelech's son, escaped the massacre and ran to David to report what had just happened. David took full responsibility for the tragedy, and promised Abiathar protection.

The death of Ahimelech, Eli's great-grandson, fulfilled the curse God pronounced through Samuel on the family of Eli.

Prophecy

Keilah
city in Judah near
Philistine border

Ziph
a barren wilderness
between the hill
country and the
Dead Sea

En Gedi
an oasis east of
Hebron

Run, Run, Run, and Run Some More

the big picture

1 Samuel 23

Saul pursued David all over the map of Judah. Important events include:

1. David delivered **Keilah**. The Philistines continued to be a threat, so when David heard they were doing some looting in Keilah, a city in Judah near the Philistine border, he and his men saved the city from the invaders, took the Philistines' livestock, and inflicted heavy losses.
2. David continued to run. In spite of David's kindness to them, the people of Keilah betrayed him to Saul. When David learned of Saul's plot to seize him, David and his followers—a group that now numbered about six hundred—escaped into the desert of **Ziph**.
3. David and Jonathan met one more time. While David was in Ziph, Jonathan paid him a visit, encouraging him and assuring him that everything would be okay. The pair renewed their friendship covenant yet again before parting for a final time.
4. The pursuit resumed. Saul chased David out of the desert and into the Wilderness of Maon, where Saul nearly caught up with David. However, as Saul and his men were closing in, the king was suddenly called away on an emergency. David ran from there to live in safety in a lush area called the **En Gedi**.

A Leader Emerges

As David fled from Saul and his men, he wasn't cowering in caves in fear. He was practicing and polishing his leadership skills as he took his place at the helm of the band of men who had joined him at Adullam. The way David handled the "Keilah question" demonstrates his leadership skills at their best. His success in that operation didn't stem from a mogul-sized portion of self-confidence, superior weaponry, slick speaking skills or cunning strategy; it found its source in his constant—almost childlike—persistence in seeking God's instruction.

He didn't want to take even one step outside God's plan.

When David began to consider whether to rescue Keilah, he immediately asked God for guidance and received a "yes," so he

key point

ordered his men to move into action. But the men brought up a concern: They were afraid to go there! Their fears weren't unfounded: Their rescue of the city would likely stir up the hornet's nest of angry Philistines and, as if that wasn't dangerous enough, it would make David and his band easy targets for Saul's hit men. But rather than stomping his foot into the ground and refusing to back off his decision to take the city, David listened carefully to the counsel of his men. He considered their advice, then asked God for direction a second time.

In doing so, he wasn't doubting God's direction or showing a lack of faith; he was simply making sure he had heard God's answer correctly and wasn't acting on his own impulse or misguided feelings. When David received a second "yes," he knew it was time to step up to the authoritative role God had ordained for him: He insisted that his men move into Keilah, which they delivered with tremendous success, as God had promised.

David and Saul: Different Schools of Leadership

David	Saul
He cared for his "sheep"—his people.	He cared for the "shepherd"—himself.
He was a visionary, fully understanding that he had a role in a plan much broader than his own life.	He had tunnel vision, seeing nothing more than the here and now.
He focused his attention on God.	He craved attention for himself.
He accepted full responsibility, remorse, and repentance for his sins.	He refused to take responsibility for his sin; showing only empty bouts of remorse and demonstrating no real repentance.

A Close Call for Saul

the big picture

1 Samuel 24

By now, David and his 600 men were being pursued by Saul and his 3,000. The proportions were making it reminiscent of David and Goliath's uneven match back in the Valley of Elah! Saul almost caught up with David at En Gedi, but when the king had to make a rest stop in a cave, the tables were turned. David and his men happened to be hiding in the far recesses of that same cave, and they had the king in a very vulnerable position: He was alone, unarmed, and preoccupied. David's men couldn't believe their good fortune. They had Saul right where they wanted him. Rather than ambush Saul, however, David simply got up and secretly snipped off a corner of Saul's robe, possibly to use as evidence that he had been close enough to kill the king but had spared his life. But even that unthreatening move bothered David, who was immediately conscious-stricken about his presumptuousness and insubordination against the king, the Lord's anointed. As Saul left the cave, David followed him, called out to him, and then bowed before him. David stated his case plainly to Saul, speaking with humility and authority.

1. He rebuked the king for believing those who told Saul that David meant to harm the king.
2. He reminded the king that he had spared his life even though he had the motive—and the opportunity—to murder him.
3. He respected the king's position as the Lord's anointed.
4. He declared his own innocence, stating he harbored no evil or rebellious intentions.
5. He relinquished judgment and vengeance to the Lord.

Saul broke down in apparently genuine—albeit temporary—remorse. He wept as he acknowledged David's righteousness and admitted that he realized that David was the one Samuel had said would replace him. David swore care and treatment of Saul's family legacy, and they went their own ways.

A Pair of Psalms

David is credited with writing two prayers for help—Psalms 57 and 142—during this time in his life. Each prayer stresses his sense of distress, his plea for help, his confidence that God would save him, and then his praise of God for doing so.

When David, the innocent, bowed before Saul, the guilty, David positioned himself as Christ would later position Himself before His accusers. It was a risky move for David! Saul could have ordered his men to seize him. Yet David was confident of God's hand on his life and he understood the power of humility.

Consider what this chapter reveals about each man's leadership abilities. When Goliath had been pacing the opposite bank of the streambed, Saul—the king of the land—couldn't pay his men to step forward to fight, much less motivate them to do so of their own volition. Yet David's followers—clearly the underdogs based on both their numbers and their résumés—couldn't wait to get their hands around the king's neck to avenge their ill-treated leader. Yet they obeyed David. His example of self-control and patience must have been rubbing off on them.

Chapter Wrap-Up

- After a brief pause in his pursuit of David, Saul resumed the chase with a vengeance, forcing David to escape from his home and run to Samuel's town. He was closely followed by three sets of Saul's thugs, who were stopped in their tracks by the Holy Spirit. They were powerless to do the evil they had originally planned.

- David fled from Samuel and the company of prophets to meet his closest ally, Jonathan. After executing a plan the two devised to find out Saul's true motives, they determined that Saul indeed was still set on killing David. The two then parted after reconfirming their friendship covenant.

- David then ran to Nob where, after telling the puzzled chief priest Ahimelech that he was on a mission for the king, he secured provisions for his flight. One of Saul's men, Doeg, was eavesdropping on the conversation.

- David fled to the Philistine town of Gath, where he feigned madness to save his life, and then to the caves of Adullam, where he was joined by his family and a band of about four hundred followers.

- Doeg told Saul what he had overheard in Nob, prompting Saul to have the priests there executed. Only one person, Abiathar, Ahimelech's son, escaped the massacre.

- Saul continued to chase David all over the map of Judah. When the king had to make a rest stop in a cave at En Gedi, David and his men had a chance to kill him, but they didn't because David honored Saul as the Lord's anointed king.

- Saul, in apparently genuine but temporary remorse, acknowledged David's righteousness and affirmed David as God's choice for king before the two parted ways.

Study Questions

1. How did Jonathan's friendship with David place Jonathan in danger?

2. How did David escape when Saul's men ambushed his home?

3. What kept Saul's men from killing David in Samuel's hometown of Ramah?

4. What missteps did David take at Nob, the city of priests?

5. Why did David flee to the enemy city of Gath in Philistia?

6. What kind of reception did he receive there?

7. Who joined David when he was a fugitive seeking refuge in the caves of Adullam?

8. What were the consequences of David's visit to Nob?

9. What positive results emerged from the time David spent running from Saul?

10. Why did David spare Saul's life?

1 Samuel 25: David and Abigail

Chapter Highlights:
• What David's Doing
• Sheepshearing Time!
• Mismatched Mates
  from Maon
• The Danger of Anger
• Divine Intervention

Let's Get Started

The way David's story illuminates what it means to become a person after God's own heart doesn't depend on David's characteristics alone, nor does it rely solely on how he responded to his remarkable circumstances. It's also about the people—both allies and enemies—God placed in David's path. In his dealings with friends such as Samuel, Jonathan, and his band of men, David learned much about loyalty, leadership, and, most important, faith. And his encounters with people like Saul and Goliath offered David treacherous but vital testing grounds for that faith.

Tucked away in the narrative of the time David spent with his band of men as they dodged into caves and fled across the countryside to evade Saul's attacks is yet another extraordinary encounter. This time, David, stomping angrily down the path toward a lethal mistake, was stopped in his tracks by a woman who seemed to turn all stereotypes of ancient womanhood upside down. She was brave, independent, assertive, fast-acting, and forward thinking. And as she was preventing the future king from jeopardizing his future, she was captivating his heart.

Samuel's Legacy

> 1 SAMUEL 25:1 *Then Samuel died; and the Israelites gathered together and lamented for him, and buried him at his home in Ramah. And David arose and went down to the Wilderness of Paran. (NKJV)*

Samuel died at age ninety-eight after faithfully serving his God and his nation as Israel's thirteenth judge and first prophet. The conversation among the Israelites who gathered in Ramah to mourn the priest's death and bury him on the grounds of his home there surely included references to his many accomplishments and his legacy of faith. Samuel had:

go to

Shiloh
1 Samuel 2:11

first king
1 Samuel 10:1

school of prophets
1 Samuel 19:20;
1 Kings 18:4

procedures
1 Chronicles 9:22

treasures
1 Chronicles
26:27–28

promises God made to David
2 Samuel 7:1–29

treasures
special gifts

intercessor
one who prays on
behalf of others

- spent his early life at <u>Shiloh</u> in the service of the Lord;
- ushered in the new form of government, the monarchy, and anointed Israel's <u>first king</u>;
- established the first <u>school of prophets</u>;
- organized various <u>procedures</u> for the tabernacle, systems that would later be used in the temple;
- collected some of the **treasures** that would later be placed in the temple of David.

His legacy included several later mentions in Scripture, which noted him as:

- a man of God (Psalm 99:6)
- an **intercessor** for Israel (Jeremiah 15:1)
- a man of great faith (Hebrews 11:32–33)

Samuel's ministry was comparable to that of John the Baptist. Both were lifelong Nazirites and both had much to do with the coming of a king. Samuel served the first divinely appointed king of Israel; John served Jesus, the last of the lineage and the culmination of the <u>promises God made to David</u>.

What David's Doing

By now, Saul was a lame-duck king. He was still in office, but his days there were numbered. God had proclaimed it; the king knew it, David knew it, and many of the people of Israel knew it. Just the same, David—still unwilling to strike down Saul with his own hands—had the tedious job of waiting for Saul's demise. Knowing fully well Saul still couldn't be trusted not to try to kill him again, David and his men were forced to remain in hiding. So, after mourning the loss of his mentor and friend, David and his entourage retreated again—this time into the wilderness in the land of Maon. There, they established an existence that was a far cry from what a person would expect life to be like for God's king-elect. Instead of living in a castle, David and his followers lived in caves. Instead of feasting at royal banquets, they were forced to forage for food. And instead of having bodyguards to protect them from enemies and intruders, they fought off enemies and intruders for themselves—and for neighboring farmers as well.

The Waiting Game

It would have been easy for David to look around at his less-than-majestic circumstances and fret over the possibility that God had forgotten all about His promise to make him king. And it might have been just as easy for David to keep checking the time and waste away the hours doing little more than daydreaming about what it would be like to finally become king of Israel. But by all indications, David was a wise and patient waiter. As he waited for God's promise to become a reality, he spent time focusing not on his circumstances or his goal, but on what mattered most: his moment-by-moment relationship with God.

something to ponder

what others say

John Indermark

How long did you wait—long enough to wonder whether you could trust it? Long enough to doubt it would ever come to pass? A day, a week, a month . . . a lifetime? . . . Several things can happen in vigils. We can exchange the look forward for a look backward by questioning the promise or the promise maker. We can exchange the look forward for a blindfold by refusing to see what does not conform to our expectations or by retreating into self-absorption. Or the look forward can be maintained. The promise of fresh beginnings can be tenaciously held even though day after day the eagerly anticipated seems only the agonizingly delayed.[1]

Jennifer Rothschild

The prize is often what keeps us faithful while we wait, but consider that our joy isn't reserved for the awards ceremony, that there is something deeply joyful in the in-between time. If we focus on the prize alone, we'll see the waiting as a trial, missing the joy of the journey and overlooking the treasures along the way. Learning to wait teaches us that our joy doesn't depend on whether we get those things for which we've waited. It teaches us to experience the strengthening effect of *in-all joy*, not just *end-all joy*.[2]

Sheepshearing Time!

1 SAMUEL 25:2 *Now there was a man in Maon whose business was in Carmel, and the man was very rich. He had three thousand sheep and a thousand goats. And he was shearing his sheep in Carmel.* (NKJV)

go to

fool
Psalms 14:1; 53:1;
Proverbs 10:23;
26:12; 28:26

wise
Psalms 19:7; 107:43;
111:10;
Proverbs 1:7; 3:7

Nabal
wealthy farmer of
Maon

Abigail
Nabal's wise and
beautiful wife, who,
after her husband's
death, became
David's wife

key point

When David and his men heard it was sheepshearing time on the nearby estate, they must have been ecstatic. This was a festive time punctuated by merriment, celebration, and feasts. The mouths of the starving boys in David's band were beginning to water already as they anticipated the delicious food they would soon eat. It would be theirs for the asking, they assumed, because any farmer in this tribal society would, as a matter of honor, gladly offer hospitality to those who had protected his family and his flocks from the marauders who roamed the countryside. But David and his men would soon learn that Nabal wasn't just any farmer.

Mismatched Mates from Maon

1 SAMUEL 25:3 *The name of the man was **Nabal**, and the name of his wife **Abigail**. And she was a woman of good understanding and beautiful appearance; but the man was harsh and evil in his doings. He was of the house of Caleb. (NKJV)*

This verse succinctly sums up the differences between the man and woman from Maon: Nabal, whose name sounds like the Hebrew word for "fool," was harsh and dishonest; and Abigail, whose name means "joy of her father," was a wise woman, beautiful inside and out.

The Bible defines a <u>fool</u> as one who does not know God and a <u>wise</u> person as one who fears God, thus Nabal was ungodly and Abigail was godly.

Opposites may attract, but given their huge differences, it's unlikely that Abigail ever would have chosen to walk down the aisle to Nabal.

She only did so because, as custom of the day dictated, her father had arranged the marriage. Even though Abigal may have been the apple of her father's eye, he apparently had in mind his pocketbook and prestige rather than her personal happiness when he offered her hand to the wealthy and powerful Nabal.

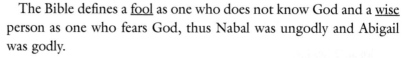

what others say

Ann Spangler

Abigail must have felt suffocated, having been paired with just such a husband. Her father may have thought the wealthy Nabal a catch, little realizing the man's domineering attitude might one day endanger his daughter's well-being.[3]

David: Finally at the End of His Rope?

1 Samuel 25:4–13

David sent ten men to ask Nabal for provisions. Ever the word-smith, David told his messengers exactly what words to use in order to convey the most appropriate impression: a kind greeting, a reminder of their diligence and honesty, and a request for the favor of their hospitality. Their eloquence didn't impress Nabal. He responded by insulting David, questioning his parentage, and accusing him of rebellion against Saul. When David heard the report of Nabal's answer, the previous poster boy for self-control exploded with violent rage. He ordered four hundred of his men to take up arms and prepare to kill Nabal as well as every member of his household.

David had been patient for so long! As mentioned earlier, he had been waiting without tapping his toes or checking the time.

- After being anointed king as a young man, anyone else would have surely tossed aside his staff in anticipation of a scepter. But David went right back to the sheepfold to wait *patiently* for something to happen.

- After being summoned to the palace to become the king's musician, anyone else might have notified the mail carrier of a permanent change of address. But David had continued to divide his time between the palace and the sheepfold as he continued to wait *patiently* for God to determine when he would move to the royal residence.

- After killing Goliath and becoming a celebrated warrior and leader, anyone else might have thought the only appropriate honor for his military accomplishments would be a crown. But David waited *patiently* for God to work out the timing of that event—even passing up the opportunity to kill the one he was destined to replace.

- After hearing the current king confess that he himself knew David was to become his replacement, anyone else might have thought the keys to the castle would be jangling in his pocket by nightfall. Yet once again, David returned to what he had been doing before to *patiently* wait for God to say "when."

go to

Jesus was without sin
2 Corinthians 5:21

He expressed anger
Matthew 21:12–13;
Mark 11:15

in danger of committing sin
Psalm 4:4

fool
Proverbs 29:11

strife
Proverbs 29:22;
30:33

befriending those who are angry
Proverbs 22:24–25

foothold for the devil
Ephesians 4:27

anger interferes
James 1:20

anger
Ephesians 4:26

Don't go to bed angry
Ephesians 4:26

Further, David had endured insults before without drawing his sword in anger. So what was up with the sudden storm of rage? Nabal's rudeness, it seems, was the last straw for David, who appeared to be ready to stop waiting and start taking matters into his own hands, even though doing so would put him in political peril (murdering one of his own people would give Saul and Saul's supporters a legitimate excuse to condemn him) and immerse him in spiritual sin (the Law drew a clear line between killing in war and killing in retribution). Blood on his hands was not something this king-to-be could have.

The Danger of Anger

Anger isn't a sin, it's an emotion. It can't be a sin because <u>Jesus was without sin</u>, and the Bible clearly states that He <u>expressed anger</u> on at least one occasion. However, anger is a volatile emotion. It can cause physical problems ranging from high blood pressure to stomach ulcers, and can wreak emotional havoc in the form of depression and addictions. It also puts people <u>in danger of committing sin</u>. Solomon described the one who gives in to anger as a "<u>fool</u>"; he said that nothing but sin and <u>strife</u> result from unchecked anger; and he warned against <u>befriending those who are angry</u> because their anger might be contagious. The apostle Paul described anger as a <u>foothold for the devil</u> in that it gives Satan an opportunity to unleash any number of sinful attitudes and behaviors. And James said that <u>anger interferes</u> with one's ability to live a righteous life.

Anger Management

The Bible offers many strategies for dealing with anger:

1. Be alert to the danger of anger. When you find yourself seething, make a deliberate effort to avoid taking the treacherous step from <u>anger</u> to sin.

2. Handle anger promptly. <u>Don't go to bed angry</u>; you'll fume and the fury will only intensify the longer you leave it untended.

3. Acknowledge your anger to God. He <u>knows what's in your heart</u> already anyway, but admitting your anger to Him will help you invite His help in getting it under control.

4. Ask the <u>Holy Spirit</u> to give you the power to overcome your anger.

5. <u>Forgive</u> the person who made you angry.

go to

knows what's in your heart
Psalm 139:1–4

Holy Spirit
John 14:16

forgive
Matthew 6:12,
14–15

women as property
Exodus 20:17

Divine Intervention

the big picture

1 Samuel 25:14–19

One of Nabal's servants saw trouble brewing in David's hot-headed behavior. He knew he couldn't report the news to the master of the estate, because he was a "scoundrel" no one could talk to, so he headed straight for someone he could trust: Abigail. He gave her an accurate report of what had transpired, and she wasted no time taking action. Without a word to her husband, she gathered the makings of a sumptuous feast—bread, wine, meat, grain, raisins, and figs—and loaded it onto donkeys as gifts for David and his men. She sent the servants ahead of her with the provisions then mounted a donkey herself to travel to David's camp.

The Hebrew word for husband is *ba'al*, or "owner" or "master," and for wife the word is *be'ulah*, or "owned," illustrating the Old Testament regard for <u>women as property</u>. However, many women apparently enjoyed considerable freedom and exerted a tremendous influence on their families, their communities, and even on the affairs of their government. Clearly Abigail was one such woman. It's already plain that she was wise and beautiful, but this passage offers even more insight to her character. She was approachable. She had won the respect of her servants. She acted with authority. She was a problem-solver. Moreover, she was a quick thinker, an action-taker, and independent. She wasn't stifled by her husband's station as a fool; she apparently had been free to establish her own reputation as a fair and trustworthy woman. And she understood the truth expressed in Proverbs 21:14 that a gift can pacify anger.

Gracious Words

1 SAMUEL 25:20–24 So it was, as she rode on the donkey, that she went down under cover of the hill; and there were David and his men, coming down toward her, and she met them. Now David had said, "Surely in vain I have protected all that this fellow has in the wilderness, so that nothing was missed of all that belongs to him. And he has repaid me evil for good. May God do so, and more also, to the enemies of David, if I leave one male of all who belong to him by morning light."

Now when Abigail saw David, she dismounted quickly from the donkey, fell on her face before David, and bowed down to the ground. So she fell at his feet and said: "On me, my lord, on me let this iniquity be! And please let your maidservant speak in your ears, and hear the words of your maidservant." (NKJV)

The caravan met David's procession on the road. Before David saw her, Abigail saw him—still muttering, fuming, and threatening Nabal and his household under his breath as he and his men made their way down the road. Slipping off her donkey, the beautiful woman bowed on the ground before him to make one of the longest speeches by a woman recorded in the Bible. Her words to David included:

key point

1. A humble greeting. She fell at his feet and asked him to hear her out.

2. Assumption of responsibility. Of course the refusal of hospitality wasn't her fault; it was her husband's! But as the woman of the house, she accepted accountability by saying she hadn't seen David's men who had brought the request and she asked David for forgiveness.

3. Acknowledgment of Nabal's true character. She called him a scoundrel and stated that he was as foolish as his name implied.

4. A reminder that the Lord's hand was upon David.

5. An accurate assessment of the situation at hand; she stated that the action David was about to take was about personal vengeance.

6. A summary of David's role in carrying out God's plan.

7. A reference to David's past victory over Goliath through the power of God.

8. A reminder of David's future as ruler over Israel.

9. A request that David remember her.

go to

gentle tongue
Proverbs 25:15

calm a person's anger
Proverbs 15:1

Abigail's speech has much to teach about effective communication. She carefully chose her words to convey respect (even when David wasn't behaving in a way that earned it!), honesty, spiritual understanding, tact, confidence, and assertiveness. But perhaps the more powerful lesson to be learned from Abigail's encounter with David doesn't come from her speech at all. It lies in her understanding that she had a responsibility to nurture the spiritual health of a fellow believer.

something to ponder

what others say

Rick Warren

Given the right situation, you and I are capable of any sin. God knows this, so he has assigned us as individuals the responsibility of keeping each other on track . . . "Mind your own business" is not a Christian phrase. We are called and commanded to be involved in each other's lives. If you know someone who is wavering spiritually right now, it is your responsibility to go after them and bring them back into the fellowship.[4]

What a Mouthful!

the big picture

1 Samuel 25:32–35

If "a gentle tongue breaks a bone," it can also calm a person's anger. Abigail proved that, and David was ever so grateful for the favor. So grateful, in fact, that he praised God for putting Abigail in his path, he profusely thanked her, he graciously accepted her gift, and then sent her on her way with a blessing.

Insubordinate. Rude. Out of line. Presumptuous. Pushy. David could have labeled Abigail with those or many other words, but he didn't. If the key lesson from Abigail's example is her willingness to speak her mind to keep a fellow believer from sinning, the big lesson in David's reaction is that he was willing to hear her out. In doing

so, he allowed God to use her words as a splash of cool water to douse his burning rage.

Remember, this is a guy who didn't really want to sin; his passion was to please God. He was grateful that a fellow believer had run interference for him.

Nabal Had a Stroke

the big picture

1 Samuel 25:36–38

Certainly Abigail had headed home feeling confident and relieved, maybe even joyous, as she realized she had acted as the Lord's mouthpiece in accomplishing His plans for David. To be used by God—nothing could be sweeter! But her heart must have fallen as she remembered her husband probably wouldn't understand the magnitude of what God had just done through her. He would likely become even angrier, she must have reasoned. It was no surprise when she arrived home to find him drunk; however, even if he had been sober she knew he would not have understood. It's a common saying today: "He'll have a stroke when I tell him the news." If those were Abigail's thoughts as she made her way toward her Carmel estate, they were prophetic: After she told him the news the next morning, he suffered a stroke that paralyzed him for ten days, then he died.

God tells men and women not to partner with unbelievers: "Do not be unequally yoked together with unbelievers. For what fellowship has righteousness with lawlessness? And what communion has light with darkness?" (2 Corinthians 6:14 NKJV). In spite of this warning, godly women continue to marry ungodly men, and vice versa, every day. If you're in that type of marital relationship, it helps to remember the following principles:

1. *You are personally accountable to God, so it's important not to let your unbelieving husband or wife obstruct your relationship with God or your obedience to Him.* Abigail serves as a vivid example of this truth in action. She understood her husband's spiritual blindness, but rather than letting his handicap hinder her, she remained obedient to God, demonstrating trust that He would protect and provide.

2. *You have influence, not control.* You can affect but not dictate your spouse's spiritual condition. Maximize your influence through your prayers, your words, and most important, through your example—never through nagging, coercion, or mind games.

3. *You may not be your spouse's only doorway to a relationship with Christ.* If you think it's all up to you to lead your mate to a relationship with Christ, think again; God is perfectly capable of drawing your mate to Him through a number of other avenues, including other people and other circumstances.

4. *God is sovereign and can work out every situation for the ultimate good.* He can use the tests and trials of being married to an unbeliever to teach important lessons about love, forgiveness, and trust, and to shape a heart to become more like His.

5. *A mate's need for Christ can be a magnet that pulls you closer to him or her in love rather than a wedge that inserts emotional distance between the two of you.*

6. *You need not let your unbelieving spouse keep you from fellowship with other believers.* In fact, you need the support, <u>encouragement</u>, and prayers of your Christian friends all the more since you don't have that from your spouse.

what others say

Kathy Collard Miller and D. Larry Miller

A Christian marrying someone who doesn't know God is like trying to mix oil and water. It makes for an incompatible union. The apostle Paul wrote that such relationships can draw a person away from their devotion to God.[6]

encouragement
Hebrews 10:25

Abigail's Reward: Thin Ice for David?

the big picture

1 Samuel 25:39–41

When David heard that Nabal had died, he praised God for intervening and avenging David. Then he asked Abigail to marry him, a proposal to which she responded with her characteristic humility and eloquence: Then she arose, bowed her face to the earth, and said, "Here is your maidservant, a servant to wash the feet of the servants of my lord" (v. 41 NKJV). This passage also reveals that David took yet another wife, Ahinoam of Jezreel, who would have become his third wife had Saul not for some unnamed reason given Michal to another man.

God transformed the wife of a fool into the wife of a king. To a woman like Abigail, however, the peace of becoming the wife of a man of God would have been far more exciting than the prestige of becoming the wife of a king. After enduring Nabal's folly day after day, how refreshing Abigail would find it to be married to a man whose passion for the Lord matched her own.

Polygamous Marriages: Are They Made in Heaven?

Do the math: David had one wife, Michal. Then he took two more, Abigail and Ahinoam. But in David's absence, Saul took Michal from David and gave her to another man, leaving David with two wives, Abigail and Ahinoam. Simply put, the king-to-be was now a polygamist.

Men in ancient Hebrew culture often took more than one wife for any of several reasons:

1. Because sons were valuable, having multiple wives meant producing multiple offspring and improving their chances to father more male children.

2. Because wives were considered possessions, having multiple wives meant prestige; they were like trophies lining the living room shelf.

3. And because family was important, having multiple wives enabled men to bring widowed relatives into the care and protection of an established household.

go to

wife
Proverbs 5:18;
Ecclesiastes 9:9

monogamous
Deuteronomy 17:17

Larry and Sue Richards

In Old Babylonian law, when a man married two women one was the primary wife, and the other had a lower status. Typically this status was spelled out in a marriage contract, a number of which have been recovered by archaeologists[7]

A discussion of polygamy raises two key questions:

1. *Was—is—polygamy okay with God?*

To answer this question, it's important to find out what Scripture has to say about marriage, and the beginning of marriage is the best place to start. Genesis 2:24 says, "Therefore a man shall leave his father and mother and be joined to his wife, and they shall become one flesh" (NKJV). This verse and several others use the singular "<u>wife</u>" rather than the plural "wives," strongly suggesting that polygamy is not part of God's plan for marriage. Other evidence that marriage is meant for two people, and not three, or four, or even hundreds (as in Solomon's case) includes the New Testament use of marriage to describe the relationship between Christ and the church; Christ is said to have one bride, not several.

strengthen your family

Mosaic Law ordered kings to be <u>monogamous</u> and discouraged polygamy among other men; nevertheless, it presented instructions for the treatment of multiple wives . . . which leads to the next question.

2. *If polygamy wasn't—isn't—okay, why has God allowed it?*

First, note that the instructions regarding polygamy were posed with "if," not "when": "*If* he takes another wife, he shall not diminish her food, her clothing, and her marriage rights" (Exodus 21:10 NKJV, emphasis added). God knows how people operate, and He knows that because He gave them a free will, they will not always follow His guidelines.

Second, an absence of God's recorded condemnation does not imply His approval. For reasons people may not understand, He simply chose not to reveal the details about consequences or condemnation for every action and attitude in the Bible.

Elkanah's household
1 Samuel 1:1–8

Sarah and Hagar
Genesis 16:1–6

Rachel and Leah
Genesis 29:18,
27–28

And third, several examples in Scripture make it clear that participants in polygamy pay a hefty penalty, most often in the form of family strife. Elkanah's household was in discord because of the conflict between his two wives, the childless Hannah and the sharp-tongued Penninah. Polygamy also brought grief and pain into the homes of Sarah and Hagar; and Rachel and Leah.

what others say

Larry and Sue Richards

Rachel's and Leah's life as sisters married to a single man was further complicated by a competition to give their husband sons. In this competition each also gave Jacob her slave ["maid"] as a surrogate. . . . the complex relationships this created caused extreme pain for each of the women, and undoubtedly for Jacob as well.[8]

Chapter Highlights

- Samuel died at age ninety-eight after faithfully serving his God and his nation as Israel's thirteenth judge and first prophet.

- Saul was still in office, but his days there were numbered. David—still unwilling to strike down Saul with his own hands—and his men were hiding in the Wilderness of Maon.

- When David heard it was sheepshearing time on the nearby estate of the wealthy but foolish farmer Nabal, he sent ten men to ask Nabal for provisions. Nabal responded by insulting David, questioning his parentage, and accusing him of rebellion against Saul.

- When David heard the report of Nabal's answer, he ordered four hundred of his men to take up arms and prepare to kill Nabal as well as every member of his household.

- One of Nabal's servants saw trouble brewing in David's hotheaded behavior and he told Nabal's beautiful and wise wife, Abigail, what had happened. She intercepted David, who was struck by her beauty and wisdom, and persuaded him to call off his planned attack.

- After Abigail told Nabal what had happened, he suffered a stroke that paralyzed him for ten days, then he died.
- When David heard that Nabal had died, he praised God for intervening, then asked Abigail to marry him.

Study Questions

1. What were some of Samuel's accomplishments?

2. Where did David go after Samuel died?

3. Why was David cheered to hear that it was sheepshearing time at the neighboring estate of Nabal?

4. Why did David expect Nabal's hospitality?

5. How did David respond to Nabal's insults?

6. Why did Nabal's servant go to Abigail rather than Nabal?

7. What effect did Abigail's intervention have on David?

8. Why did Abigail wait until the next morning to tell her husband the news?

9. What did David do when he heard of Nabal's death?

1 Samuel 26–31; 1 Chronicles 10: David's Deliverance

Let's Get Started

When David mulled over his situation, he must have found it increasingly difficult to see a bright side. First, there was Saul, who hated him for no apparent reason. Then, there was the king's army of 3,000 top-notch men: not exactly an even match for his band of 600 discontented and discouraged misfits. Which led to another matter: David was responsible for making sure his men's wives and children—plus his own two wives—had enough food, water, and provisions. That couldn't be easy in the inhospitable terrain of the Middle Eastern desert. As the pressure continued to build, it began to wear away David's physical, emotional, and spiritual stamina. Doubts began to dominate his thoughts, and he began to believe that he really would die at the hand of Saul. But in the meantime, all he knew to do was keep running for his life, and the only place he figured he could go to find any hope of safety was in enemy territory, where Saul and his friends would not dare to go.

As for Saul, he was struggling with thoughts of his own mortality, too. While David's fear of Saul was driving him into the false security of the enemy's backyard, Saul's fear of a looming attack from the Philistines was driving him to take extreme measures. He soon learned that his choice to leave God out of his life left him nowhere to look but down.

Ziphites
1 Samuel 23:19–23

Saul's Last Close Call

the big picture

1 Samuel 26

The last time Saul's name appeared in Scripture, he had broken down before David and in so many words said he would halt his pursuit. As David had suspected, those words were empty. When Saul learned from the <u>Ziphites</u>—who seemed to enjoy keeping tabs on David for the king—where David was hiding, he launched another pursuit with his elite troop.

troubled temper
1 Samuel 16:23

Goliath
1 Samuel 17:32–58

Abishai
David's nephew and
a skilled soldier

Abner
Saul's commander
and bodyguard

David discovered Saul was hot on his trail again, so he sent out a spy to find out the king's whereabouts. Then he and his nephew—his skilled and faithful soldier, **Abishai**—went to the king's camp, where he found Saul asleep, with his spear in the ground by his head and his commander, **Abner**, resting nearby. Abishai saw the circumstance as providential and begged David to let him kill the king. Once again, David refused to murder Saul, restating his confidence that God would handle it. David took the king's spear and water jug before slipping out with Abishai; they left undetected because the men had been in a God-induced sleep. The pair left the camp and headed for a hilltop some distance away. From there, David began chiding Abner for his failure to guard the king.

Saul awoke, instantly recognizing the voice that by now he knew as well as he knew the voices of his own sons. This was the voice that had soothed his <u>troubled temper</u>, that had earnestly sought his permission to fight <u>Goliath</u>, and that had asked him once before why the king was after his life. He heard similar words now as David spoke across the ravine to the sleepy enemy, demanding to know why Saul was pursuing him. And again Saul confessed his guilt, acknowledged David's position as Israel's next king, and pledged to end the chase. The two went their separate ways.

Who Spared Whose Life?

Picture the scene: a military encampment populated with enough soldiers to fill a high school football stadium. As was customary, Saul and his highest officers were situated in a central, circular clearing. They were surrounded by the rest of the men, the baggage and wagons.

These guys had been hand-picked by the king because of their outstanding military prowess. They were first-rate militia, but they had had it up to here with the slippery renegade David. The longer the manhunt remained unsuccessful, the angrier—and crazier—Saul became. Nothing would have pleased them more than to capture or kill David and put an end to the madness so they could go home to their families or at least land another, undoubtedly more rewarding, assignment fighting the Philistines or other enemies.

Yet when the fugitive whose head these men sought came tiptoeing across their pallets by the light of the moon, not even one of the snoring soldiers stirred. They were sound asleep on the job.

Was it sloppy soldiering? Too many hours on the job? Were they coming down with something? Hardly.

The reason Saul's elite were dead to the world was because of God. He had caused them to fall into a deep sleep, one described by the same word used when God anesthetized Adam so He could carve a rib from his side to create Eve. So even though this episode in David's life is usually referred to as the second time David spared Saul's life, a more accurate headline for the incident might be "God Spares David's Life—Again."

what others say

Matthew Henry

How helpless do Saul and all his forces lie, all, in effect, disarmed and chained! and yet nothing is done to them; they are only rocked asleep. How easily can God weaken the strongest, befool the wisest, and baffle the most watchful! Let all his friends therefore trust him and all his enemies fear him.[1]

Seeing Double?

Some scholars believe the accounts of David sparing Saul's life in the cave at En Gedi and here are so similar that they must be two versions of the same event. The resemblance is in fact striking. In both passages,

- The Ziphites revealed David's whereabouts to David.
- Saul was in pursuit with three thousand men.
- David's men made similar remarks.
- David had a chance to kill Saul, but refused.
- David took a "trophy" from Saul to prove his proximity.
- Saul recognized David's voice.

Other Bible researchers, however, believe the details are just too different to assume both reports refer to a single incident. They point out that:

- The locations were too different—a cave was the site of the first account and a large open camp of the second.
- Saul *always* had <u>3,000 men</u> with him, so this wasn't an unusual coincidence.

3,000 men
1 Samuel 13:2; 24:2; 26:2

- In the first incident, Saul wandered into David's hideout; in the second one, David sought Saul.

- In the first incident, Saul was separate from his men, and in the second, Saul was surrounded by them.

Lost!

1 SAMUEL 27:1–4 And David said in his heart, "Now I shall perish someday by the hand of Saul. There is nothing better for me than that I should speedily escape to the land of the Philistines; and Saul will despair of me, to seek me anymore in any part of Israel. So I shall escape out of his hand." Then David arose and went over with the six hundred men who were with him to Achish the son of Maoch, king of Gath. So David dwelt with Achish at Gath, he and his men, each man with his household, and David with his two wives, Ahinoam the Jezreelitess, and Abigail the Carmelitess, Nabal's widow. And it was told Saul that David had fled to Gath; so he sought him no more. (NKJV)

As the narrative shifts to follow the activity of David, the interior monologue in the opening line, "And David said in his heart," gives readers their first recorded glimpse of his thoughts.

This time, Saul had told the truth. Never again would he seek David's life. Problem was, David didn't know it. All he knew was that twice before, Saul had made similar promises, and twice before, the king's word had been worthless. How was he to expect this time to be any different? He didn't.

key point

But it was God's words, not Saul's, that should have mattered most to David. God had promised to remove Saul from power to make David king of Israel. (And if David had forgotten that promise, he could have reviewed a long list of affirmations of his coming kingship from people including Samuel, Jonathan, Abigail, the Philistines, and even Saul himself.) With just ten words—"Now I shall perish someday by the hand of Saul"—David displayed an attitude shockingly uncharacteristic of this man after God's own heart. The usually optimistic guy revealed a dark pessimism by assuming the worst-case scenario and blatantly expressing distrust in God. The Lord suddenly didn't seem faithful enough to fulfill promises or strong enough to overcome enemies.

David let doubt distort his vision and damage his ability to make good decisions. To take the spiritual high road, David would have "waited on the Lord." But he took the low road when he decided to take matters into his own hands, shocking his family, his men, and their families with the unthinkable announcement: "Pack your bags, we're moving to Gath."

go to

waited on the Lord
Psalms 27:14; 37:7, 34; 130:6

What's Up with Him?

That's what David's men must have wondered as they began to break down tents and pack up their provisions to set up housekeeping in a new neighborhood right in the middle of their worst enemy's territory. They had been glad to sever their alliance with the compromising, cowardly King Saul when they had seen the fire in David's heart for fighting for God's people God's way. Even though it had meant living under hardship and poverty in the desert, David had earned their loyalty with his uncompromising passion and courage to do what was right, even in the face of adversity. But now they must have wondered whether they had sorely misjudged their leader. The man who had asked God for direction not once but twice before leading them into the operation at Keilah hadn't even bothered to consult God on this big decision! Maybe he wasn't as outstanding as they had first thought.

something to ponder

what others say

Alan Redpath

I ask you to notice how dishonoring this was to the Lord. Hadn't God promised David he would be king? Hadn't the Lord said that He would cast out David's enemies like a stone out of a sling? Hadn't every word of God been confirmed to David . . . ? David, Are all God's promises to be discarded?[2]

Achish Gains a Warrior

"I already have enough crazy people around here," Achish had said the last time David had come knocking at the city gate, drooling into his beard and scratching against the gate like a madman. But the striking shepherd boy "cleaned up pretty good," so to speak. So good, in fact, that Achish figured the giant-killer must not be crazy after all. He figured he could use the illustrious warrior's skills—and

Ziklag
small settlement on
the southern frontier
of Philistia between
Gaza and Beersheba

his band of soldiers—to his own advantage, making Israel's loss his gain. When the king opened the gate to let David and his men move in, he established a lord-and-vassal relationship with David. In other words, the man who was supposed to be king of Israel went to work for Israel's most despised enemy.

Gath at a Glance

- *Big Five*—Gath was one—and possibly the most important—of five Philistine cities (along with Ashkelon, Ashdod, Ekron, and Gaza) called the "Philistine Pentapolis."

- *Wine Country*—Gath's name is taken from the Hebrew word *gat*, which means "winepress." The area around Gath was very fertile and a likely site for many winepresses.

- *White Mound*—Gath is identified with the modern city of Tell es-Safi, Arabic for "the white mound," in reference to white chalky cliffs nearby. With approximately one hundred acres, it is one of the largest biblical sites in Israel.

Moving to Ziklag

1 SAMUEL 27:5–7 *Then David said to Achish, "If I have now found favor in your eyes, let them give me a place in some town in the country, that I may dwell there. For why should your servant dwell in the royal city with you?" So Achish gave him Ziklag that day. Therefore Ziklag has belonged to the kings of Judah to this day. Now the time that David dwelt in the country of the Philistines was one full year and four months.* (NKJV)

Considering how many people were in David's entourage, it's no wonder Gath soon began to feel crowded, prompting David to ask Achish for somewhere else to live. Imagine that: the inheritor of the throne to the land God had promised the Isrealites asking an enemy for a scrap of real estate he could call his own! Achish agreed to give David his own fiefdom, sending David and his people to a city named **Ziklag**.

Ziklag held little value to the Philistines. They had captured the Canaanite city that had been allocated to Judah when Joshua had entered the Promised Land, but had never moved in. It was now occupied by descendants of <u>Simeon</u>, and it suited David's purposes because it was far from Saul's territory and fairly isolated from Gath.

Simeon
Joshua 15:31; 19:5;
1 Chronicles 4:30

worshipped idols
2 Samuel 5:21

what others say

Alan Redpath

These people were living in territory that had been given to them by God, but it was controlled by the enemy and they were living in subjection.[3]

Living with the Enemy

Thus began a distinctly dismal period of David's life, one in which he moved from living by faith and honor in the land of Israel—even though he was on the run from Saul—to living by fear and deceit in the land of the enemies.

Truly, Philistia was enemy territory in more ways than one. Not only were the Philistines formidable military foes, they were significant spiritual foes as well. On the outside they may not have appeared to be evil: with roots in Greek culture, they were sophisticated and attractive, with all the latest bells and whistles that made life easier and more pleasurable. But beneath all the finery were hearts darkened by godlessness and immorality. Perhaps their most disturbing trait was that they <u>worshipped idols</u>.

David had moved in with the Philistines because he thought he would be safe there. And for a time he was. Physically safe, that is. But any time a godly person spends time with ungodly people, he or she is likely to experience some uncomfortable consequences. Wasn't David aware that by aligning himself with the Philistines he not only was helping the enemy's cause, but he was dishonoring the God he so longed to please? No one can know the answer to that question because David's thoughts on the matter aren't recorded in the Bible—either in 1 Samuel or in the psalms. But then again, his silence may in fact be a clue to his frame of mind during that time, considering that the man who had composed psalms of prayer, peace, and praise during some of his darkest moments put down his pen during his entire sixteen-month stay among the Philistines.

go to

joined David's company
1 Chronicles 12:3–7

what others say

Charles Swindoll

The sweet singer of Israel was mute. He wrote no songs when he was in this slump. He couldn't sing the Lord's song in a foreign land governed by the enemy's influence! As the Jewish captives in Babylon would later ask, "How can we sing the Lord's song in a foreign land?" (Psalm 137:4). There is not much joy flowing out of David's life during this carnal interlude in Gath.[4]

One for All

When David dared to move into the land of the enemy, directly disobeying God's instructions that His people "remain separate," he didn't rent a one-room flat. He brought an entire village of people with him, including his wives, his family, his friends, and his militia. In doing so, he exposed them to the same godless Philistine influences he received.

apply it

Not everyone leads a band of soldiers, but we're all leaders. When we venture outside the boundaries God sets for us, it's not just our own safety we're compromising; we drag our spouses, our children, our colleagues, our extended family members, and countless others within our sphere of influence into the danger zone as well!

God Never Stops Working

Even though David and his followers were firmly planted outside the will of God, God continued to provide protection and work out His ultimate purpose for David's future. He even continued moving David's future troops into place; during this time in Ziklag, twenty-three of Saul's relatives <u>joined David's company</u> of "mighty men."

Take No Prisoners!

the big picture

1 Samuel 27:8–12

As a vassal for Achish, David had to pledge the king military muscle as well as loyalty. That meant he had to stay busy in battle from his Ziklag headquarters. Unable to stomach a fight against his own people, he instead launched a series of raids against Israel's ancient enemies, the Geshurites, Girzites, and Amalekites. Since these nomad desert tribes were allies of the Philistines, David was forced to lie whenever Achish would ask about his recent raids. And to further ensure word of his traitorous activity would not reach Achish, he had to implement a particularly harsh policy: slaughter every member of each tribe, including women and children, so that no one would be left alive to report his activities. Achish believed the deception and read David's so-called diligence as a sign of his break with Israel and his wholehearted alliance with the Philistines. So when the Philistines began organizing to fight Israel once again, Achish counted on being able to use David as his personal bodyguard in the battle.

To try to justify the puzzling actions of David, it might be tempting to applaud his stubborn refusal to attack his own people. Yet virtually nothing about his behavior during this time is worthy of praise. He was a leader placing his followers in physical and spiritual jeopardy; he was an Israelite acting as a traitor to his own nation; and he was a man of God clearly living outside the will of God. Doubt had faded his firmly fixed faith; lies and cover-ups had become everyday practice; and his deceit was forcing him to harm innocent people. Some scholars say this episode in David's life compelled him to write Psalm 119:28–29: "My soul melts from heaviness; strengthen me according to Your word. Remove from me the way of lying, and grant me Your law graciously" (NKJV).

something to ponder

what others say

Burton Coffman

There is no way to gloss over David's sin in this. He lied continually about what he was really doing. Achish who believed David, trusted him and aided him was shamefully betrayed and deceived by David.[5]

Saul's Super-Sized Sin with a Medium

1 SAMUEL 28:3 *Now Samuel had died, and all Israel had lamented for him and buried him in Ramah, in his own city. And Saul had put the mediums and the spiritists out of the land. (NKJV)*

The focus of chapter 38 suddenly shifts back to Saul, beginning with a reminder of Samuel's death. The repetition of the fact that Samuel died underlines the important role Samuel had played in Saul's life—and highlights the void he left behind. The king had enjoyed a close, if turbulent, relationship with the prophet, who had anointed him, helped him set up the monarchy, mentored him, stood up for him, and prayed for him. It had likely been under Samuel's direction, in the early days of his reign, that Saul had demonstrated obedience to God by driving all the **mediums and spiritists** from the land.

Saul Got the Silent Treatment

1 SAMUEL 28:4–6 *Then the Philistines gathered together, and came and encamped at Shunem. So Saul gathered all Israel together, and they encamped at Gilboa. When Saul saw the army of the Philistines, he was afraid, and his heart trembled greatly. And when Saul inquired of the LORD, the LORD did not answer him, either by dreams or by Urim or by the prophets. (NKJV)*

Saul had known for some time now what was going to happen: God was going to remove him from power so that David could take the throne. He just hadn't known exactly how these things might come about. When Saul saw the Philistines gathered for another fight, they looked bigger, better armed, and more frightening than ever. Even though his fears and paranoia frequently clouded his thoughts, it must have been in a moment of perfect clarity that Saul wondered: Would this confrontation be the way God would erase him from the scene so that David could take the throne?

The severity of his predicament was unmistakable: Samuel no longer was able to help him by giving him advice or praying for him, and David's military might was out of reach since he had driven him into an alliance with the enemy. The only two people on earth who could have possibly helped were beyond his reach.

Worst of all, God was silent.

When God Stops Talking

God wants to talk. His words <u>instruct</u>, protect, <u>encourage</u>, <u>guide</u>, <u>nourish</u>, and <u>empower</u> those who hear them and act upon them. They are even <u>flawless</u>. Because His words are so invaluable, God delights in people who crave His words and cling to them as if they were life itself. Consider how Samuel, as a boy, "let none of [God's] words <u>fall to the ground</u>"; how David wrote that he <u>longed for God's instructions</u>; how the prophet Jeremiah said he "ate" God's words, which were the "joy and rejoicing of [his] heart" (Jeremiah 15:16 NKJV), and how Job said he would rather have <u>God's Word</u> than his daily bread. Yet the opposite is true for those who continually disregard what He says. God disapproves of people who don't listen or who hear His words but discard them as if they were worthless.

When people stop listening, God stops talking:

- "Behold, the LORD's hand is not shortened, that it cannot save; nor His ear heavy, that it cannot hear. But your iniquities have separated you from your God; and your sins have hidden His face from you, so that He will not hear" (Isaiah 59:1–2 NKJV).

- "'Yes, they made their hearts like flint, refusing to hear the law and the words which the LORD of hosts had sent by His Spirit through the former prophets. Thus great wrath came from the LORD of hosts. Therefore it happened, that just as He proclaimed and they would not hear, so they called out and I would not listen,' says the LORD of hosts" (Zechariah 7:12–13 NKJV).

In his selfish determination to repeatedly do what he wanted to do rather than what God instructed him to do, Saul had tuned out God long ago. Now, when he was finally ready to seek God's help, God wouldn't answer his call. God had "hidden His face" from Saul, and would not hear his cry.

go to

instruct
Psalms 119:104, 129–130;
Colossians 3:16;
2 Timothy 3:14–17

encourage
Micah 2:7b;
Acts 20:32

guide
Psalm 119:105

nourish
Deuteronomy 8:3b;
Job 23:12;
Psalm 119:103

empower
Psalm 119:11

flawless
2 Samuel 22:31;
Psalm 19:7

fall to the ground
1 Samuel 3:19

longed for God's instructions
Psalm 119:131

God's Word
Job 23:12

key point

what others say

Beth Moore

Unconfessed, unrepented sin can easily be the reason for God's silence in our lives. Remember, Saul continued in disobedience to God. He relentlessly sought the life of an innocent man, and even attempted to spear his own son! . . . We've seen some regrets, but we've never seen him truly turn from wickedness to righteousness.[6]

go to

Joseph's dreams
Matthew 1:20; 2:13

Nebuchadnezzar
Daniel 2 and 4

urim and thummim
Exodus 28:29–30;
Leviticus 8:8

breastplate
Exodus 28:15–30

mediums
Deuteronomy
18:10–11;
1 Samuel 28:3, 7;
Isaiah 8:19

teraphim
Judges 17:5;
18:13–20;
Hosea 3:4;
Zechariah 10:2

pagan deities
2 Kings 1:2–3, 16;
Zephaniah 1:5

divination
ways of determining
God's will

How God Speaks

When Saul asked God for help, the king looked for an answer in three sources:

- *Dreams.* Scripture records many times when God revealed His word to someone through a dream. Sometimes messages revealed in dreams were simple; they did not need special interpretation, as in the case of Joseph's dreams regarding Mary and Herod. Other types of dreams used symbols that were clear enough to be easily understood, as with the patriarch Joseph's dreams in Genesis 37. Still other dreams—as those of Babylonian king Nebuchadnezzar—featured complex symbols and required interpretation by someone with a special ability.

- *Urim (and thummim).* A system of communication established by God Himself, the urim and thummim were objects that fit into a pouch inside the breastplate worn by the high priest. Details about their construction and how they were used are sketchy. Some scholars believe they were a pair of stones—one light and one dark—used to indicate a "yes" or a "no" from God. The difference between this and other methods of **divination**, such as consulting mediums, teraphim, and pagan deities, is in the source. The urim and thummim were established by God and therefore were holy; other forms of seeking God's will were instituted by people and were therefore unholy and forbidden.

- *Prophets.* People who spoke about or for God were prophets. Samuel, of course, had been the first prophet and was accredited with beginning a school of prophets. In a sense, he had established a seminary for those whom God had chosen to become His mouthpieces.

Seeking His Fortune

the big picture

1 Samuel 28:7–25

One characteristic setting God's nation, Israel, apart from the godless nations across its borders was the Israelites' refusal to participate in witchcraft and magic. God had clearly <u>prohibited</u> <u>those practices</u>, which were commonly used in other pagan nations. In fact, in Deuteronomy 18:12, God called these practices "abominations," one of the strongest terms He used to express His disapproval. Saul knew this well; after all, he himself had driven many of the mediums and spiritists from the land. Yet he was desperate for some kind of direction regarding his current dilemma, so absent a word from God of the holy way, he put on disguise and set out on a dangerous trip to En Dor to consult one of the few fortune-tellers who remained in the area. Assuring the witch that he would make sure she wouldn't get into trouble for her illegal practice, Saul asked her to bring up Samuel from the dead. When, much to her surprise, the prophet did appear, she realized who Saul must be, but continued her task.

Samuel, whose appearance prompted Saul to bow, facedown, on the ground before him, obviously wasn't happy to be disturbed. Saul asked Samuel for instruction but received no reassurance or advice. Instead, he got a sound scolding for his past disobedience and a blood-chilling piece of news:

Saul and his sons would die at the hands of the Philistines the next day. The king collapsed in fear, and the medium then tended to him, preparing a "last meal," of sorts, which he and his companions ate before returning home.

go to

prohibited those practices
Deuteronomy 18:10–12;
Leviticus 19:31;
20:6, 27;
Exodus 22:18;
Isaiah 8:19

stripped
1 Samuel 19:24

fabric
1 Samuel 24:4–8

prophecy

what others say

David Guzik

Things such as tarot cards, palm readers, horoscopes and Ouija boards are modern attempts to practice forms of spiritism. They are dangerous links to the demonic, even if undertaken in a spirit of fun.[7]

What Saul Wore

What a story clothes tell about Saul's life and character! The king had <u>stripped</u> off his royal robe and lay naked and vulnerable as he prophesied in Ramah with the other prophets, painfully aware that he was outside God's will and protection. The breakdown of his reign was further symbolized by the piece of <u>fabric</u> David had snipped from his robe in the cave at En Gedi. He degenerated from mere nakedness and vulnerability to blatant disguise as he deliberately trod onto the forbidden turf of the underworld. The absence of his royal regalia foreshadowed his coming death.

something to ponder

David's Dilemma

go to

Eli's sons
1 Samuel 4

the big picture

1 Samuel 29 and 30

The narrative backtracks to describe events that took place before Saul made his midnight journey to meet the medium. Before the Philistines had moved northward toward Shunem, Achish had gathered his troops into a camp at Aphek, the same place they had gathered before the Philistines had routed the Israelites during the battle that had claimed the lives of <u>Eli's sons</u>. Achish had grown to trust David, who now served as Achish's vassal as well as his bodyguard, but his men weren't so sure. They convinced the king to order the Israelite company back to Ziklag. David and his men struck out for home, probably feeling very relieved not to have to face their fellow countrymen in battle. However, their sighs of relief turned to cries of grief when they discovered that the Amalekites had burned their city and taken captive their families—including David's wives, Ahinoam and Abigail. David and his men wept until they had no more strength. Then David found himself in even more trouble as the hurting men began looking for someone to blame for their grief and talked of stoning him. Just when things began to look their grimmest, a glimmer of hope appeared. David found strength in God, and asked Him what to do next.

As David found himself caught up in the hubbub of preparing to stand shoulder-to-shoulder in battle against his own people, his heart must have been heavy. How had things become so complicated? His flight into enemy territory had seemed harmless enough at first; it had been a temporary refuge, a place to settle down for a few months to pass the time in peace and safety until Saul simmered down. But it had been impossible to stay among the violent people without being pulled into their ranks. Through deception he had managed to dodge their expectation that he would harm his own people, but what trick could he possibly use to get out of the predicament he was in now? But for divine intervention, there would be no safe way out of this dilemma. He would either fight alongside the enemies and be forced to kill his own countrymen, or refuse to fight, unveiling his true loyalty and bringing a death sentence upon his head.

When the powers that be in Achish's army put their feet down against allowing David to fight with them against the Israelites, God's tender care of David couldn't have been more evident.

(Maybe they remembered some of the things David had done in the past through God's power—even if David didn't!)

David Hit Rock Bottom

prodigal son
Luke 15:22–24

David had hit some low valleys of despair before, but this had to be the absolute bottom of the pit of depression. The king with the shepherd's heart had returned to the sheepfold to find the pasture charred and smoldering, and the sheep taken away. Grief surged over him in waves as the David the soldier was sickened by the physical loss of property, David the man mourned the painful personal loss of loved ones, and David the leader grieved over the "if onlys" and "should haves" that might have spared his people and property. And as if that weren't enough, the people he considered his strong allies and loyal friends were considering mutiny. Things were going wrong, really wrong.

At this point, he had two choices: he could keep gazing downward, head hung low, paralyzed by shame, regret, and fear. Or he could look up and ask for help.

Being a man after God's own heart, he chose to look up. He "strengthened himself in the LORD his God" (1 Samuel 30:6 NKJV).

The Prodigal Before the Parable

A headstrong, proud son leaves home to make his own way in the world, where he finds nothing but poverty, loneliness, and danger. Feeling desperate, discouraged, and most of all unworthy, but longing for home, he takes one step in the right direction—one step toward home. That's all it takes. As he moves toward home, he sees his father running to greet him with arms wide open and dinner in the oven.

It's the parable of the prodigal son, but it's also a good summary of David's return to God's care after being away for sixteen months. David, like the prodigal son, began thinking he could make it just fine outside his father's care and provision. But he couldn't. One bad decision gave way to another, and before long he had strayed so far from the shelter of God's love and care that he surely must have wondered whether he was too far away to be rescued. But that couldn't have been farther from the truth.

God had been watching and waiting for the moment when David would turn back to Him.

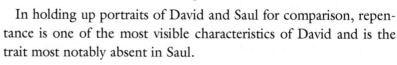

what others say

Max Lucado

The child may have been out of the house, but he was never out of his father's heart. He may have left the table, but he never left the family. Don't miss the message here. You may be willing to stop being God's child. But God is not willing to stop being your Father.[8]

A Pattern of Repentance

While the Bible doesn't say "David repented" in this passage, his actions make it obvious that "repent" is exactly what he did as he gazed at the smoldering ruins of Ziklag and heard his distraught men mention the possibility of stoning him. Without repentance, he couldn't have found strength in God. Without repentance, he wouldn't have asked God for help.

In holding up portraits of David and Saul for comparison, repentance is one of the most visible characteristics of David and is the trait most notably absent in Saul.

key point

Recovery!

1 SAMUEL 30:15–20 *And David said to him, "Can you take me down to this troop?" So he said, "Swear to me by God that you will neither kill me nor deliver me into the hands of my master, and I will take you down to this troop."*

And when he had brought him down, there they were, spread out over all the land, eating and drinking and dancing, because of all the great spoil which they had taken from the land of the Philistines and from the land of Judah. Then David attacked them from twilight until the evening of the next day. Not a man of them escaped, except four hundred young men who rode on camels and fled. So David recovered all that the Amalekites had carried away, and David rescued his two wives. And nothing of theirs was lacking, either small or great, sons or daughters, spoil or anything which they had taken from them; David recovered all. Then David took all the flocks and herds they had driven before those other livestock, and said, "This is David's spoil." (NKJV)

Once David had "strengthened" himself in the Lord, he snapped into action. He summoned Abiathar the priest to help him learn what God wanted him to do next. David asked God whether he should pursue the Amalekites and God, answering via the ephod, responded with a "yes," promising certain victory. So David and his six hundred men set out to obey. When they arrived at Brook Besor, a third of his men were so weary that they stayed behind at the Besor Ravine, about twenty miles south of Ziklag, but David and the remaining four hundred continued the pursuit. They met and aided an abandoned and ailing Amalekite servant, who led them to the Amalekite camp, where a victory celebration was in full swing. David launched a twenty-four-hour attack that resulted in the rescue of every person held captive and the recovery of every piece of property the Amalekites had taken as well as the flocks and herds the Amalekites had stolen from other cities and towns of Judah. Establishing a principle he would implement thereafter, he distributed the recovered items among the men who had remained behind as well as among the four hundred who had fought with him in battle. Further, he shared the booty with other cities and towns of Judah that had been raided by the Amalekites.

There had been a time when David hadn't taken even one step without asking for God's permission and direction. Yet beginning with his hot-tempered threat to attack Nabal's household, David had slipped into the bad habit of failing to seek heavenly counsel before springing into action.

That practice had transformed him from being an arrow-proof king-to-be to being a miserable fugitive whose family had been kidnapped and whose friends had begun to turn on him. Once David decided to turn to God for help, he kicked the old, bad habit and resumed the good one: Seek God's direction first.

Saul Dies

the big picture

1 Samuel 31:1–13 and 1 Chronicles 10

Just as Samuel had prophesied during Saul's late-night visit to the medium, the Philistines fought and easily defeated Israel in the Valley of Jezreel, where they also killed Jonathan, Abinadab, and Malchishua, three of Saul's sons. (His fourth son, Ish-bosheth, will be mentioned beginning in 2 Samuel 2:8.) Then, just as Saul had feared, the Philistines overtook him and the

go to

temple of Dagon
1 Samuel 5:2

people of Jabesh Gilead
1 Samuel 11:1–11

Ashtoreth
pagan goddess often associated with Philistines

archers hit him, leaving a mortal wound. Afraid of being found alive and tortured by the Philistines, he asked his armor bearer to kill him. The armor bearer refused, so Saul thrust himself on his spear, committing suicide in violation of yet another Israelite taboo. When the Israelites found out their king was dead, they scattered and hid out in the wilderness. The Philistines found Saul, cut off his head, and stripped off his armor. They put his armor in the temple of the goddess **Ashtoreth**, fastened his body to the wall of Beth Shan, on the eastern slopes of Mount Gilboa overlooking the Jordan Valley, and put his head in the temple of Dagon. The people of Jabesh Gilead—whom Saul had rescued from the Ammonites forty years earlier—were so upset by what the Philistines had done to Saul that they traveled by night to retrieve the bodies of Saul and his sons. Most likely because the remains were so badly mutilated, the people of Jabesh Gilead burned the bodies, buried the bones, then fasted seven days.

Saul's Legacy

No one summed up Saul's downfall more concisely than he himself when he lamented in 1 Samuel 26:21: "I have played the fool" (NKJV). That covers a lot of territory, but the king indeed made many foolish choices:

- He was unfaithful to the Lord.
- He neglected and refused advice from his godly friend, Samuel.
- He failed to ask God for direction.
- He disobeyed God.
- He failed to see—and remember—God's work in his life.
- He tried to disguise his sin as religion.
- He allowed himself to be controlled by his emotions—jealousy and hatred, in particular.
- He turned from God.
- He participated in witchcraft.
- He continually refused to repent.

The apostle Paul, who would have known well the ancient history of his people, may have had Israel's first king—or someone much like him—in mind when he described people who merit condemnation in his letter to the Romans: "Although they knew God, they did not glorify Him as God, nor were thankful, but became futile in their thoughts, and their foolish hearts were darkened. Professing to be wise, they became fools" (Romans 1:21–22 NKJV). Paul then listed some of the characteristics of such a person, whom he calls "without excuse" (1:20 NKJV). He said they worship idols, they don't acknowledge God, they have a debased mind, and they are unrighteous, wicked, covetous, malicious, envious, murderous, argumentative, deceitful, evil-minded, violent, proud, undiscerning, untrustworthy, unloving, unforgiving, and unmerciful. "Those who practice such things," Paul said, "are deserving of death" (1:32 NKJV).

Suicide in Scripture

How significant that Saul, who determined to act independently of God in virtually everything he did, even tried to take his own death into his own hands! He is one of six people in the Bible who committed suicide. The others are:

- Abimelech (Judges 9:50–54)
- Samson (Judges 16:23–31)
- Ahithophel (2 Samuel 17:23)
- Zimri (1 Kings 16:15–20)
- Judas (Matthew 27:3–5)

what others say

International Bible Encyclopedia

No special law is found against this crime, for it is included in the prohibition against killing. Contrary to the practice and the philosophy of paganism, the act was held in deep abhorrence by the Hebrews because of the high value placed on human life. It was held inexcusable that any but the most degraded and satanic should lay hands on their own lives. Only the remorse of the damned could drive one to it, as witness Saul (1 Samuel 31:4) and Judas (Matthew 27:5).[9]

Chapter Wrap-Up

- David and his nephew Abishai discovered Saul's whereabouts and went to the king's camp, where David passed up yet another opportunity to kill him. Saul confessed his guilt, acknowledged David's position as Israel's next king, and pledged to end the chase before the two went their separate ways.

- Deeply discouraged, David moved his family and followers into the enemy territory of Gath in Philistia, beginning a distinctly dismal period of David's life, one in which he moved from living by faith and honor in the land of Israel—even though he was on the run from Saul—to living by fear and deceit in the land of the enemies.

- Saul, with Samuel gone, God's guidance withdrawn from his life, and the Philistines closing in, was desperate for some kind of direction, so he consulted with a witch, who conjured up Samuel from the dead.

- The prophet scolded Saul for his past disobedience and said that Samuel and his sons would die at the hands of the Philistines the next day.

- David hit the bottom of the pit of depression after returning to Ziklag to find his family and friends taken captive, the livestock seized, the settlement in smoking ruins, and his men considering mutiny.

- In his grief, he turned to the Lord, who restored his soul. David found strength in God and then recovered the lost people and property.

- Just as Samuel had prophesied, the Philistines fought and easily defeated Israel in the Valley of Jezreel, killing three of Saul's sons, including Jonathan. Saul, mortally wounded, killed himself after his armorbearer refused to kill him to save him the humiliation and pain of being tortured or maimed by his enemies.

Study Questions

1. Why did David move into Philistine territory?

2. What characteristics marked David's life during his stay in the enemy's land?

3. Why was Saul feeling so desperate?

4. What happened to surprise the Witch of Endor?

5. What news did the prophet Samuel give Saul?

6. What devastating event sent David into despair?

7. How did David find his way out of that despair?

8. Why did Saul ask his armorbearer to kill him?

9. What did the Philistines do to Saul's body?

10. What did the people of Jabesh Gilead do after Saul's death, and why?

Part Five
DAYS OF GLORY

2 Samuel 1–5; 1 Chronicles 11: God's Man Takes the Throne

Chapter Highlights:
- Messenger with a Motive
- Heading for Hebron
- Civil War!
- Abner's Assassination
- King of Israel!
- Taking Jerusalem

Let's Get Started

The day David's brother fetched the suntanned teen from the sheepfold to meet Samuel in his father's home had been a long time ago. The timeline connecting that day's activity to the events that occur next can only be described as turbulent. During the past fifteen or so years, David had experienced the highs of victories and successes as well as the lows of defeat and failure. Each experience had helped shape David into the man he would need to be for the next season of his life. And with Saul's death, it became apparent that the latest season—the season of running—was coming to an end. He was on the threshold of becoming the second king of Israel. However, before his coronation, he would face a few more tests, most having to do with how to deal with difficult, deceitful, unpredictable, and ungodly people—all while the nation was watching his every move.

go to

his sons' fate
1 Samuel 4:12–18

Messenger with a Motive

the big picture

2 Samuel 1:1–10

David had been in Ziklag for two days after routing the Amalekites and subsequently restoring and recovering all the people and possessions they had seized. In a scene reminiscent of the one that took place the day Eli received devastating news about his sons' fate during the battle in which the Philistines had seized the Ark, David saw a figure approaching. The person—a messenger, he could assume—was wearing torn clothes and had dust on his head, so he knew the news couldn't be good; these were expressions of mourning. As the man fell to the ground at his feet, David demanded to know details. He learned that Saul and three of his sons were dead. Pressing for more information, David listened as the Amalekite described happening onto the injured Saul, who begged him to show him mercy by killing him. The Amalekite, seeing that Saul's injuries were so severe he would not have lived anyway, claimed to have complied with Saul's request.

The Amalekite's Discovery

Saul and his sons were dead; that much was true. But the rest of what the Amalekite told David contradicted the details provided in 1 Samuel 31:3–5. So, which account is the accurate one? Many scholars believe the Amalekite lied in order to earn his way into David's good favor.

- *What the Amalekite Said Happened:* The Amalekite said Saul had been alive but mortally wounded when he happened by. Saul had asked him to kill him. The Amalekite, convinced the king wouldn't have lived anyway, consented. He killed the king and took his crown and bracelet.

- *What the Amalkite Thought Would Happen:* The Amalekite couldn't believe his good fortune as he realized the identity of the figure on the ground in front of him. Being the first person to come across the body of the fallen king presented amazing possibilities. He acted quickly to turn the extraordinary discovery into self-serving advantages. Slipping the heavy crown off the dead king's head and the engraved bracelet off his arm, he concocted a story that would handily transform him from a hungry, homeless refugee from Saul's camp into a celebrated hero in David's. He guessed David would at least pay a handsome reward to the one who killed Saul. He might even do more than that. Would he offer him a position in his army? Give him a parcel of land? The Amalekite's imagination must have run wild as he considered the possibilities. No doubt he rehearsed what he would say all the way to David's camp.

- *What Really Happened:* According to 1 Samuel 31:1–6, Saul committed suicide after being mortally wounded by the Philistines. His armorbearer, who had refused Saul's request to kill him, witnessed his death and then killed himself.

what others say

Robert Alter

Having come upon Saul's body, [the Amalekite] sees a great opportunity for himself: he will bring Saul's regalia to David, claim personally to have finished off the man known to be David's archenemy and rival, and thereby overcome his marginality as resident alien . . . by receiving a benefaction from the new king—perhaps a portion of land at David's disposal.[1]

Whether or not the Amalekite killed Saul, he is a reminder of one of the chief reasons for Saul's demise: the king's failure to obey God's orders to totally annihilate the Amalekites. (Had Saul obeyed that order, this man wouldn't even have been alive at this time, either to slay Saul or to say that he did!)

The Amalekite's Reward

the big picture

2 Samuel 1:11–16

If the Amalekite thought his news of Saul's death would compel David to kick up his heels in elation, he thought wrong. Instead of congratulating the messenger on a job well done and expressing good riddance to the man who had made his life miserable, David was instantly grieved by the news. He tore his clothes, mourned, wept, and fasted for Saul and his son Jonathan, David's beloved friend. He even mourned for all the people of Israel whose anointed king—albeit an ineffective one—had been taken from them by violence.

David knew firsthand what it was like to face a decision about whether to take the life of the Lord's anointed, and he couldn't believe the Amalekite had dared to kill the king. He ordered the messenger executed for the transgression.

Dealing with the Death of the Enemy

David's reaction to the Amalekite's "confession" could be considered one of the first tests God would put him through in the series of passages leading up to his coronation as king over all of Israel. Apparently he passed with flying colors. His response to the Amalekite exposed wisdom and goodness in David's heart.

- *David understood that placing kings on thrones—and removing them from thrones—is God's job, not man's.* This applied to Saul and, he knew, it would apply to him as well. That's why he never attempted to contrive his own way onto the throne. He trusted God as the one and only kingmaker.

giver and taker of life
Job 1:21;
Colossians 1:16–17

murder
Exodus 20:13;
Deuteronomy 5:17;
Proverbs 6:16–17

loving one's enemies
Matthew 5:43–47;
Luke 6:32–33

guilty of murder
1 John 3:15

Book of Jasher
Joshua 10:13

lamentation
elegy or dirge

Book of Jasher
ancient non-
canonical history
book

- *God—and God alone—is the <u>giver and taker of life</u>.* His laws are to be followed. God's law prohibited <u>murder</u>. The Amalekite had violated God's sacred law, and David determined to enforce the legal consequences.

- *David loved Saul.* In spite of Saul's hatred for David, David loved Saul and his family. Jesus said loving those who return the love is common human behavior. But loving those who don't reciprocate, including <u>loving one's enemies</u>, is a feat that can be accomplished only with the power of the Holy Spirit. David's deep and heartfelt grief demonstrated his true feelings toward Saul. A love like that can only have one source: God. Further, had David not loved Saul, but hated him, he would have been <u>guilty of murder</u> anyway, according to New Testament teaching.

The Song of the Bow

the big picture

2 Samuel 1:17–27

David expressed his grief through a beautiful **lamentation** over Saul and Jonathan, a song said to be recorded in the **Book of Jasher**. The song conveyed his admiration of Saul's heroism and leadership, articulated his genuine regret over Saul's fate, and presented a moving tribute to his brother-like friend.

The passing of Israel's first king was a monumental event and David, wordsmith as well as warrior, shepherd, and musician, believed it important to compose an appropriate elegy. He carefully crafted a poem called "The Song of the Bow."

- It spoke the truth about Saul without weaving into it any kind of bitterness or condemnation (obviously deciding to leave recording the less stellar details of the king's life to the historians).
- It described his love for Jonathan.
- It expressed concern for the honor of God.
- It acknowledged the public nature of the loss.

What the men of Jabesh Gilead had done with their actions—respectfully moving the remains of their mutilated king to a place of honor in Jabesh—David did with these words. Saul's behavior during his life, from fits of depression and paranoid tirades to obsession with killing David and failing to adequately fulfill the responsibilities of being king, certainly could have been fodder for a verbal dismemberment of the king. But David, by example and with his words, steered the people away from that kind of behavior. His lament guided the public down the high road of forgiveness, respect, and love rather than the low road of grudge-holding, disrespect, and contempt.

Heading for Hebron

His children
John 1:12; 11:52;
Romans 8:16–17,
21; 9:8;
1 John 3:1–2

obedient children
Ephesians 5:1;
Philippians 2:15

seek His direction
Jeremiah 6:16;
Matthew 6:33

> **2 SAMUEL 2:1–3** *It happened after this that David inquired of the LORD, saying, "Shall I go up to any of the cities of Judah?" And the LORD said to him, "Go up." David said, "Where shall I go up?" And He said, "To Hebron." So David went up there, and his two wives also, Ahinoam the Jezreelitess, and Abigail the widow of Nabal the Carmelite. And David brought up the men who were with him, every man with his household. So they dwelt in the cities of Hebron.* (NKJV)

There was a vacancy in the throne room of Israel and David had been divinely appointed to fill it. Yet before he loaded his camel and headed to Israel to get on with his exciting new job, he took an important step many in his position might have overlooked: He asked God what he should do next.

As parents or anyone who works with kids quickly discovers, some children are obedient by nature. They ask permission before making a move, they seek direction, and they want to avoid doing things that displease those who are caring for them. Other children are more headstrong. They act on impulse and don't seem to give a thought to asking for permission or guidance. They just do it. Scripture frequently refers to God's followers as <u>His children</u>; and He wants us to be <u>obedient children</u> who <u>seek His direction</u> before we act.

When God Doesn't Seem to Make Sense

Was David surprised when God directed him to Hebron instead of Israel? The assignment couldn't have made much sense to him. But

friend of God
2 Chronicles 20:7;
James 2:23

the Lord's promise
Genesis 18:1–15

destruction of Sodom
Genesis 19

burial place
Genesis 23:19–20

David didn't doubt. He simply obeyed God's instructions, confident that if God's plan for his becoming king over all of Israel included a side trip to his tribal homeland to rule over Judah, then that was the best plan possible.

Imagine the sense of relief David must have felt as he moved his family from the ruins at Ziklag to a place they could finally call home after spending years running for his life and hiding out in caves!

Upon hearing Saul had died, David's family and followers may have wondered whether David was "settling for less" by going to Judah instead of storming the gates of the palace to take his rightful place as king of Israel. But apparently their trust in David had been restored; they must have started to breathe much easier with each step they took away from Ziklag. They had experienced nothing but temptation, unrest, and heartache in the pagan Philistine land, and were eager to settle their families into the beloved city of Hebron. Indeed, their time of service and loyalty to David—even though at least once they had been tempted to turn against him—was finding its reward.

what others say

Matthew Henry

They had accompanied him in his wanderings, and therefore, when he gained a settlement, they settled with him. Thus, if we suffer with Christ, we shall reign with him (2 Timothy 2:12). Nay, Christ does more for his good soldiers than David could do for his; David found lodging for them—They dwelt in the cities of Hebron, and adjacent towns; but to those who continue with Christ in his temptations he appoints a kingdom, and will feast them at his own table.[2]

Hebron's History

The city of Hebron, even at this ancient date, had a rich history. The Hebrew word comes from the Hebrew word for "friend," a description for the patriarch Abraham, who was considered to be a friend of God. Hebron was where the ninety-nine-year-old Abraham received the three angelic visitors who confirmed the Lord's promise that his barren wife would bear a son named Isaac. Abraham witnessed the destruction of Sodom. It was also the site of the cave Abraham bought as a burial place for his wife Sarah and where Abraham, Isaac, Jacob, Rebekah, and Leah—patriarchs and matriarchs of the Jewish people—were all later buried as well. That cave is known today as the Tomb of the Patriarchs and remains among the Jews' holiest sites.

After Joshua took possession of the Promised Land, he gave Hebron to Caleb, who, when he was eighty-five, drove out the Anakim who still resided in Hebron, and settled there. It became one of forty-eight cities where the Levites were assigned to live and one of six levitical cities designated as **cities of refuge**.

A Practice Reign in Judah

go to

possession of the Promised Land
Joshua 10:36–37

gave Hebron to Caleb
Joshua 14:6–15;
15:13;
Judges 1:20

drove out the Anakim
Joshua 15:14

Levites were assigned to live
Numbers 35:2–5

cities of refuge
Numbers 35:9–34;
Joshua 20:1–9,
21:11

Anakim
race of giant people

cities of refuge
safe places for awaiting trial

Ishbosheth
Saul's youngest son; temporary and powerless ruler of Israel between Saul's death and David's reign

Mahanaim
city in Gilead, east of the Jordan River; seat of Saul's government

the big picture

2 Samuel 2:4–11

The men of Judah anointed David as their king and pointed out the men of Jabesh Gilead who had buried Saul. David thanked them and pledged to return the kindness. Abner, Saul's general, was the man who wielded the most power over the remaining eleven tribes after Saul's death. He quickly installed **Ishbosheth**, Saul's youngest and only surviving son, as Saul's replacement. Ishbosheth ruled from **Mahanaim**, located in the eastern-central part of Transjordan, for two years. David's reign in Judah lasted seven and a half years.

David's move to the city of Hebron in his homeland of Judah proved valuable, diplomatically speaking, in many ways. It's as if God were saying, "If you can prove to be faithful with this smaller portion of power, I will later bless you with a larger portion of it." Truly, David was faithful with this mission. He made the most of his leadership of Judah, and while there he handily accomplished at least three valuable diplomatic feats:

1. He formalized his break from his ungodly alliance with the Philistines.

2. He made friends with the people of Jabesh Gilead, who had kindly treated Saul's remains (1 Samuel 31:11–13). Earning their favor helped him draw support from northern Israel.

3. He subtly began to position himself in the people's minds as Saul's replacement: "for your master Saul is dead, and also the house of Judah has anointed me king over them" (2 Samuel 2:7 NKJV).

Joab
David's nephew and
army commander

The Bible Knowledge Commentary

This was a decisive and important move, for it immediately alienated him from the Philistines with whom he had taken refuge and made an alliance; it signified the quasi-independence of Judah from Israel, an attitude which would find complete expression at the division of the kingdom after Solomon's death (1 Kings 12:16), and it asserted David's reign as being in rivalry with that of Saul's son, Ish-Bosheth, who succeeded his father in the North.[3]

The discrepancy between the length of time each of the kings served could be explained by the fact some time may have passed after Saul's death before Abner was able to succeed in establishing Ishbosheth as king; further, David's reign over Judah didn't necessarily end when Ishbosheth died.

David's Life, Defined According to His Three Anointings

Anointing	Scripture	Defining Event
1	1 Samuel 16:13	Samuel privately anointed David; marked the beginning of the years spent running from Saul.
2	2 Samuel 2:4	Men of Judah publicly anointed David as king of Judah; marked the beginning of David's seven-and-a-half-year reign as king of Judah, during which there were civil wars and political intrigue.
3	2 Samuel 5:3; 1 Chronicles 14:8	Men of Israel anointed David to mark the beginning of his reign as king over all of Israel.

Civil War!

2 Samuel 2:12–32

Abner and David's military leader, **Joab**, met for "peace talks" at the pool of Gibeon (Gibeon was in Benjamin, where Saul was likely to have lots of support), between elite troops of twelve men per side. All twenty-four men were killed and the episode escalated into a bloody battle, which David's men won. Asahel, Joab's brother and one of David's nephews, continued to chase Abner until the seasoned general, irritated by the young man's pursuit, killed Asahel. Joab and his surviving brother Abishai pledged revenge, but eventually gave up the chase and called all fighting to a halt. Abner went home to Mahanaim, and Joab returned to Hebron. David lost 20 soldiers, but Abner lost 360. Joab and his men then returned to Hebron.

If Israel was to become a united monarchy, the people were going to have to submit to the rule of one man. Yet two kings were now seated on royal thrones: David—selected by God—reigned in Judah, and Ishbosheth—chosen by man—reigned in Mahanaim.

The conflict was clear, and the two factions determined to resolve it. In an earlier day, Saul's impressive army would have appeared to have the upper hand. But the fallen king's troops had suffered losses during the Philistine attack, and the violent power struggle in the upper ranks no doubt had taken a toll on morale. Meanwhile, David's troops, though smaller, were gaining in strength, in numbers, and in spirit. God was on their side, and there was no surer source of confidence than that. The casualty report said it all.

key point

Power Struggles

the big picture

2 Samuel 3:1–19; I Chronicles 3:1–4

The civil war continued, and in fact became a long-term power struggle between Saul's dynasty in the north and David's in Judah, in the south. As the years passed, David's position grew stronger. He continued to take additional wives, bringing the total count to six, and he fathered six sons: Amnon (his first), Chileab, Absalom, Adonijah, Shephatiah, and Ithream. Meanwhile, Saul's position continued to weaken. Abner continued to wield the real power, while Ishbosheth remained nothing more than a figurehead. Conflict arose between the two when Abner took **Rizpah**, one of Saul's **concubines**, as his own. The gesture indicated he thought he would next be king. When Ishbosheth questioned his motives, Abner became angry and switched his loyalty, telling David he would help him secure Saul's kingdom. All David demanded from Abner was the return of his former wife, Michal. Abner traveled around the land meeting with the elders of Israel and convincing them to accept David as their king.

go to

remarry
Deuteronomy
24:1–4

Rizpah
one of Saul's
concubines

concubines
slave women often
employed to
provide heirs

David again resorted to the prohibited practice of polygamy in order to forge and cement political alliances. During his reign in Judah, he brought his total number of wives to six. He committed yet another breach of God's will when he asked to <u>remarry</u> Michal.

These violations could be considered marks against his score on his practice run as king of Judah, but God continued to bless David in spite of his sins. (However, they would weaken him, as powerfully proved in later episodes of David's life.)

what others say

Richard D. Phillips

The significance of this is clear: with David acknowledged again as Saul's son-in-law, it would be that much easier for the rebel faction to recognize him as king.[4]

David's Children Born in Hebron

Wife	Children
Ahinoam	Amnon
Abigail	Chileab (Daniel)
Maacah	Absalom and Tamar
Haggith	Adonijah
Abital	Shephatiah
Eglah	Ithream

Abner's Assassination

the big picture

2 Samuel 3:20–38

When Joab learned of the agreement between David and Abner, he was furious; he had many reasons to hate Abner, from his being the enemy's commander-in-chief to being the murderer of his brother, Asahel. Joab confronted David, accused Abner of spying, and then—without David's knowledge—devised a way to draw Abner aside so that he and his brother Abishai could assassinate him to avenge their brother's murder. David was appalled by the news of Abner's death. He pronounced a dreadful curse on Joab and his family, led the nation in public mourning of the fallen general, and buried him with great honor.

vengeance
Deuteronomy 32:35;
Psalm 94:1;
Romans 12:19;
Hebrews 10:30

tongue
James 3:5–8

Burton Coffman

The incredible damage to the entire history of Israel which resulted from this shameful assassination of Abner could hardly be overestimated. The eventual division of the kingdom in the reign of Rehoboam was due in part to the mistrust and hatred that followed this terribly unjust action of Joab and Abishai.[5]

Joab Let David Down

Why was David enraged rather than elated to hear that the man who had given him fits for so many years had been killed at the hands of his own general?

- Politically, the murder could have jeopardized the support from the northern tribes so recently drawn by Abner. The strength of the curse David pronounced against Joab, the degree of grief he expressed over Abner's death, and the passion with which he mourned kept David at a safe distance from any speculation that he might have been behind the murder.

- Personally, David was mortified that the most prominent leader in his army had so blatantly violated God's laws.

- <u>Vengeance</u> was the Lord's job, not man's. David had demonstrated his understanding of this law time after time in his own dealings with Saul, and couldn't fathom how his closest colleague and family member could disregard God's instructions.

- Legally, Hebron was a city of refuge where such revenge was not permitted. That one of David's own men would cross that holy boundary line must have been unimaginable.

Trouble from Within

As if conflict with the enemy weren't presenting enough difficulty, Joab was causing even more problems—from within David's own camp! The same thing often happens in a Christian's life. Many of the biggest challenges come from within his or her own camp. From a <u>tongue</u> that can corrupt the entire person, and deep-seated

envy
James 4:1

wicked
Jeremiah 17:9

envy that causes strife rather than unity to a heart that is desperately wicked, people, it seems, can get into plenty of danger on their own turf without even setting a foot onto the enemy's soil.

Ishbosheth's Death

the big picture

2 Samuel 4

The death of Abner panicked Ishbosheth, who no doubt could see his already loose-knit reign rapidly unraveling. Abner's death also shook up the already unstable nation of Israel. On the heels of the turmoil, while Ishbosheth was taking a midday siesta, two Benjamite assassins—Baanah and Recab—snuck up on him and killed him the same way Abner had been killed—with a stab to the stomach. They also beheaded him and carried his head to David, who ordered the two to be executed for murdering a defenseless man. The account of the murder of Ishbosheth in chapter 4 is interrupted by an introduction to Jonathan's son, Mephibosheth, who is referred to as Merib-Baal in 1 Chronicles 8:34. The boy was Jonathan's five-year-old son, who was lame because of injuries that had occurred when his nurse dropped him while carrying him from danger just after the deaths of his father and grandfather. The boy's name and more of his story will appear in 2 Samuel 9.

When God is in control, there is no need to fear. When men are in control, fear takes over. This is seen clearly in the fear of Ishbosheth—a king placed on the throne by a man—and of Israel—a nation led by a man chosen by themselves, not by God.

"Stop the violence!" the frightened people of Israel must have been murmuring as they heard the news that their king had been assassinated in the wake of the violent death of their general. They were without a leader and more vulnerable than ever to attacks by the Philistines and others.

"Stop the violence!" King David must have been thinking, too, as he heard yet more dreadful news that would test his abilities to take wise and decisive action before the eyes of all who were watching him closely.

God had assured David he would one day be king, but He hadn't said the journey would be easy. Even now, with one foot practically inside the entrance to the palace, it seemed David was having to struggle his way to the promised position.

The parallels relevant to Christians are clear:

- Just as David endured danger and persecution before he could reign as king of Israel, Christ endured danger and persecution before He could reign as King of His church.
- Just as the people of Israel suffered pain and death while the old, sinful regime was being torn apart in order to make way for a new, godly king to be placed on their throne, Christians suffer pain and death as their old, sinful nature is destroyed in order for Jesus to take His place as King of their hearts.

apply it

David: King of Israel!

the big picture

2 Samuel 5:1–5; 1 Chronicles 11:1–3; 12:23–40

The people of Israel had been watching the way David handled the deaths of Abner and of Ishbosheth, and apparently they liked what they saw. Rather than seeing a man focused on personal retribution and revenge, they saw a man who was striving to live out a set of high and holy principles—a man who appeared to be focused on pulling together former enemies into a single, united nation. Convinced it was time to follow David's lead, a delegation from all the tribes from the North went to Hebron to encourage David, now thirty-seven years old, to rule over them. David made a covenant with them—likely involving his pledge to follow the requirements of kings set forth in Deuteronomy 17:14–20—and they installed him as their king, confirming the occasion with his third anointing. First Chronicles 12 goes into great detail concerning the thousands of men who rallied behind David to help make him king: "All these men of war, who could keep ranks, came to Hebron with a loyal heart, to make David king over all Israel; and all the rest of Israel were of one mind to make David king" (1 Chronicles 12:38 NKJV).

After he was anointed as king of Israel, David wasted no time on speeches or parades. He got right to work by presenting his followers with a challenge: securing a headquarters for his new government.

Jebusites
Joshua 15:63

David needed to find a location well-suited to becoming the center of Israel's new government, and he knew exactly where it was: Jerusalem. He favored that city for several reasons. It was:

- centrally located

- easily defended—situated on a ridge surrounded by valleys in all directions

- easily accessible to the sea via the port at Jaffa

- well-watered by abundant rainfall and by the Gihon spring

- in neutral territory—Jerusalem had been in the control of the <u>Jebusites</u> since Joshua's day and therefore was considered politically neutral. By living there, David could demonstrate his tribal impartiality.

what others say

Richard D. Phillips

Jerusalem had long been on David's mind. It was not only a prominent and strategically vital location right in the heart of Israel but its ability to hold out against the Israelites was a centuries-old symbol of their failure, faithlessness, and mediocrity. Other brave men had tried to take Jerusalem . . . and they had ultimately shrunk back from the task. Jerusalem was the ideal defensive position . . . So to take Jerusalem would be more than a coup, it would be the kind of success around which a new identity is forged. For Israel, a future in Jerusalem meant the fulfillment of its past and the promises such fulfillment held for tomorrow.[6]

Alfred J. Kolatch

Jewish history and Jewish tradition is linked to Jerusalem more than to any other place on earth. From about 1000 B.C.E., when David captured the city from the Jebusites (of whom there is no longer any trace) and set it up as his capital, Jerusalem has been sacred to Jews. When Solomon built the First Temple there, it became a holy city, often called "the Eternal City." Jews lived in Jerusalem and prayed for its well-being for 1,000 years before there were Christians on the face of the earth, and for 1,600 years before Islamic nations came into being.[7]

Taking Jerusalem

2 Samuel 5:6–25; 1 Chronicles 11:4–9; 14

There was only one problem with establishing Jerusalem as the capital: The **Jebusites** who lived there were strong people, and they had attitude! So David issued a challenge: Whoever found access to the city would be promoted to commander-in-chief. Joab, David's disgraced general, snuck in through the city's water tunnels. Thus David's men made Jerusalem as well as some of the surrounding areas the capital, calling the entire tract the City of David.

David's great power and success made it clear to everyone watching that God's hand was upon him. Particularly striking evidence of this was being recognized by Hiram, king of the Phoenician city-state of Tyre, who sent gifts in the form of supplies to be used to build David's palace. David, already a polygamist, continued to increase his family's size and his government's power by acquiring a large harem in keeping with the ancient Near Eastern custom of cementing alliances through gifts of princesses.

The capture of Jerusalem cued the Philistines to David's success. They now completely understood that in spite of his brief tenure of service for them, he was their enemy. Twice they made offensive moves into the nearby Valley of Rephaim, about three or four miles southwest of Jerusalem, twice David sought God's direction about how to proceed against the enemy, and twice David led Israel's troops to victory, finally driving the Philistines from Gibeon to Gezer, fifteen miles away.

Chaim Herzog and Mordechai Gichon

Joab's exploit cannot be sufficiently appreciated until we are cognizant of the fact that he and his men had to ascend a fifty-foot-high vertical shaft between the tunneled approach from the town and the channel which led the spring waters to its bottom. These waters were drawn up in pails through the shaft, but it seems that an additional reason for its construction was to prevent a penetration into the town via its water-inlet—exactly as was amazingly achieved, in spite of this precaution.[8]

Charles Swindoll

David's accomplishments were marvelous. Territorially, he expanded the boundaries of Israel from 6,000 to 60,000 square miles. Incredible! He set up extensive trade routes that reached throughout the known world. And from that, wealth came into Israel like the nation had never known before.[9]

Chapter Wrap-Up

- A messenger told David that he had happened upon Saul and killed the mortally wounded king upon his request. David, instantly grieved by the news, ordered the messenger executed for the transgression and expressed his grief through a beautiful lamentation.

- At the Lord's direction, David, his family, and his followers moved to his homeland of Judah, where he was anointed as their king. He made the most of his leadership of Judah and used his time there to do important diplomatic work.

- Abner, Saul's general, wielded the most power over the remaining eleven tribes after Saul's death. He quickly installed Ishbosheth, Saul's youngest and only surviving son, as Saul's replacement.

- Civil war developed into a long-term power struggle between Saul's dynasty in the north and David's in Judah, in the south. As the years passed, David's position grew stronger. He continued to take additional wives, bringing the total count to six, and he fathered six sons.

- Joab learned of a peace agreement between David and Abner and in his fury had him killed. David, appalled by the news, pronounced a dreadful curse on Joab and his family, led the nation in public mourning of Abner's death, and buried the general with great honor.

- The death of Abner panicked Ishbosheth and shook up the already unstable nation of Israel. Two Benjamite assassins snuck up on him and killed him.

- The people of Israel, who had been watching David as he had handled the deaths of Abner and of their king Ishbosheth, were convinced it was time to follow David's leadership. They sent a delegation from all the tribes of the north to Hebron to install him as their king.

- David immediately secured Jerusalem as headquarters for his new government.

Study Questions

1. When Saul died, why didn't David make an immediate move to replace him as king of Israel?

2. What kind of a leader was Saul's son Ishbosheth?

3. What did David accomplish during his reign as king of Judah?

4. What caused Abner to switch his loyalty to David?

5. How did Joab react to the agreement between Abner and David?

6. How was Ishbosheth killed?

7. How did the people of Israel confirm David's installation as king?

8. What was David's first action as king of Israel?

2 Samuel 6; 1 Chronicles 13-16: Dancing King

Chapter Highlights:
• How NOT to Move the Ark
• Getting It Right
• Michal Missed the Point
• David's Defense

Let's Get Started

The men and women of Israel had long endured the uncomfortable and often violent consequences of their demand to have their own king their own way and according to their own schedule. But the future had suddenly become brighter. No doubt they felt overwhelmed by relief as they watched God's man, David, take his rightful place on their throne. If their faltering sense of national security and patriotic pride had been restored by David's swift and effective move to establish Jerusalem as the flourishing hub of politics and government, how much more their faith in God was fortified as David revealed his plans to make Jerusalem the religious center of the nation. They could see that David understood a truth they had long ago forgotten: political power and military might are impossible apart from God.

Where Is the Ark?

During Saul's reign, the king had done little to run the nation according to God's guidelines. He had practically abandoned practicing the model of tabernacle worship outlined by God and as a result, Israel's relationship with God had become mediocre. The Ark of the Covenant—the focal point of tabernacle worship—has not even been mentioned in the biblical narrative since Saul, trying to look spiritual when the Philistines were closing in, asked his priest to bring it to the battlefront for him (see 1 Samuel 14:18). With the possible exception of that brief time, the Ark had rested for the past twenty or more years at the house of Abinadab in Kirjath Jearim.

But David was about to change that. As a man whose heart hungered for God's presence, he wanted to reestablish for his nation worship, God's way. That meant fetching the piece of sacred furniture from Abinadab's home and putting it back where it belonged: in the tabernacle.

David's Proposal

Baale Judah
Joshua 15:9

Baale Judah
another name for
Kiriath Jearim

the big picture

2 Samuel 6:1–2; 1 Chronicles 13:1–6

Speaking to throngs of Israelites, David presented his proposal to retrieve the Ark of the Covenant, and the people whole-heartedly agreed. So David and about thirty thousand Israelites went to **Baale Judah** to retrieve the holy vessel.

what others say

Charles Swindoll

David unified the nation under Jehovah God, creating a national interest in spiritual things. He was not a priest; he was a king . . . but he lifted up the role of the priesthood so that Judaism could operate openly and freely in the land.[1]

David's Speech

In looking for lessons on leadership taught by the life of David, it's helpful to study closely the words he used in his brief speech regarding retrieving the Ark of the Covenant:

1 CHRONICLES 13:2–3 *And David said to all the assembly of Israel, "If it seems good to you, and if it is of the LORD our God, let us send out to our brethren everywhere who are left in all the land of Israel, and with them to the priests and Levites who are in their cities and their common-lands, that they may gather together to us; and let us bring the ark of our God back to us, for we have not inquired at it since the days of Saul." (NKJV)*

David was an excellent communicator! Notice how:

- He addressed the entire nation rather than a few close advisers.

- He clothed the proposal with concern for the hearers' opinions.

- He acknowledged God's authority.

- He affiliated himself with the people.

- He took full responsibility for neglecting the matter of the

Ark in national worship, even though it had been under Saul's leadership that proper worship had deteriorated.

How NOT to Move the Ark

go to

Obed-Edom
1 Chronicles 26:4

Koath
Numbers 4:15

the big picture

2 Samuel 6:3–10; 1 Chronicles 13:5–13

Celebrate! That was the word of the day when David and his followers had retrieved the Ark and placed it on the cart they had custom-built for the job. David and the Israelites marked the occasion with music by playing their harps, lyres, tambourines, cymbals, and trumpets as Abinadab's sons, **Uzzah and Ahio**—who were not sons of Kohath—slowly guided the cart toward Jerusalem. But when the parade hit a bump in the road—literally—the oxen pulling the cart stumbled, the cart tipped, and the holy Ark shifted. Uzzah automatically did what any conscientious person carrying precious cargo would do: reach out to steady the Ark and prevent it from crashing to the ground. But by doing so, Uzzah's touch violated the sanctity of the vessel and God instantly struck him dead. David immediately realized what had happened: He had failed to follow God's specific instructions for handling the Ark. He was angry; at whom, it's not stated. Perhaps he was angry at Uzzah for making the deadly error. Perhaps he was angry at God for demonstrating His righteous judgment. Most likely, however, David was angry at himself for allowing the tragedy to happen. Whatever the focus of his anger, the king was filled with fear of the Lord and called off the whole operation. Temporarily storing the Ark at the nearby home of **Obed-Edom**, he abandoned his effort to bring the Ark to the City of David.

Uzzah and Ahio
Abinadab's sons who unlawfully moved the Ark from Kirjath Jearim

Obed-Edom
Levite of the family of **Koath**

Koath
the Levite family responsible for moving the Ark

Only Koathites may carry the Ark, and they may only carry it on their shoulders by using the specially designated poles and rods. The vessel is never to be transported on a cart and above all, it is never to be touched by human hands.

What Was David Thinking?

Nothing in the text suggests that David intended to disobey God when he decided to build a new cart upon which to tote the Ark home. Nor does it say his actions were deliberately rebellious or irreverent. David was simply single-mindedly careening toward one goal: getting the Ark home. It was a good goal, one of which God certainly approved. Yet in David's enthusiasm to get the job done, he didn't bother to check the "how-to" guide before taking his first step. He acted on an impulse prompted by passion, expedience, and speed—and his oversight cost a man his life.

key point

That brings up again the uncomfortable yet important point so emphatically expressed throughout David's life: The person who sins is rarely the only one who suffers the consequences. Many times, inevitable effects spill over into the lives of other people—including those who, like Uzzah, are also guilty of sin as well as those who are innocent.

what others say

Mark Buchanan

Uzzah's willingness to carry the ark on an ox cart was in clear breach of divine command. God had given detailed instruction about how the ark was to be transported: slung on poles and hefted by priests. Freighting the ark on an ox cart was a Philistine notion. It must have seemed to Uzzah—maybe it was even his idea to bring it over from the Philistines—more convenient, efficient, elegant. The latest fashion in worship accoutrements. Why didn't God think of it? Well, we'll amend that. It was always the hankering of the Israelites to be like the other nations. It's always been the hankering of the church, too. If everybody's doing it out there, it must be an improvement on what we do in here.[2]

apply it

There's an old saying, "The road to hell is paved with good intentions," and this episode illustrates the truth that while God often chooses to show mercy instead of judgment, certain absolutes do not change according to a person's intentions or feelings. When God said in Numbers 4:15, "Whoever touches the ark will die," that's exactly what He meant. It was David's responsibility—and Uzzah's, too—to follow God's law. Regardless of our good intentions, doing God's work but refusing to do it His way thwarts even the best of plans and usually brings disastrous consequences.

what others say

Kay Arthur

No matter how much time has elapsed since God gave His commandments, His instructions, the revelation of His heart, and His desire in various matters, we have ample evidence that He expects us to "seek Him according to the ordinance" (1 Chronicles 15:13). We are not to choose our way above His way. No matter how noble our intentions, even as David's were noble in restoring the ark of the covenant to its proper status in the life of the nation, what we do must be done God's way. God is a holy God, and when we do not comply with His way we are not treating Him as holy.[3]

They Got It Right the Second Time

go to

dancing
Ecclesiastes 3:4

victory celebrations
Exodus 15:20–21;
Judges 11:34;
1 Samuel 18:6;
30:16

weddings
Judges 21:1;
Psalm 45:14–15;
Song of Solomon
6:13

entertainment
Matthew 14:6;
Mark 6:22;
Job 21:11;
Matthew 11:17;
Luke 7:32

personal celebration
Luke 15:25

the big picture

2 Samuel 6:11–19; 1 Chronicles 15

When David heard the news that the household of Obed-Edom was experiencing great blessing because the Ark of the Covenant had been stored there for the past three months, he decided it was time to try the move again. This time he wanted to get it right, so he oversaw the appropriate steps. He prepared a place for it, he assembled the correct people—the priests—to transport it, and he made sure the priests carried it the correct way. The result made the moving-day road trip a joy-filled praise party attended by thousands of Israelites playing music, dancing, and offering praise. King David was no exception; he was twirling in ecstatic abandon and embracing the priestly privileges God granted kings. He donned the linen ephod, the official priest's uniform, administered burnt offerings and fellowship offerings, blessed the people and gave them individual gifts of food. Little did David know that while he was dancing, his wife, Michal, had been watching his every move from her window seat. She found David's delight despicable.

The kind of dancing David did wasn't what preteens practice in front of the full-length mirror in the bedroom. This was a physical expression of the soul-deep praise and adoration spilling out of his heart. His dancing—probably similar to today's traditional folk dances—may have taken Michal aback, but it shouldn't have; after all, dancing was an integral part of the Hebrews' life. They also danced for:

- victory celebrations
- weddings
- entertainment
- personal celebration

David's Dance Attire

As significant as the fact that David danced is what he was wearing while he did it. Second Samuel 6:14 states he wore a linen ephod. First Chronicles 15:27 states he wore a linen robe and ephod, and was dressed like other priests and Levites. Why would a newly crowned king cast off his royal regalia and put on such simple garments for this praise-and-worship session? Because David the king wasn't the one worshipping the Lord; it was David, God's humble servant, who was doing the worshipping. He donned the garments of pure linen worn by those who served with humility before the Lord. This offers an apt example of the New Testament charge that believers should "be clothed with humility" (1 Peter 5:5 NKJV).

David was a king, not a priest. However, God's law authorized him to step into the role of a priest.

Ordering Worship

> the big picture
>
> ### 1 Chronicles 16:4–43
>
> David did more than dance on the special day the Ark arrived at its new home in Jerusalem. He also arranged for future worship.
>
> 1. David organized the Levites into an administrative structure, appointing Asaph, Heman, and Jeduthun as chief musicians.
> 2. He assigned each priest specific instruments to play.
> 3. He put together a psalm of thanks in honor of the Lord.
> 4. He provided for the continuation of organized worship by appointing some priests to continue ministering before the Ark of the Lord in Jerusalem on alternating shifts.
> 5. Because the tabernacle was still in Gibeon, he arranged for worship to continue there, with Zadok serving as priest of that tabernacle.

Liner Notes for the Psalm

priest
1 Kings 8:62–65;
1 Samuel 2:35;
Deuteronomy
18:15–19

The hymn of thanksgiving offered that day was actually a medley of other psalms, including Psalms 105:1–15; 96:1–13; and 106:1, 47–48. It featured a call to worship, an expression of God's greatness and glory, and praise that proclaimed God's superiority over the other nations' gods. It also highlighted His creative power and included an invitation for everyone to turn to God.

Worship: What's Your Style?

Alternative, experiential, contemporary, formal, casual, traditional. The ways people worship God vary not only from denomination to denomination and church to church but often from person to person as well. Some worshippers express adoration of God with full-out physical motion like David; others remain much more reserved, rarely lifting a hand or tapping a toe. So what makes worship worship?

apply it

1. It's all about God—not about the people in the next pew, the pastor, or the music leader—and it focuses on God's character, His greatness, and His presence.

what others say

Max Lucado

Worship is the act of magnifying God. Enlarging our vision of him. Stepping into the cockpit to see where he sits and observe how he works. Of course, his size doesn't change, but our perception of him does. As we draw nearer, he seems larger. Isn't that what we need? A big view of God? Don't we have big problems, big worries, big questions? Of course we do. Hence we need a big view of God. Worship offers that.[4]

2. It's a matter of the heart. Jesus taught that "true worshipers will worship the Father in spirit and truth" (John 4:23 NKJV). The heart truly involved in worship is bowed in humility, awed by God's greatness, and reverently submitted to His service.

what others say

Rick Warren

Surrendering to God is the heart of worship. It is the natural response to God's amazing love and mercy. We give ourselves to him, not out of fear or duty, but in love, "because he first loved us."[5]

go to

personal
Romans 12:1

corporate
Psalms 34:3; 95:6–7

changes the
worshipper.
Isaiah 6:1–8

corporate
carried out with
other people

bless
express good wishes
for and/or offer
prayer for

3. It's both <u>personal</u> and **corporate**.

4. It's fueled by faith rather than by emotion, rituals, or surroundings and rests on the principle that the only doorway to God's presence is His grace.

5. It <u>changes the worshipper</u>.

what others say

Max Lucado

God invites us to see his face so he can change ours. He uses our uncovered faces to display his glory.[6]

Michal Missed the Point

2 SAMUEL 6:20 *Then David returned to **bless** his household. And Michal the daughter of Saul came out to meet David, and said, "How glorious was the king of Israel today, uncovering himself today in the eyes of the maids of his servants, as one of the base fellows shamelessly uncovers himself!"* (NKJV)

David probably couldn't remember a happier occasion. The Holy Ark had been returned, and he had spent the past few hours celebrating its arrival in the City of David, giving thanks to God and giving gifts to his people. And the day wasn't even over yet! David headed home with a spring in his step and a heart full of satisfaction with the intention of sharing his joy by blessing his own family.

How quickly his elation was extinguished, however, when Michal slipped off her window seat to meet him at the door with mean-spirited sarcasm. With just one venom-filled sentence, she accused her husband of being unkingly, undignified, and even immodest.

what others say

Liz Curtis Higgs

The truth is, Michal missed the point. She didn't comprehend the purpose of David's dancing. She saw it as a passion of the flesh, when David knew it was a spiritual passion for God that set his feet in motion.[7]

Michal: Victim or Vixen?

From where did Michal's bitterness erupt? It came from the same spot that David's unharnessed joy had originated: the heart. In all fairness, she had reason to harbor bitterness in her heart:

- She had fallen in love as a young girl only to be married to the man of her dreams as a convenient political pawn instead of as a coveted princess.
- Her husband had abandoned her soon after they married.
- Her father had developed a murderous hatred of her husband.
- Her father had taken her away from her husband and given her to another man.
- Her father and brothers had died violent deaths.
- She had been torn from her second husband—a man who apparently truly loved her—for political advantage.

Much of the tragedy in Michal's life was wrought by the two men who were supposed to be looking out for her: her father, Saul, and her first husband, David. Little wonder the lovestruck princess standing at the window of their first home, relieved to watch her husband <u>escape</u> his pursuers, now stood at a window as an embittered queen planning to ambush her husband with abrasive words! The intervening events had made her love grow cold and her heart become hardened.

It's easy to sympathize with Michal and identify her as a victim of her circumstances. However, it's also important to remember that she didn't have a corner on the market of reasons to be resentful. Everyone has plenty of reasons to be bitter, whether it's a bad boss, chronic allergies, a wayward child, or a soured business deal. David himself had just emerged from a season full of reasons to cultivate a sour attitude, as had Michal's "co-wife," Abigail. Yet David and Abigail apparently had learned something Michal didn't understand. Michal missed the point of David's display because she, like her father before her, had come to view the world not through God's eyes, but through the eyes of a human with very selfish motives and very limited understanding.

escape
1 Samuel 19:12

Ann Spangler

Michal's story is tragic. Throughout the difficult circumstances of her life, we see little evidence of a faith to sustain her. Instead, she is tossed back and forth, her heart left to draw its own bitter conclusions . . . The story of Michal seems to indicate that she grew to be more like Saul than David. As such, she reminds us that even victims have choices. No matter how much we've been sinned against, we still have the power to choose the attitude of our heart. If we cast ourselves on God's mercy, asking him to help us, he cannot refuse. Even in difficulty, he will dwell in us, shaping our own wayward hearts into the likeness of his own.[8]

Two Wives, Two Responses

Abigail	Michal
Married to an ungodly, foolish man of tremendous wealth and influence.	Married to a godly, wise man of tremendous wealth and influence.
Woman with potential for influencing many people around her.	Woman with potential for influencing many people around her.
Met David on the road as he was coming to bring disaster to her home.	Met David on the road as he was coming to bring blessing to her home.
Used words chosen to soothe anger.	Used words chosen to incite anger.
Demonstrated her understanding of David's high calling in God's plan for Israel.	Demonstrated her ignorance of David's high calling in God's plan for Israel.
Acted without regard for what onlookers might think.	Based her opinion of David largely upon what onlookers might think.
Ultimately was rewarded by David.	Ultimately was punished by the king.

David's Defense

2 SAMUEL 6:21–23 *So David said to Michal, "It was before the LORD, who chose me instead of your father and all his house, to appoint me ruler over the people of the LORD, over Israel. Therefore I will play music before the LORD. And I will be even more undignified than this, and will be humble in my own sight. But as for the maidservants of whom you have spoken, by them I will be held in honor." Therefore Michal the daughter of Saul had no children to the day of her death.* (NKJV)

If Michal had deliberately chosen her words to provoke a reaction from David, she succeeded. However, instead of shaming David into an apology, she invited a well-deserved dressing-down: David let her know in no uncertain terms that the Lord, not Michal, was his audience; that he was acting as the Lord's chosen ruler of Israel, and that he would gladly undergo even more indignities in his service to the Lord. In other words, "You haven't seen anything yet!"

go to

Lucifer
Isaiah 14:12–15

However, even in his anger David retained humility. In contrast to the proud, presumptuous words used by the fallen angel <u>Lucifer</u> to proclaim his intent to usurp the Lord's exalted position, David's words passionately proclaimed his intent to further humiliate himself in service to the Lord.

In a sad conclusion to the episode, readers learn that Michal lived the rest of her days under the shadow of the most shameful disgrace that could befall a Hebrew woman: she bore no children. The Bible doesn't state that this was a specific judgment of barrenness from God; most scholars agree that her failure to bear children was a natural result of David's anger: he most likely had no desire to be intimate with the hateful woman and banished her from his bedroom.

Like Father, Like Daughter

The family resemblance is uncanny! Just like her father, Michal was terribly concerned with what others thought of her, and she seems to have chosen suspicion, paranoia, and cynicism over trust in people and in the Lord. Just as Saul's reign as king was largely barren of producing any good for the nation of Israel, her reign as queen was barren of producing any good for the nation of Israel—or for her own lineage.

something to ponder

what others say

Mark Buchanan

Michal, at great personal cost, teaches us another valuable lesson about God. God is not the safe-keeper of our reputations. God is not some priggish domestic deity, a heavenly Miss Manners intent on prescribing the etiquette that maintains polite society, aghast by any outbursts of fervor. And our role on this Earth, be it prophet, king, priest, or homemaker, is not to keep ourselves from embarrassment. We must come before the King, dignified or undignified, robed or disrobed, in the presence of the elite or in the company of slave girls, and worship with all our might.[9]

Liz Curtis Higgs

As King David's first wife, Michal had the opportunity to learn true worship from a flawed but passionate man after God's own heart. Instead, she threw away such blessings with both hands, then shoved her manicured fists inside the folds of her costly tunic, determined to be miserable forever. And so she was.[10]

Chapter Wrap-Up

- David wanted to reestablish for his nation worship, God's way. That meant fetching the Ark of the Covenant from Kirjath Jearim and putting it back where it belonged: in the tabernacle.

- David and his followers retrieved the Ark and placed it on the cart they had custom-built for the job, marking the occasion with much celebration. When the oxen pulling the cart stumbled, the cart tipped, and the holy Ark shifted. Uzzah reached out to steady the Ark but was stricken dead for touching the holy vessel.

- David, immediately realizing that he had failed to follow God's specific instructions for handling the Ark, stored it at the nearby home of Obed-Edom, temporarily abandoning his effort to bring the Ark to the City of David.

- David tried the move again, getting it right the second time by making sure the Ark was handled appropriately.

- The Ark's arrival in Jerusalem was marked by great celebration, with David twirling in ecstatic abandon.

- Michal, who had been watching his every move from her window seat, found David's delight despicable and gave him a scathing rebuke.

- David let her know in no uncertain terms that the Lord, not Michal, was his audience; that he was acting as the Lord's chosen ruler of Israel, and that he would undergo even more indignities in his service to the Lord.

Study Questions

1. Why was it important to David to have the Ark of the Covenant brought to Jerusalem?

2. How was David's first attempt at moving the Ark in error?

3. What were the consequences of the error?

4. How did David show his delight that the Ark was finally brought into Jerusalem?

5. How did Michal misread his expression of joy?

6. What are some possible reasons she didn't understand David's actions?

7. How did David respond to her rebuke?

2 Samuel 7; 1 Chronicles 17: David's Deep Desire

Chapter Highlights:
- Peace in the Palace
- The Big Idea
- God Says No
- A House of a Different Kind
- David's Response

Let's Get Started

David's running was over, his reign was established, his residence was built. As he glanced around at the magnificence of his surroundings, he felt ashamed: The Creator of the universe was living in a tent while he lived in a splendid palace. The disparity sparked inspiration: He would build a home—a temple—worthy of God! The thought of erecting an elaborate dwelling place for the Lord may have been a good idea, but it wasn't God's idea. God said, "no," and turned the tables on David by saying that, instead, *He* would build a house for David. David didn't let the disappointment of hearing a heaven-sent "no" get him down; instead, his spiritual eyes trained on God's will alone, he chose praising over pouting and gratitude over grumbling.

gift
2 Samuel 5:11;
1 Chronicles 14:1

Peace in the Palace, the Family, and the Nation

> **2 SAMUEL 7:1** *Now it came to pass when the king was dwelling in his house, and the LORD had given him rest from all his enemies all around . . . (NKJV)*

That David was living in a house at all is no small detail in his biography, considering his history. His homes had ranged from a room in the palace of a king who kept trying to kill him, to the recesses of cramped, damp caves in the wilderness. His current address wasn't a typical starter home: After David had been anointed king of Israel, Hiram, the neighboring king of Tyre, had given the new ruler a lavish <u>gift</u>: the supplies (expensive cedar from Lebanon) and the manpower (skilled craftsmen) to build a place literally fit for a king.

On the domestic front, David was happily married, and at least one of his wives (Abigail) shared his passion for the Lord. His wives heaped honor after honor upon him with each male child they bore. Times were very good indeed for the family flourishing within the walls of David's home.

Times were good outside the palace, too. The uniting of the nation had unleashed a fresh surge of patriotism and an unprecedented sense of security. Israel's longtime enemies had retreated, giving the men of Israel a rare break from battle. Spirits were high, as was the king's approval rating. David truly had much to be thankful for.

The "Rest" of the Story

The kind of "rest" David was enjoying in the great chambers of his exquisite new digs didn't come from afternoon power naps on a chaise in the courtyard. Oh, to be sure, David probably was physically drained after the years spent dodging spears and fighting Philistines. But this "rest" meant much more than eight to ten hours of sleep a night. The Hebrew word used here—*nuach*—suggests settling down, remaining still, and being quiet. It is the same word used in Joshua 21:44 to explain the rest God gave the Israelites after He escorted them into the Promised Land. In other words, *nuach* meant breathing a deep sigh of relief. It meant not having to constantly scan the horizon for enemies approaching. It meant not having to look back to see who might be in hot pursuit. Most important, it meant enjoying the blessing of seeing God's promises fulfilled.

In Jeremiah 6:16, the Lord promises *margoa*—a "resting place"—for the souls of the people who follow His guidelines for living; and in Matthew 11:28, Jesus Christ promises His people *anapauo*—a refreshing "rest"—for the souls of those who stay close to Him.

The Big Idea

2 SAMUEL 7:1–2 (See also 1 Chronicles 17:1b–2.) *The king said to Nathan the prophet, "See now, I dwell in a house of cedar, but the ark of God dwells inside tent curtains." Then Nathan said to the king, "Go, do all that is in your heart, for the LORD is with you."* (NKJV)

Often, when a person experiences sudden idleness after a long period of busyness, the body stops its motion but the mind keeps moving. That certainly was the case with David, and his racing thoughts couldn't have been loftier. He looked around at the solid, cedar-lined walls of his own spectacular surroundings, compared them to the spindly poles and billowing draperies that sheltered God's Presence in the tabernacle, and decided to do something about the disparity: He would build a temple suitable for the Lord.

David couldn't wait to tell Nathan about his monumental idea, and the prophet responded just as he had hoped, with an enthusiastic, "Get with it, then."

Stephen
leader in the early church

what others say

Matthew Henry

> When God by his providence has given us rest we ought to consider how we may honour him with the advantages of it, and what service we may do to our brethren who are unsettled, or not so well settled as we are. When God had given David rest, see how restless he was till he had *found out a habitation* for the ark.[1]

No wonder David didn't believe the tabernacle was big enough or magnificent enough for the Lord! Perhaps one of David's greatest assets was his ability to see himself for who he was—and to see God for who He is. David, after all, wrote Psalms 19, 24, and 29, which, among other things, express the magnificence of God's presence.

something to ponder

God Says No

the big picture

2 Samuel 7:4–7; 1 Chronicles 17:1–6

Nathan may have given David a thumbs-up on the building proposal, but God didn't. Not right away, at least. That night, God gave Nathan a two-part message for David. The first part answered David's proposal. It wasn't exactly a harsh rebuke, but it did harbor a stern tone:

1. **"Are you the one to build me a house to live in?"** God wanted David to remember *who was in charge*. Choosing a builder for the temple—if there was to be one—was God's responsibility, not David's.
2. **"I don't need a house."** God wanted David to remember *who He was*—a God who is everywhere, all the time. As **Stephen** told the high priests at the Sanhedrin: "The Most High does not dwell in temples made with hands" (Acts 7:48 NKJV).

promise of land
Genesis 15

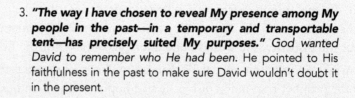

3. *"The way I have chosen to reveal My presence among My people in the past—in a temporary and transportable tent—has precisely suited My purposes."* God wanted David to remember who He had been. He pointed to His faithfulness in the past to make sure David wouldn't doubt it in the present.

Even though God denied David permission to build the temple, He did give him credit for his good intentions. Speaking at the dedication of the temple, David's son Solomon said:

> 1 KINGS 8:17–20 *Now it was in the heart of my father David to build a temple for the name of the LORD God of Israel. But the LORD said to my father David, "Whereas it was in your heart to build a temple for My name, you did well that it was in your heart. Nevertheless you shall not build the temple, but your son who will come from your body, he shall build the temple for My name." So the LORD has fulfilled His word which He spoke; and I have filled the position of my father David, and sit on the throne of Israel, as the LORD promised; and I have built a temple for the name of the LORD God of Israel. (NKJV)*

A House of a Different Kind

the big picture

2 Samuel 7:8–17; 1 Chronicles 17:7–15

The second part of God's response to David was a staggering promise: One of his descendents eventually would rule over Israel and the world forever.

The promise God gave David is called the Davidic Covenant. It not only reaffirmed the <u>promise of land</u> that God had made to Israel; it also outlined in great detail what David and Israel could expect in the near and distant future.

In the near future, God promised:

- *A dynasty of kings:* God guaranteed that David's own offspring would succeed him as king of Israel.

- *A construction delay:* God stated that David's heir, not David, would be the one to build a house for God.

224 ——————————— **The Smart Guide to the Bible** ———————————

In the distant future God promised:

- *An everlasting kingdom:* God promised that David's dynasty would never end.

- *A coming Messiah:* God pointed to the coming eternal reign of the Messiah, a Savior who would enter the history of humankind through the lineage of David and the tribe of Judah. The angel Gabriel referred to this never-ending reign when he said to Mary, "He will be great, and will be called the Son of the Highest; and the Lord God will give Him the throne of His father David. And He will reign over the house of Jacob forever, and of His kingdom there will be no end" (Luke 1:32–33 NKJV).

abrogated
abolished

what others say

Larry Richards

This Davidic Covenant is the foundation of much Old Testament prophecy, which describes an era of world-wide peace under David's promised descendant. The New Testament gospels make it clear that the person the promises refer to is none other than Jesus Christ. Jesus Christ, the only living descendant of David, will fulfill God's promise and rule an eternal kingdom.[2]

Tim LaHaye

Over a period of 500 years, the promise that the Davidic line would continue forever was repeated many times: to David himself, to Solomon, in the Psalms, and by the prophets Isaiah, Jeremiah, Amos, Micah and Zechariah. While individual kings were chastised for disobedience, the covenant was never **abrogated**. From David a direct line of descent continued for over one thousand years, until Jesus, the Son of Abraham, the Son of David, was born.[3]

Prophecies About the Messiah

God's covenant with David is just one instance in the Old Testament of a prediction about the coming Messiah. Others include:

Predictions About the Messiah to Come

Prophecy	Old Testament Reference	New Testament Fulfillment
The Messiah would be born in Bethlehem.	Micah 5:2	Matthew 2:1
The Messiah would be born to a virgin.	Isaiah 7:14	Matthew 1:18–23
Herod would attempt to murder the Messiah.	Jeremiah 31:15	Matthew 2:16–18
The Messiah would be betrayed by a friend.	Psalm 41:9	John 13:18–19, 26
The Messiah would be sold for thirty silver coins.	Zechariah 11:12	Matthew 26:14–16
The Messiah would be crucified.	Zechariah 12:10	John 19:16–18, 37
Lots would be cast for the Messiah's clothes.	Psalm 22:18	Matthew 27:35
None of the Messiah's bones would be broken.	Psalm 34:20	John 19:31–36
The Messiah would be buried in a rich man's tomb.	Isaiah 53:9	Matthew 27:57–60
The Messiah would arise from the dead on the third day after His crucifixion.	Hosea 6:2	Acts 10:38–40

fathers of kings
Genesis 17:6, 16;
35:11

promised Judah
Genesis 49:10

<u>No Strings Attached</u>

The covenant God made with David was unconditional, meaning there was nothing David or the people of Israel could do—or fail to do—to lose God's promises. In fact, this covenant marked the fulfillment of previous promises God had made to His people. He had promised the patriarchs that they would be the <u>fathers of kings</u>, and He had <u>promised Judah</u>, the great-grandson of Abraham, that a ruler would come from his tribe.

what others say

J. Dwight Pentecost

Like the other of Israel's covenants, it is called eternal in 2 Samuel 7:13, 16; 23:5; Isaiah 55:3; and Ezekiel 37:25. The only way it can be called eternal is that it is unconditional and rests upon the faithfulness of God for its execution.[4]

The Covenant's Key Points

While God's promises to David certainly are the crux of this passage, the events of 2 Samuel 7 and 1 Chronicles 17 address at least two other important issues:

1. *God sometimes says "no."*

It's hard to fathom, and even seems a little unfair, that God would not approve of David's proposal. After all, the gift—the temple David had in mind to build—would be designed to honor God, plus, the giver's intentions were nothing but the best. People can never fully understand the reasons God does the things He does because <u>His ways are higher</u> than humans' ways. However, sometimes a look back can reveal many possible reasons He sees fit to say "no."

For example, sometimes a "no" from God stretches and increases believers' faith. Other times it refines their character, making His followers more Christlike. And often it paves the way for a much bigger "yes" that will better serve God's plans for His people and for His kingdom. In David's case, God said "no" for at least a couple of reasons that are revealed in Scripture. First, He wanted the temple to be built by a <u>man associated with peace, not war</u>. Second, He had better plans that far overshadowed David's: David wanted to build God a temporary structure, a temple of stone and wood; God wanted to build David a permanent structure, an everlasting dynasty.

go to

His ways are higher
Isaiah 55:9

man associated with peace, not war
1 Chronicles 22:8–10

apply it

what others say

Charles Swindoll

When God says "no" it is not necessarily discipline or rejection. It may simply be redirection.[5]

John MacArthur

God removed from him one great joy and in return God gave to him one great promise and said in Second Samuel 7, though you will not build My house, through your loins will come a child and of that child shall be built a kingdom which shall never end.[6]

seek advice
Proverbs 1:5; 11:14;
12:15; 15:22; 19:20

apply it

2. *God's people sometimes give bad advice.*

Nathan is a case in point. Prophets, as God's official spokesmen, were charged with dispensing God's words of instruction, prophecy, and judgment to the ancient Hebrews. Since Nathan gave David advice that God contradicted, does that mean he was not trustworthy? Scholars vary in their opinions. Some say that, as a prophet, he was "on duty" all the time, and spoke out of turn by offering his own advice and blessing before he sought God's opinion. Others suggest that when Nathan told David, "Sounds like a good idea to me," he wasn't on "official business" from God; he was simply responding to David based on what he knew to be true: that the Lord was with David. (The Lord Himself confirmed that in verse 9.)

Either way, this episode is a reminder that even men and women called by God to teach and preach His Word can be wrong. While it's not a bad idea to seek advice from godly friends and counselors, it's not a good idea to do so without seeking direction from God Himself.

what others say

Thomas L. Constable

Notice that it was not because God was disciplining David or had rejected him that He prohibited David's good intention. God was simply redirecting His servant. He was to be a ruler, not a temple builder. Similarly God does not always permit us to carry out our desires to honor Him, such as becoming a pastor or missionary. He sometimes makes this impossible because He wants us to serve Him in other ways. A realization of this fact would relieve many Christians from false guilt and shattered dreams.[7]

Alan Redpath

When God has said "No" to the ambition of your life, to something that is very precious to you, He brings you close to His heart and shows you that every need of your soul is met by His promises. He wants to teach you, in the face of His negative answer, to learn to make your own every possible promise in the Book.[8]

John Wesley

For the holy prophets did not speak all things by prophetic inspiration, but some things by an human spirit.[9]

David's Opening Lines

2 SAMUEL 7:18 (See also 1 Chronicles 17:16). *Then King David went in and sat before the LORD; and he said: "Who am I, O Lord GOD? And what is my house, that You have brought me this far?" (NKJV)*

God had opened His reply to David's proposal with a question. Now David, his physical position conveying the state of his heart, sat down to pray—a posture that varied from the usual kneeling or standing in prayer. As he did, he began his response to God with a question of his own: "Indeed, who am I?"

David acknowledged that he had done nothing to deserve God's favor; in fact, he didn't even have a "house" or family background valuable enough to make him worthy of the blessings God had given him. The first words of his discourse set the tone of humility and gratitude—a fitting foundation for his remaining words.

key point

what others say

Charles Stanley

Notice the phrase, David "sat before the Lord." Now he wasn't sitting in a chair as we would. He was kneeling and sitting back on his heels, listening, and talking to the Lord. David was meditating.[10]

Warren Wiersbe

The posture of prayer is different in various places throughout the Bible—sometimes people stand to pray. Solomon stood and lifted his hands to God in his praying when he dedicated the temple. Sometimes people would kneel to pray. Our Lord fell on His face and prayed. Dr. Oswald J. Smith used to pace up and down in the room to pray. David "sat" before the Lord. It's a picture of a child coming and sitting before the Father.[11]

The Rest of David's Prayer

the big picture

2 Samuel 7:19–29; 1 Chronicles 17:16–27

The rest of David's prayer spoke of:
1. **David's Humility.** David referred to himself as "Your servant" ten times in his prayer to God. Just as he demonstrated when he wore the simple ephod—garments worn

by God's servants—rather than the royal regalia during the celebration accompanying the Ark's arrival in Jerusalem, David preferred to emphasize his status as a servant rather than as a king.

2. **God's Greatness.** David referred to God's greatness by recalling His past awesome deeds and proclaiming His present majesty.

3. **Israel's Identity.** David expressed that he understood his people's unique, everlasting relationship with the Lord.

4. **David's Compliance.** In the face of apparently conflicting agendas, David didn't try to force his own plans upon God. Instead, he instantly realigned his desires to match up to God's perfect plans. His "do as you have said" is echoed later in Mary's response to Gabriel and in Christ's "thy will be done" in the Garden of Gethsemane.

what others say

Warren Wiersbe

Notice his humility: "Who am I, oh Lord? What is my family?" And notice in verse 20, David uses his own name. Children often refer to themselves in this manner, and here we have David like a little child sitting before God, thanking God, using humility of spirit to let God know how grateful he is. In fact, this same verse says David even ran out of words—(vs. 20) "And what can David say more to thee?" David was not usually at a loss for words but here he was coming as a child to a father in humility.[12]

The Bible Knowledge Commentary

David's response to this magnificent revelation concerning the nature of his kingship was to acknowledge the Lord's goodness in bestowing it and to extol God's incomparable sovereignty.[13]

Robbie Castleman

How often do we run ahead of God and decide what should happen in our lives? Sometimes out of zeal, sometimes out of fear, we charge ahead with our agendas and then feel disillusioned or angry when things don't turn out the way we had planned. David experienced a similar desire to make something happen. He wanted to honor God in a specific way, a way that seemed good and right. As he became aware of God's perspective on the matter, he learned that God's sovereign plans are better in the long run.[14]

Chapter Wrap-Up

- After years spent in homes ranging from caves to military camps, David was living in a magnificent house and enjoying the peace that had settled over the land.

- As he eyed his sturdy, spectacular surroundings and compared them to the temporary, timeworn tabernacle that sheltered God's presence, he got the idea to build a temple suitable for the Lord.

- David shared his idea with the prophet Nathan, who enthusiastically approved.

- That night, God gave Nathan a two-part message for David saying that He didn't need a house; in fact, He would build David a house.

- The house God would build David would be an everlasting dynasty that would produce the coming Messiah; in other words, one of David's descendants eventually would rule over Israel and the world forever.

- David responded to God's words by acknowledging that he had done nothing to deserve God's favor; in fact, he didn't even have a "house" or family background valuable enough to make him worthy of the blessings God had given him.

Study Questions

1. What caused David to want to build a temple for the Lord?

2. What was the prophet Nathan's initial response to David's idea?

3. How did the Lord let David know He had different plans for the king?

4. What reasons did the Lord give David to explain why He did not need him to build a temple?

5. What promise did the Lord make to David?

6. What were the conditions of the Davidic Covenant?

7. To whom did the Davidic Covenant point?

8. How did David respond to the Lord's promise?

2 Samuel 8-10; 1 Chronicles 18-21: The King's Conquests and Kindnesses

Chapter Highlights:
- Finally, the Philistines
- Mastering the Moabites
- For Jonathan's Sake
- An Unwanted Invitation
- Back to Battle

Let's Get Started

After establishing Jerusalem as the political center of the nation, David had brought the tribes of Israel together under a single banner by reminding them of their unique standing as God's chosen people. He brought their most sacred object, the Ark of the Covenant, to the forefront of the nation's attention to symbolize their restored spiritual vision. But the king wasn't about to settle into domestic complacency. Much work remained, and he got right to it by launching a series of campaigns to drive out the enemies of God's people.

(Incidentally, these events predate those of 2 Samuel 7 [see preceding chapter].) The map of the nation draped across a table in Israel's military headquarters must have been updated frequently as David and his troops vanquished first one enemy, then another. The register of peoples brought under Israel's subjection grew longer while the nation's borders were pushed and stretched until the people of God finally—completely!—possessed the entire tract of land God had promised His people.

However, the passages covered in this chapter aren't limited to demonstrating the power God wielded through His mighty warrior and gifted administrator David. Tucked within the broad-sweeping narrative describing the magnitude of the king's public conquests is a report highlighting the measure of the king's personal commitment to the covenant he made with Jonathan.

Finally, the Philistines

the big picture

2 Samuel 8:1

David defeated the longtime enemy, the Philistines, at Metheg Ammah.

go to

killed him
1 Samuel 31

The Philistines had been a menacing enemy of Israel during the reigns of both Saul and David. Why, with his tremendous resources and vast army, had Saul not been able to overcome them? The Philistines had in fact been Saul's undoing many times, right until they finally <u>killed him</u> on Mount Gilboa.

Part of the reason David, not Saul, grabbed this victory over the Philistines may have had something to do with this: Saul, with his limited vision, regarded the Philistines as a political foe, a "goliath" of aggression, arrogance, and superior weaponry. They were simply the people to beat in the political arena of the day. David, however, with his God's-eye view, regarded these people as much more than the reigning heavyweight champions of the Middle East. He wasn't out to destroy them solely because they were longtime enemies; he wasn't out to conquer them so he could add their name to his list of victories. He wanted to subdue them because of what they embodied. Their idolatry and godlessness represented everything the king hated; thus, his goal was to put them to an end.

key point

Saul repeatedly failed against the Philistines because he used flawed strategy based on human logic rather than God's guidance, and because he relied on ineffective, physical weapons. David's stunning victories can be attributed to his understanding of the words recorded in Psalm 60:11–12: "Give us help from trouble, for the help of man is useless. Through God we will do valiantly, for it is He who shall tread down our enemies" (NKJV).

what others say

Robbie Castleman

Being a man of his times, David led his share of battles to protect and enlarge his kingdom. But the foundation of David's reign was his faith in God and his knowledge that God was with him and the people of Israel. Because of this conviction, he could respond aggressively when necessary and with kindness when it was right.[1]

Alan Redpath

The thing that fascinates me about this complete victory is the utter contempt with which David treated the great power of his adversaries. The Philistines, for instance, who had occupied part of the land and harassed the Israelites for so long, had their chief city taken away from them. In 2 Samuel 8:1 it is called Metheg-ammah, but that is another name for Gath, "the bridle of Ammah." This implies that the city was a curb of a bridle, and it had been that very thing to the people of Israel. David simply took it out of the hands of the Philistines and then used it against them.[2]

Mastering the Moabites

Moabites
1 Samuel 14:47;
Genesis 19:37

Ruth
Ruth 1:4

parents
1 Samuel 22:3–4

Moabites
descendants of Lot through an incestuous union between Lot and his daughter

the big picture

2 Samuel 8:2

David defeated the Moabites, putting two out of every three of them to death. The survivors were placed in bondage to Israel.

Saul had attacked, but not subdued, the **Moabites**. Although discord existed between Moab and Israel, it's still hard to understand why David treated the Moabites so severely. After all, his great-grandmother <u>Ruth</u> had been from Moab; further, David himself had placed his own <u>parents</u> in the care of the Moabites when he had fled from Saul in the wilderness.

If for no other reason, one alone would have been more than sufficient explanation for David's severe treatment of the Moabites: He was claiming for the people of Israel what was rightfully theirs. As king and as a man of God, David would settle for nothing less than securing the full extent of God's land grant to His people.

Think of all the promises God has made to those who follow Him! He pledges safety, protection, blessing, power, and countless other benefits to believers. But He doesn't say these things will come without some effort or struggle. Just as David had to wage war against the people who had staked a claim to the land God had promised the Israelites, Christians must wage war against a long list of spiritual "intruders" that rob them of God's promises.

apply it

The Aramaeans and Edomites

the big picture

2 Samuel 8:3–15

Having conquered the Philistines and the Moabites, David next turned his attention to the Aramaeans, or Syrians, in the north,

treasury of the temple
1 Kings 7:51

horses
Deuteronomy 17:16

treasury
spoils from wars and
gifts from neighbor-
ing nations

along the Euphrates River, and the Edomites, who lived in the mountainous area south of the Dead Sea. David easily overcame both. In the process, he acquired more men, more chariots, and more valuables. He set up garrisons throughout the conquered territories. Their inhabitants then became subject to Israel. During these battles, David acquired an abundance of riches: gold shields, supplies of bronze, and other items of great worth. He added the articles to the growing supply of goods he had been collecting from other nations he had subdued. His son Solomon would later place the articles he had dedicated to the service of the Lord in the **treasury** of the temple.

David Kept His Head on Straight

David had endured a lion's share of periods of trials, testing, and troubles, but this certainly wasn't one of those times. Victories were coming easily, and wealth was pouring into the national treasury from all fronts. His fame and fortune, reach and responsibilities had never been greater, yet the man after God's own heart didn't let the success go to his head. In fact, he kept his head on straight as he let his heart lead the way toward mercy, obedience, and faithfulness to God:

- *Mercy to the Moabites.* David allowed a third of the Moabites to live, giving them not only the dignity of continuing their lineage but also granting them the possibility of turning their hearts to God.

- *Obedience about the horses.* David could have increased the horsepower of his military machine by returning from the conflict with the Syrians with thousands of horses; yet he only brought home one hundred in compliance with God's law stating that kings should not horde excessive numbers of horses. (What a contrast to Saul's record of disobedience to the Lord's instructions!) David outlined his philosophy concerning the true nature of military strength in Psalm 20:7–8: "Some trust in chariots, and some in horses; but we will remember the name of the LORD our God. They have bowed down and fallen; but we have risen and stand upright" (NKJV).

- *Faithfulness with his possessions.* David wasn't amassing wealth in anticipation of a day he could retire and sit in his chamber counting gold coins; as stated earlier, he dedicated the spoils of war to the Lord to be used in the future temple. (This also demonstrated his obedience to God's instructions that kings should not accumulate excessive wealth.)

Kerethite and Pelethite troops soldiers hired from Crete to serve as the king's bodyguard

what others say

Beth Moore

David left a remnant among the nations. David exhibited hope for the nations to bend their knees to the King of all kings.[3]

David's Administration

the big picture

2 Samuel 8:15–18

An empire as expansive as David's couldn't run itself, so "administrator" is yet another title in the list of attributes describing God's chosen king. David organized his inner circle in the following way:
- Military commander: Joab
- Record keeper: Jehoshaphat
- Chief priests: Zadok and Ahimelech
- Secretary: Seraiah
- Leader of the elite **Kerethite and Pelethite troops**: Benaiah
- Royal advisers: David's sons

what others say

The Bible Knowledge Commentary

The mention of Zadok and Ahimelech together (8:17) indicates the transition that was occurring in the office of priest. "Ahimelech, son of Abiathar, was a descendant of Eli . . . , whose priestly line Samuel had said would come to an end (1 Samuel 3:10–14). Zakok was a descendant of Aaron through Eleazar (1 Chronicles 6:4–8). Through Zadok the line of priests eventually continued through the remainder of OT times.[4]

For Jonathan's Sake

go to

covenant of friendship
1 Samuel 20:14–17

2 SAMUEL 9:1–5 Now David said, "Is there still anyone who is left of the house of Saul, that I may show him kindness for Jonathan's sake?" And there was a servant of the house of Saul whose name was Ziba. So when they had called him to David, the king said to him, "Are you Ziba?" He said, "At your service!" Then the king said, "Is there not still someone of the house of Saul, to whom I may show the kindness of God?" And Ziba said to the king, "There is still a son of Jonathan who is lame in his feet." So the king said to him, "Where is he?" And Ziba said to the king, "Indeed he is in the house of Machir the son of Ammiel, in Lo Debar."

Then King David sent and brought him out of the house of Machir the son of Ammiel, from Lo Debar. (NKJV)

David had promised Jonathan he never would forget the <u>covenant of friendship</u> the two had made, so he asked whether any of Saul's family members were still alive. Saul's servant, Ziba, told him Jonathan's lame son, Mephibosheth, was living in Lo Debar. David had the man brought to him right away.

What an exciting time to be living and working in the capital of the nation of Israel! The king's to-do list must have included such exhilarating tasks as planning military strategy, overseeing his administration, establishing foreign relations, and supervising the construction of new cities. Why, then, would he take a break from the action to turn his attention toward an issue as mundane as searching for a long-lost relative of a long-ago friend?

To understand what motivated David to issue this inquiry, recall his meeting with Jonathan many years earlier. David, discouraged by Saul's tireless pursuit, had confided to his friend that he was more fearful than ever of Jonathan's father: "But truly, as the LORD lives and as your soul lives, there is but a step between me and death" (1 Samuel 20:3 NKJV).

Jonathan, one of just a few people who truly understood David's coming role as God's anointed king of Israel, had reassured David with a pledge of loyalty: "Whatever you want me to do," he had said. The two had then devised a plan to determine Saul's intentions toward David. But before they parted, Jonathan—recognizing the danger his friendship with David might present his family—had

key point

asked David to show kindness to future generations: "And you shall not only show me the kindness of the LORD while I still live, that I may not die; but you shall not cut off your kindness from my house forever, no, not when the LORD has cut off every one of the enemies of David from the face of the earth" (1 Samuel 20:14–15 NKJV).

Perhaps those very words were scrolling through David's thoughts as he heard the servant Ziba saying that Jonathan did have a son, one who was still alive. This would give David the privilege of putting his promise into action! He could honor the heir of his fallen friend with *hesed*, the kindness of God.

As Good as His Word

Incidentally, Jonathan wasn't the only one to whom David had made a promise. When David had spared Saul's life in the cave at En Gedi, Saul had asked David to "swear now to me by the LORD that you will not cut off my descendants after me, and that you will not destroy my name from my father's house" (1 Samuel 24:21–22 NKJV). David had agreed. Even if David hadn't pledged kindness to Jonathan's offspring, he would have done so to keep his word to Saul—regardless of the circumstances or of his personal feelings toward the man.

An Unwanted Invitation

2 SAMUEL 9:6–7 Now when Mephibosheth the son of Jonathan, the son of Saul, had come to David, he fell on his face and prostrated himself. Then David said, "Mephibosheth?"

And he answered, "Here is your servant!"

So David said to him, "Do not fear, for I will surely show you kindness for Jonathan your father's sake, and will restore to you all the land of Saul your grandfather; and you shall eat bread at my table continually." (NKJV)

Custom dictated that members of a new dynasty were to completely annihilate any traces of the former one. So if any of Saul's relatives still were alive, they certainly wouldn't have volunteered to reveal their existence to David. Because Mephibosheth had no way of knowing David wasn't out to eliminate possible rivals to the throne, he must have been terrified when the king's couriers came knocking on his door to escort him back to the palace.

When Mephibosheth was brought before David, the young man fell before the king with his face to the ground. He was, with good reason, afraid for his life, having no idea that plans for his care had long ago been put into place between David and Jonathan. David immediately called Mephibosheth by name and set him at ease. He made several promises:

- Kindness
- Restoration of the land that was rightfully his as the heir of Saul's estate
- An ongoing income from the yield of that land, and
- A seat at the royal dinner table

David and Mephibosheth: A Snapshot of God and Sinners

Few stories in the Bible offer such a vivid illustration of the character and grace of God and the way He relates to His people as the exchange between David and Mephibosheth. For starters, Mephibosheth's name, residence, and condition are rich with meaning and symbolism:

- *His name:* "Mephibosheth" comes from two Hebrew words:
  paah: "to break into pieces, or shatter"
  bosheth: "greatly ashamed, shameful thing" and "confusion"
- *His residence:* Mephibosheth was living in Lo Debar, a place-name derived from the Hebrew words:
  Lo: "nothing"
  Dober: "no promise"

- *His condition:* Mephibosheth's feet had been crippled when his nurse dropped him as she and the boy fled for safety after the deaths of Saul and Jonathan.

go to

poor and needy
Psalms 72:13; 113:7

The words that characterize Mephibosheth aptly describe a person before he or she comes to know Jesus Christ as Savior. Broken, shamed, and without direction, they live in an earthly version of "Lo Debar"—a barren, desolate place offering no source of spiritual nourishment. All people are "crippled" by sin because of mankind's fall in the Garden of Eden.

Just as Mephibosheth serves as an example of a sinner, David, in many ways, symbolizes God:

- *God is a pursuer.* David actively sought out a relative of Jonathan's; God pursues people to call His own.

- *God is a covenant-keeper.* David had a covenant with Mephibosheth through Jonathan; God has a covenant with His people through Jesus Christ.

- *God is a grace-giver.* Mephibosheth had done nothing to earn David's favor (in fact, there was nothing he *could* do about his parentage and his crippled condition); likewise, a sinner can do nothing to earn God's gifts. These are grace gifts, freely given to those who will accept them.

- *God is a restorer.* Just as David restored the land to Mephibosheth that was rightfully his, God restores blessings to His followers. Through David, He restored the Promised Land to Israel; through Jesus Christ, He restores all of His spiritual promises back to believers.

- *God accepts people as they are.* David didn't discount Mephibosheth because he was lame. In fact, many scholars note that seating Mephibosheth at his table gave David the opportunity to graciously hide his crippled feet from sight, illustrating the irrelevance of their condition.

- *God desires fellowship with His people.* David didn't invite Mephibosheth to take a seat at the king's dinner table one night only; he gave Jonathan's son a permanent place setting. That meant the two would have the opportunity to form a lifelong friendship.

God's invitation isn't extended to those who have reached perfection; it's offered to those who are <u>poor and needy</u>.

key point

John Vawter

The ethic in the kingdom of God is not "survival of the fittest" but "service to the neediest." We bring people into that kingdom by serving their needs.[6]

Just as David found joy in striking up a personal relationship with his newfound family member, God finds joy in personal interaction with those He loves.

Burton Coffman

Not only were Mephibosheth's basic needs met, he was given the honor of eating continually at the king's table. Jesus doesn't just want to supply our needs, he wants our fellowship.[7]

Humility Before Honor

2 Samuel 9:8–12

Mephibosheth responded to David's staggering promises with a question: "What is your servant, that you should look upon such a dead dog as I?" (v. 8 NKJV). David then instructed Ziba, his family, and his servants to oversee the administration of the land restored to Mephibosheth, who ate with the king thereafter.

Mephibosheth not only called himself a "dog"—a scathing insult in both ancient and modern Hebrew—but he intensified his self-deprecation with the word "dead." The tone of his remark echoes that of David's prayer when God had promised him an everlasting kingdom, and reinforces that the only appropriate response to God's grace is humility.

Charles Spurgeon

If Mephibosheth was thus humbled by David's kindness, what shall we be in the presence of our gracious Lord? The more grace we have, the less we shall think of ourselves, for grace, like light, reveals our impurity.[8]

Over-the-Top Blessings

Within moments, Mephibosheth transformed from a crippled man who had been forced to hide out in a borrowed residence into a wealthy, respected landowner with an invitation to dine with the king. Surely these blessings were more than he could have ever <u>asked</u>, and were a sampling of what the apostle Paul described in Ephesians 2:7: "the exceeding riches of His grace in His kindness toward us . . ." (NKJV).

something to ponder

what others say

Charles Spurgeon

Mephibosheth was no great ornament to a royal table, yet he had a continual place at David's board, because the king could see in his face the features of the beloved Jonathan. Like Mephibosheth, we may cry unto the King of Glory, "What is thy servant, that thou shouldst look upon such a dead dog as I am?" but still the Lord indulges us with most familiar intercourse with himself, because he sees in our countenances the remembrance of his dearly-beloved Jesus.[9]

Back to Battle

After relating the account of David's interaction with Mephibosheth, the Bible's narrative resumes its focus on the wars David fought to protect and expand the nation of Israel. While the details of the king's armies aren't specifically mentioned at this point in Scripture, this is a good place to stop and take a look at their makeup.

David's Armies at a Glance

With Saul's coronation had come the institution of a fledgling <u>standing army</u> divided into three units. Under David's reign, the Israelite military went through a tremendous amount of change and refinement.

The king's regular army consisted of two divisions:

1. *Professional Soldiers*, including:

go to

asked
Ephesians 3:20

standing army
1 Samuel 13:2

Amasa
2 Samuel 20:4–5

Benjamites
1 Chronicles 12:2

Gentiles
those who are not a
part of the Jewish
race

Israelites—This group of "mighty men" included the first band of loyal followers that had rallied around David, as well as those who had stepped forward to serve when he received the crown of Judah. These men were placed under Joab's command and, once David became king, landed top positions in the army.

Foreign Mercenaries—This group of mostly **Gentiles**, including some Philistines, were commanded by Ittai the Gittite. They were excellent fighters who were armed more heavily than most of the Isrealites.

2. *Militia*—This drafted army, likely commanded by <u>Amasa</u>, was organized into 12 divisions of 24,000 each, with each division serving one month a year. Apparently David was able to build a strong and diversified militia by capitalizing on the particular strengths of each of the twelve tribes. For example, the <u>Benjamites</u> were highly skilled archers who also happened to be ambidextrous, and the people of the tribe of Issachar apparently specialized in military intelligence, since they had an "understanding of the times, to know what Israel ought to do" (1 Chronicles 12:32 NKJV).

> **what others say**
>
> **The Bible Almanac**
>
> These men had probably been recruited at the time that David fled from Saul into Philistia and served as a mercenary to Achish, the king of Gath.[10]

Ammonite Animosity

> **the big picture**
>
> **2 Samuel 10:1–14**
>
> To repay an unnamed kindness shown by Nahash, king of Ammon, David dispatched a group of ambassadors to convey his sympathy to the late king's son, Hanun. However, Hanun's men misjudged the Israelites' motives and advised the king to regard them as spies out to cause them harm. They then greatly shamed David's servants by shaving off half their beards and trimming their robes to an immodest length, leaving them humiliated. When David learned what had happened, he first

sent word to the men to stay put until their beards grew back. Then he sent in Joab and his army, who fought and defeated the thousands of Syrians the leaders of Ammon had recruited for battle once they had realized their derisive act was, essentially, a call to arms.

Lot
Genesis 19:36–38

treaty with Israel
1 Samuel 11:2–11

David had reclaimed the Promised Land to the fullest extent of its borders, but he also needed to tend to Israel's relationship with the Gentiles, the nations outside the boundary lines of Israel. His first conflict with one such nation was with Ammon.

The Ammonites, of the family of <u>Lot</u>, had threatened the Israelites during the early days of Saul's reign. Back then, Nahash had offered to make a <u>treaty with Israel</u> on one condition: that he be allowed to gouge out the right eye of each Israelite warrior. The wicked cruelty was rewarded by an overwhelming defeat. However, the Ammonites' inherent evil apparently remained, as seen in their demeaning treatment of David's servants. There could hardly be an act more insulting or humiliating to an ancient Israelite than indecently exposing his body or shaving off part of his beard.

what others say

Easton's Bible Dictionary

The mode of wearing [the beard] was definitely prescribed to the Jews (Leviticus 19:27; 21:5) . . . It was a part of a Jew's daily toilet to anoint his beard with oil and perfume (Psalm 133:2). Beards were trimmed with the most fastidious care (2 Samuel 19:24), and their neglect was an indication of deep sorrow (Isaiah 15:2; Jeremiah 41:5).[11]

<u>More of the King's Kindness</u>

Note David's concern for the dignity of his men. Rather than allowing them to suffer further public dishonor on a return journey home, he sent word that they should stay put until they had time for their beards to grow. He took care of their personal needs before turning his attention to political matters. How like Jesus Christ! He had only three years in which to complete His public ministry on earth, yet He consistently placed people over programs and personal relationships over public ministry.

Under Israel's Thumb

2 Samuel 10:15–19

The Aramaeans tried to avenge the Ammonite defeat. However, David and his troops met and crushed them in a short but decisive victory before they even had a chance to cross the Jordan River to attack Israel. The Aramaeans had no choice then but to submit to Israel's authority.

Chaim Herzog and Mordechai Gichon

[The Aramaeans were] a large, rich, well-established nation whose technological and strategic know-how was comparable to that of the Philistines. With a much larger population than the latter, the Arameans occupied the area now called the Golan Heights, a position that commanded the approaches to Philistia.[12]

Setting the Stage

The accounts of Israel's military campaigns may seem a little on the dry side compared to many other more colorful episodes of David's life. Yet one thing is certain: If God put it in the Bible, it is there for an important reason. While no one can know for sure all of the "whys" concerning God's reasons for doing what He does, scholars suggest that these "war stories" are important for several reasons:

1. They begin a section of the Bible (beginning in 2 Samuel 9) called the "Succession Narratives" that outline the way David succeeded Saul and set up his own dynasty.

2. They chronicle the expansion of Israel, a nation important to the rest of the world because it's important to God.

3. They illustrate David's faith in and dependence on God.

4. They give readers a sense of the political climate of the day.

Robert Alter

This whole account of military operations . . . is meant to establish the facts of continuing armed conflict with the Ammonites, which is the crucial background for the story of David and Bathsheba in the next chapter.[13]

Chapter Wrap-Up

- David launched a series of campaigns to drive out the enemies of God's people, including the Philistines, Moabites, Aramaeans, and Edomites, and lengthening the list of peoples brought under Israel's subjection and expanding its borders until the people of God finally—completely!—possessed the entire tract of land God had promised them in His covenant with Abraham.

- David had promised Jonathan he never would forget their friendship covenant, so when he learned Jonathan had a lame son named Mephibosheth who was still living, he sent for him.

- David promised Mephibosheth kindness, restoration of the lands of his grandfather King Saul, and a permanent place at the royal dinner table.

- David and Mephibosheth serve as a vivid illustration of the character and grace of God and the way He relates to His people.

- Nahash, king of Ammon, provoked war when he humiliated David's ambassadors on a mission of kindness to the king. Israel won the victory.

- The Aramaeans then tried to avenge the Ammonite defeat, but David and his troops met and crushed them in a short but decisive victory. The Aramaeans then submitted to Israel's authority.

Study Questions

1. What four enemies did David and the Israelites defeat and subdue?

2. What did David do with the spoils he accumulated from these wars?

3. Why did David ask whether Jonathan still had any living relatives?

4. Was Mephibosheth's lameness a concern to David?

5. What did David promise Mephibosheth?

6. How does David illustrate God in this account?

7. How does Mephibosheth illustrate sinners in this story?

8. How did King Nahash humiliate David's ambassadors?

9. What was David's response?

Part Six
DAYS OF SHAME

2 Samuel 11:
The King's Crimes

Chapter Highlights:
- Springtime, Wartime
- A Patio with a View
- An Unwanted Pregnancy
- A Man with a Plan
- David Spins the Sin

Let's Get Started

Once again, the biography of David shifts in scope. The last chapter gave a panoramic view of the political landscape of Israel and its neighboring nations. This one throws open the doors of the palace to give an up-close look at the suddenly scandalous personal life of Israel's king. This "meanwhile back at the palace" embellishment to the action of 2 Samuel 10—when David's soldier Uriah is out fighting beside Joab against the Ammonites—marks a turning point in the life of the man after God's own heart.

Apparently no longer a hands-on manager with scarcely a minute to spare, David has become a sedentary monarch. And he seems to have far too much time on his hands. The way he spends some of those idle moments one evening—by taking a walk on his rooftop patio—proves catastrophic. If David's defeat of Goliath was his most celebrated act of heroism, certainly his encounter with Bathsheba following that moonlit stroll was his most infamous act of sin.

The plot that begins in 2 Samuel 11 is well known. Because of that, it can be easy to speed through the text on wheels of familiarity, taking in stride the accustomed—even predictable—lessons to be drawn from the actions and consequences involved in David's wrongdoing. It's important not to let that familiarity take over, however. Reading the account of David and Bathsheba as if for the first time can lend new insight to the spiritually deep and wide truths that are as relevant to today's believers as they have been to each generation since David's reign.

Springtime, Wartime

> 2 SAMUEL 11:1 *It happened in the spring of the year, at the time when kings go out to battle, that David sent Joab and his servants with him, and all Israel; and they destroyed the people of Ammon and besieged Rabbah. But David remained at Jerusalem.* (NKJV)

This verse is packed with lots of information:

- It was spring, or, as the ancient warriors might have said, it was "fighting season." Springtime—after the harvest was gathered—was wartime because dry ground, sunny days, and mild nights replaced the cold temperatures and heavy rains of winter, giving the warriors a more suitable setting for carrying out their orders.

- David had sent his army, led by Joab, to fight the Ammonites in and around Rabbah, the modern city of Amman, the capital of Jordan.

- David had chosen to sit this one out and stay at home in Jerusalem.

You All Go On Without Me

David had been a fighter since the days and nights he had spent in the sheepfold warding away wild animals that had threatened the safety of his flocks. He had further proved his prowess against the formidable Philistine giant. He had remained in the thick of one battle or another ever since.

But for some reason, David chose not to join his men on this junket. It's left to logic—plus perhaps a little bit of imagination—to explain why. Here are some theories:

- *David was getting old.* He had seen the turn of his fiftieth year by now—and he might not have felt he had the stamina for physical combat.

- *David was getting tired.* He had led a fast-paced life running from Saul and fighting in the nation's wars to secure its boundaries and to expand its influence. As he watched his men preparing to march toward Rabbah, he may have simply thought, *I've had enough; I'm worn out and I want to stay home.*

- *David was getting spoiled.* He had been king for some time now and may have become so accustomed to the lavish meals and luxurious accommodations at his palace that he didn't think he could stomach field rations or sleep on uncomfortable pallets anymore.

Whatever the reason, Bible commentators across the board agree that staying home was the first in a spree of poor choices David made during this period of his life. Even though the Law didn't specifically prohibit kings from refraining from military duty, sitting out on this campaign ultimately placed David in graver danger than any posed by spears, arrows, or slingshots.

key point

what others say

Kay Arthur

One spring while his army went to battle, David the valiant warrior chose to stay behind. That seemingly insignificant compromise left David in a vulnerable position.[1]

Charles Swindoll

David was in bed, not in battle. Had he been where he belonged—with his troops—there would never have been the Bathsheba episode. Our greatest battles don't usually come when we're working hard; they come when we have some leisure, when we've got time on our hands, when we're bored.[2]

David Guzik

In 2 Samuel 10 Joab and the army of the mighty men were preserved against the Syrians and the Ammonites but they did not win a decisive victory. The decisive victory came when David led the battle at the end of 2 Samuel 10. Both through custom and experience God told David, "You need to be at the battle." But David remained at Jerusalem.[3]

A Patio with a View

*2 SAMUEL 11:2–3 Then it happened one evening that David arose from his bed and walked on the roof of the king's house. And from the roof he saw a woman bathing, and the woman was very beautiful to behold. So David sent and inquired about the woman. And someone said, "Is this not **Bathsheba**, the daughter of Eliam, the wife of **Uriah** the Hittite?" (NKJV)*

Maybe his conscience was nagging at him for sleeping like a king on fine linens in the palace while his faithful men were swatting away sand gnats so they could catch a few hours of shut-eye on lumpy pallets. Or maybe he just had a routine case of insomnia. Whatever

Bathsheba
the woman David committed adultery with, who later became his wife and the mother of Solomon

Uriah
one of David's mighty men; Bathsheba's husband

caused David to throw back the covers and roll out of bed, no one knows. For one reason or another, he simply decided to get up and get some fresh air.

Who David Saw

From his patio with a view, David caught a glimpse of his next-door neighbor, bathing. In that instant, he faced another choice: either to turn away or to keep staring. The Bible suggests he decided on the latter. Without so much as a blush for his boldness, he had to have gazed at Bathsheba at least long enough to see that she was very beautiful.

He Should Have Just Gone Back to Bed

David had already made a couple of blunders: not being on the battlefield where he should have been, and not tearing his eyes off the naked woman next door. Now he faced another decision: to go back to bed and forget what he had seen, or to find out more about the captivating female. Again, he chose the latter option. Instead of turning away from the vision of beauty, he set out to learn more about her. He may have intended to find out whether she was available for him to take as a new wife.

David's servant told the king that Bathsheba (whose name means "daughter of an oath") was a woman of prestige. She was the granddaughter of Ahithophel, one of David's closest advisers, and the wife of Uriah, one of David's top-ranking soldiers.

what others say

Larry and Sue Richards

While the biblical text does not say so, the fact that Uriah had a house in Jerusalem near the palace may suggest that when the nation was not at war he served in David's palace guard.[6]

It was decision time once again. David, having found out that Bathsheba was "taken," could either drop the matter or pursue it. His passion—possibly fueled by a hunger for power after discovering that something he wanted was off-limits, or possibly fueled by pride after seeing that his own officer had a wife more beautiful than any of his own—dictated his action.

key point

For the third time in just a few minutes, David chose the spiritual low road. This time it took him out of the realm of questionable behavior and placed him right in the middle of unquestionable sin.

Manhandler, Manhandled, or Somewhere in the Middle?

2 SAMUEL 11:4 *Then David sent messengers, and took her; and she came to him, and he lay with her, for she was cleansed from her impurity; and she returned to her house.* (NKJV)

purification ritual
to make herself
spiritually (i.e.,
symbolically) clean
and pure before
God

Bible commentators' assessments of Bathsheba's role in the affair range from casting her as a seductress who caused David to sin to presenting her as an innocent victim of rape:

- *Manhandler.* Some scholars propose that Bathsheba would have been well aware that her bathing pool could be seen from the king's terrace. Since modesty of the day would have called for her either to flee or to cover herself the moment she saw that a man was watching her, the fact that she continued bathing might suggest she turned bathtime into a seductive performance. After all, she might have been bored and lonely with her husband away at war. Being the king's next-door neighbor might also have given Bathsheba an up close glimpse of—and desire for—the lavish lifestyle led by those who lived behind the palace doors.

- *Manhandled.* Other scholars point out that Bathsheba was washing herself in the privacy of her own home and would have had no reason to think she was being watched. Even if she had been aware of the king's vantage point, she never would have suspected anyone—particularly any man—to be watching her while she bathed this particular evening because, after all, most of the men in town were at war. Further, this wasn't a bath as thought of in today's terms that imply bathing as a time of luxury, pampering, and sensuality. This was her monthly **purification ritual** following her menstrual period. Finally, the fact that Bathsheba complied with the king didn't indicate her consent; as a woman and as a subject of the king, she could not have possibly refused the invitation.

- *Somewhere in the middle.* It's likely that the truest assessment of Bathsheba's role in the adulterous affair falls somewhere between the two extremes, but probably much closer to "manhandled" than to "manhandler." Classifying her as a temptress with deliberate designs on landing a share of the king's wealth seems to be a biblically insupportable stretch. It also seems difficult to believe that, considering David's history and his character, the king was capable of a crime as violent as rape. However, it may be logical to conclude that Bathsheba might have realized she was being watched, that she might have ducked away for cover sooner, or that, like David's godly wife Abigail, she might have tried to convince the way-out-of-line David not to act on his passions.

Ann Spangler

But why did Bathsheba have to suffer along with the man who molested her and murdered her husband? Though the story gives us little insight into her true character, it is hardly likely that Bathsheba was in a position to refuse the king. In Nathan's parable, in fact, she is depicted as an innocent lamb. Why, then, have so many people painted her as a seductress? Perhaps Bathsheba's innocence is too painful to face. That a good person can suffer such tragedies, especially at the hands of a godly person, appalls us. Worse yet, God punishes both David and Bathsheba by taking their son. If we can believe that Bathsheba had an affair with David, we can accept her suffering more easily; her guilt makes David's sin seem less grave and God's punishment less cruel.[7]

God's Word on Adultery

Adultery is such a significant topic that it's addressed in God's top ten list of things people should and should not do: "You shall not commit adultery," He says in the seventh of the Ten Commandments (Exodus 20:14 NKJV). But the listing of Ten Commandments isn't the only place in the Bible where there's a warning against adultery and sexual immorality:

for your marriage

- **Proverbs 6:32:** Whoever commits adultery with a woman lacks understanding; he who does so destroys his own soul. (NKJV)

- **Galatians 5:19–21:** Now the works of the flesh are evident, which are: adultery, fornication, uncleanness, lewdness, idolatry, sorcery, hatred, contentions, jealousies, outbursts of wrath, selfish ambitions, dissensions, heresies, envy, murders, drunkenness, revelries, and the like; of which I tell you beforehand, just as I also told you in time past, that those who practice such things will not inherit the kingdom of God. (NKJV)

- *1 Corinthians 6:18:* Flee sexual immorality. Every sin that a man does is outside the body, but he who commits sexual immorality sins against his own body. (NKJV)

God Created Sex

God says committing adultery is wrong, but He certainly doesn't say sex is wrong. Having sex *outside marriage* is what falls outside the boundaries of His guidelines.

Safe Sex, God's Way

Precisely because sex, then, is holy, God is very concerned with how people handle it. Remember what happened when the Ark of the Covenant was handled inappropriately? There were dangerous, even deadly, consequences. Sexual misconduct can have similar results.

Those who don't follow God's guidelines for marriage and sex endanger their marriage and jeopardize the well-being of their children. For that reason, Bible teacher and author Ron Mehl has called the seventh commandment "God's fence around marriage."

Ron Mehl

Why should God be so concerned about adultery in particular? Why should purity and faithfulness in a marriage be so very important to Him? Because He knows that the home and the church are the two institutions ordained of God on earth to visibly model the love of God. It is in Satan's interest to mar and disfigure both of those models. In particular, Satan seeks the destruction of married love and the family.[10]

Matt Kaufman

The great evil (and yes, that's the right word) of sex outside marriage is that it takes something created to be holy and desecrates it. Sex can't be separated from God's order of creation, and when we try to pretend otherwise, we're trying to make God go away so we can re-order creation to suit our own lusts or other emotional desires. We may try to tell ourselves we're expressing "love." But when we seek to slice sex off from the *life* of love—lasting marriage—and to have it on the side instead, we're actually expressing a type of hatred for our Creator. We're throwing the blessings He gave us back in His face and demanding substitutes tailored to our preferences.[11]

That's Sin, Too?

Jesus pointed out that David's sin didn't begin the moment he slept with Bathsheba, or even the moment he invited her to sleep over at his place. It began the instant he desired to have her: "You have heard that it was said to those of old, 'You shall not commit adultery.' But I say to you that whoever looks at a woman to lust for her has already committed adultery with her in his heart" (Matthew 5:27–28 NKJV).

Ron Mehl

I think I could safely say that we have *all* failed in this command. Is there anyone who has never allowed an impure,

adultery
Leviticus 20:10

adulterous thought to linger on the screen of the mind? And the Lord tells us that if we have committed adultery in our mind, it is the same in heaven's eyes as if we'd already followed through on the act.[12]

An Unwanted Pregnancy

2 SAMUEL 11:5 *And the woman conceived; so she sent and told David, and said, "I am with child." (NKJV)*

The fact that Bathsheba had been bathing as part of her purification ritual following her last period left no room for doubt that David, not Uriah, had fathered this child. It's hard to imagine how many sleepless nights Bathsheba must have spent trying to figure out what she should do. Finally, with her pregnancy becoming more visible each day, she realized she had only one option: She had to tell the king.

what others say

Bob Deffinbaugh

Bathsheba informs David that she is pregnant, not that she is afraid she might be. This means that she has missed at least one period and probably another. All in all, several weeks or more have passed. It will not be long before her pregnancy will become obvious to anyone who looks at her. This is David's sin and his responsibility, and so she informs him.[13]

Richard D. Phillips

The message was simple and straightforward: "I am pregnant." That was all she said, but of course there was much more implied, such as, "What are you going to do about it, David?"[14]

No Cause for Celebration

The coming birth of a child. The news that would have made any Jewish mother or father leap with joy gave neither David nor Bathsheba any cause for celebration. In fact, the announcement of the impending birth triggered despair because, for one thing, the crime of adultery carried a heavy penalty; the levitical punishment for both parties involved in <u>adultery</u> was death.

Richard D. Phillips

Under Israelite law those convicted of adultery were to be stoned to death. Bathsheba's husband Uriah was off fighting in David's army, so this birth would raise more than a few eyebrows. Bathsheba needed David's protection, and David needed her cooperation.[15]

Billy Graham

The Bible says, "There is a way that seemeth right unto a man; but the end thereof are the ways of death" (Proverbs 16:25). Under Jewish law, adultery was punishable by death. Under God's law today, it also results in spiritual death.[16]

A Man with a Plan

2 Samuel 11:6–24

In his desperation, David figured there were only two ways out of the dilemma: either make it look like Uriah was the baby's father, or have Uriah killed so David could marry Bathsheba. Starting with the first option, David brought Uriah home from the battlefront on furlough, assuming the soldier would spend time with his wife and create the impression that he was the baby's father. But David's plans were derailed by Uriah's integrity. Out of respect and compassion for his fellow soldiers who were enduring the hardships of battle, Uriah refused himself the pleasure of sleeping indoors with his wife. That compelled David to step up his scheme. He invited Uriah to dinner, gave him too much to drink, and figured the wine would make the soldier's desire for his wife override his concern for his men. But it didn't work. Once again, Uriah refused to enjoy the comforts of home—including the bed of his beautiful wife—while his men were at war. Finally, David resorted to the most extreme strategy. He sent Joab a letter (which, ironically, Uriah delivered himself) instructing his commander to assign the soldier to the battle zone that was currently the most dangerous. As David had hoped, Uriah was killed.

The story of David's life up to this point has made it clear that he was no saint. His record of conduct had been marred by disobedience to God on several occasions. Even so, it's hard to comprehend

go to

sin nature
Romans 3:23

temptation
Matthew 26:41;
Mark 14:38;
James 1:12–14

temptation is common
1 Corinthians 10:13

resist temptation
Matthew 6:13,
26:41;
Mark 14:38;
Luke 11:4, 22:40;
James 4:7

sin nature
the desire and ten-
dency to choose to
disobey God

that this David—the one who had an innocent soldier killed in order to cover up his own crime of adultery—could possibly be the same man who had so many times before lived out his conviction that it's up to God to decide who should live and who should die.

The difference between David at his best and David at his worst speaks volumes because it brings up the troubling question: If someone who loved God as much as David did could fall this far into sin, couldn't it happen to anyone? The answer to that question is an absolute "yes," for several reasons:

1. *The inclination to sin is inherent in everyone.* It's called a "<u>sin nature</u>," and everyone is born with it. That inclination can be controlled with the power of the Holy Spirit, but it never completely goes away. So no one earns "immunity" from sin as a reward for good behavior or for living a long life, and no one can attain any kind of political or social status that places him or her "above" the reach of sin.

what others say

Alan Redpath

I want you to notice that middle life for David (for he was over fifty at this time) did not mean that there was immunity from the attacks of the enemy; there was no lessening of the need for buffeting the body and keeping it in subjection.[17]

2. *The temptation to sin is everywhere.* There's no place on earth a person can go to completely avoid <u>temptation</u>. In other words, David didn't sin solely because he chose to remain at home instead of going off to war; he might as easily have been tempted to sin on the battlefield as he was just outside his bedroom door.

But being tempted to sin and committing sin are two different things. The Bible says that <u>temptation is common</u>; it also explains how to <u>resist temptation</u> by praying and by turning away from it. David sinned because, when he faced temptation, he chose to give in to his desire rather than turn away from it.

key point

3. ***Sinning leads to more sinning.*** Scholars trace the roots of this particular sin all the way back to David's decision to practice <u>polygamy</u> many years earlier.

polygamy
1 Samuel 25:42–43;
2 Samuel 3:2–5

what others say

David Guzik

It is wrong to think that *this* was the beginning of the chain of events David followed all the way down to adultery and murder. David showed his disregard of God's plan for marriage many years before when he took more than one wife. David's practice of adding wives showed a lack of romantic restraint and an indulgence of his passions. *This* corrupt seed, sown long ago, has grown unchecked long enough and will now begin to bear bitter fruit.[18]

4. ***Sinning causes people to question and even ignore God.*** Where did David think God was while he was contriving to get Bathsheba into his bed, and while he was plotting to have her husband killed? Certainly the man who wrote Psalm 139 knew God was everywhere: "Where can I go from Your Spirit? Or where can I flee from Your presence? If I ascend into heaven, You are there; if I make my bed in hell, behold, You are there. If I take the wings of the morning, and dwell in the uttermost parts of the sea, even there Your hand shall lead me, and Your right hand shall hold me" (Psalm 139:7–10 NKJV). He also knew that God knew the condition of his heart: "O LORD, You have searched me and known me. You know my sitting down and my rising up; You understand my thought afar off. You comprehend my path and my lying down, and are acquainted with all my ways. For there is not a word on my tongue, but behold, O LORD, You know it altogether. You have hedged me behind and before, and laid Your hand upon me. Such knowledge is too wonderful for me; it is high, I cannot attain it" (Psalm 139:1–6 NKJV).

Who can know how this episode might have been rewritten had David—as he had often done in the past—turned to God for guidance before he sent his servant to summon Bathsheba to his chambers, or had he even turned to God for rescue when he realized he needed help!

David Spins the Sin

2 Samuel 11:25 *Then David said to the messenger, "Thus you shall say to Joab: 'Do not let this thing displease you, for the sword devours one as well as another. Strengthen your attack against the city, and overthrow it.' So encourage him." (NKJV)*

David knew Joab well enough—and he knew Joab knew him well enough—to anticipate the questions his behavior must have raised in the commander's mind. So, just like a smooth-talking politician trying to spin past mistakes into exemplar ethics, he tried to give Joab a thumbs-up through his messenger. "Tell him everything's just fine," David said, probably with a shrug of the shoulders and a smug "I've-got-it-under-control" look on his face. "Hey," he continued, "it's wartime—these things happen. People die on the battlefield all the time. Now just get back to what you were doing and don't worry about a thing. Like I said, I've got everything under control."

Happily Ever After, at Least for Now

> ### the big picture
> ### 2 Samuel 11:26–27
> When Bathsheba heard her husband was dead, she went into mourning. Once her period of grieving was over, David sent for her, brought her to his house and married her. Whereupon, she soon delivered a son.

Bathsheba had two reasons to be grieving. First, she had lost her beloved companion. Second, she was now alone in the world without the much-needed protection and provision of her husband. But she need not fear. David did have everything under control, at least on the surface. He was able to sweep the whole mess under the rug because, once Bathsheba's mourning period for her husband ended, the king brought Bathsheba into his house as one of his wives.

Their first child may have arrived a little earlier than people counting the months on their fingers anticipated, but, after all, the boy was born to parents who were married to one another. No one except Bathsheba, Joab, and David himself needed ever know what had really happened.

But Someone else did know what had really happened. God knew. And He stated His opinion of the affair with His own editor's note to the episode recorded in the Bible: "But the thing that David had done displeased the LORD" (2 Samuel 11:27 NKJV).

Chapter Wrap-Up

- David sent his army, led by Joab, to fight the Ammonites but for some reason he chose to break with tradition and stay at home in Jerusalem.
- On a night when he became restless, he took a stroll on his rooftop patio and spied his beautiful next-door neighbor, Bathsheba, bathing.
- Rather than turn away, David inquired about her, sent for her, and slept with her, conceiving a child and setting off a disastrous chain of events.
- In an attempt to cover up his crime, David had her husband, Uriah, brought home from the battlefront to sleep with her to make it appear the child was his. Uriah's integrity got in the way, however; he twice refused himself the pleasure of his wife's company when his fellow soldiers were undergoing the hardships of battle.
- In a second attempt to cover up his crime, David instructed his commander Joab to send Uriah into the most dangerous zone of fighting on the battlefield. Uriah was killed.
- David continued the cover-up by marrying Bathsheba to make everything appear to be on the up-and-up. God, however, was displeased with David's behavior.

Study Questions

1. What are some possible reasons David might have had for staying at home when his soldiers were off at war?

2. Name some of the opportunities David passed up to turn away from sin.

3. Was Bathsheba at fault for seducing David?

4. What revolutionary lesson about sin did Jesus teach based on David's sin with Bathsheba?

5. An ancient Jewish couple could hardly receive news any better than the announcement that a child was on its way. Why couldn't David and Bathsheba celebrate the announcement of the coming birth of this child?

6. How did David initially try to cover up his crime?

7. What foiled that attempt?

8. How did David try to have Uriah killed?

9. Does anything about David's behavior after the murder reveal that his conscience might have begun to bother him?

10. How did David appear to have everything under control?

2 Samuel 12:
Deadly Consequences

Chapter Highlights:
• A Powerful Parable
• God's Judgment
• Truth and
  Consequences
• Blessed at Home and
  on the Battlefield

Let's Get Started

Nearly a year had passed since David contrived to have Uriah killed in order to cover up his own sin with Bathsheba. David's biography as told in 2 Samuel 12 doesn't tell how he spent the intervening days. But his prayer during that time reveals that each day was longer and more miserable than the day before:

> PSALM 32:3–4 *When I kept silent, my bones grew old, through my groaning all the day long. For day and night Your hand was heavy upon me; my vitality was turned into the drought of summer. (NKJV)*

David may have created the impression that things were fine, but beneath the surface they were anything but fine; his guilt had made him sick and lifeless. He had become spiritually, emotionally, and physically ill.

Still, he was very much the king of Israel, the monarch of a nation teeming with people to see and needs to be met. So when the prophet Nathan entered the king's chambers to describe some citizens' squabble over a pet lamb, David assumed he was hearing yet another conflict that he would be expected to resolve. As he listened to Nathan's tale, it didn't initially dawn on David that the prophet wasn't really seeking his verdict on a dispute about livestock. In fact, it wasn't until Nathan looked at David and said, "You are the man," that David realized the truth: He had just been handed a judgment for his own sin from the almighty God Himself.

A Powerful Parable

> 2 SAMUEL 12:1–4 *Then the LORD sent Nathan to David. And he came to him, and said to him: "There were two men in one city, one rich and the other poor. The rich man had exceedingly many flocks and herds. But the poor man had nothing, except one little ewe lamb which he had bought and nourished; and it grew up together with him and with his children. It ate of his*

own food and drank from his own cup and lay in his bosom; and it was like a daughter to him. And a traveler came to the rich man, who refused to take from his own flock and from his own herd to prepare one for the wayfaring man who had come to him; but he took the poor man's lamb and prepared it for the man who had come to him." (NKJV)

A Persistent Parent

key point

Don't miss the significance of the action in the first line of this passage! David had spent nearly a year suffering from the physical, mental, and spiritual fallout of his sin. It's almost as if he were a guilty child hiding in a closet, his cries drowning out the words of his father trying to coax him out.

David may have withdrawn himself from God's presence, but God was not going to remove His presence from David. Since David couldn't hear the whisper of the Holy Spirit above the din of his own groaning, God chose another way of getting through to David: He sent His messenger, Nathan.

The act reveals that, rather than being a disconnected deity, God is a pursuing and persistent parent to everyone who chooses to call Him "Father."

When Speaking to a Shepherd, Talk Sheep

For the second time in the recorded history of David's life, God called on the prophet Nathan to deliver important information to the king. The first message had involved good news: After setting His own boundaries around David's temple plans, God had given David the promise that he and his descendants would enjoy an everlasting reign. Relating that kind of information to the king must have been a high point in the prophet's life. This time, however, the news wasn't so great. In fact, it was quite disturbing: Nathan had been charged with the ominous task of delivering God's message of rebuke and judgment to the king for his sin.

How does a man of God point out a superior's sin? Very carefully! Confronting the man who wielded the most power and prestige in the nation would be a challenge. It could even be dangerous. That's why Nathan used the utmost tact in delivering his message that was designed to point out the king's offenses. To get the truth across with honesty, clarity and kindness, he wrapped the message in the language of a **parable**. He made the truth even more accessible to David by placing a lamb in the starring role of his tale. David, after all, was a shepherd at heart. If anyone understood sheep talk, he would.

go to

parables
Matthew 13:1–23;
Mark 4:2–33;
Luke 8:10

parable
short, simple story
that teaches a
spiritual lesson

what others say

Holman Bible Dictionary

The teller of the story was living dangerously as he seized a teachable moment to confront the life of the most famous king of Israel. He sought to get inside David's guard and cut the iron bonds of his self-deception to strike a moral blindness from his eyes.[1]

The Potency of Parables

Jesus, a master communicator, often used parables as a teaching tool: "I speak to them in parables," He said, "because seeing they do not see, and hearing they do not hear, nor do they understand" (Matthew 13:13 NKJV). He used the simple and familiar language of stories based on everyday objects, activities, and circumstances to expose the sins of His critics, and explain spiritual truths to His followers.

something to ponder

what others say

Martin B. Copenhaver

Nathan was able to approach David with a parable because the two worshiped the same God and shared an understanding of what God expects.[2]

Judging David

2 SAMUEL 12:5–6 *So David's anger was greatly aroused against the man, and he said to Nathan, "As the LORD lives, the man who has done this shall surely die! And he shall restore fourfold for the lamb, because he did this thing and because he had no pity." (NKJV)*

The story Nathan told infuriated David, even though he hadn't yet made the connection that he, of course, was represented by the rich man with many sheep and that the poor man with just one pet lamb represented Uriah. The king—after swearing the angry oath, "as the Lord lives"—wasted no time in pronouncing judgment against the crime and against the condition of the thief's heart. Even though theft was not a capital offense according to the Law, David judged the man—whom he still very much believed to be a real person—guilty. He even called for the death penalty. Further, the king ordered restoration of the stolen property according to the guideline set out in Exodus 22:1. In declaring the man guilty, David was unwittingly declaring his own guilt.

John Indermark

> Nathan's story moves the one who acted with absolutely no pity toward Uriah to condemn this rich man "because he had no pity" (12:6).[3]

J. Vernon McGee

> It is interesting how easily you can see the sin in somebody else, but you cannot see it in your own life. That was David's problem.[4]

Robert D. D. Jamieson

> This punishment was more severe than the case deserved, or than was warranted by the divine statute (Exodus 22:1). The sympathies of the king had been deeply enlisted, his indignation aroused, but his conscience was still asleep; and at the time when he was most fatally indulgent to his own sins, he was most ready to condemn the delinquencies and errors of others.[5]

Adam Clarke

> It was construed to make David, unwittingly, pass sentence on himself. It was in David's hand, what his own letters were in the hands of the brave but unfortunate Uriah.[6]

From Tale Spinner to Truth Teller

2 SAMUEL 12:7–9 *Then Nathan said to David, "You are the man! Thus says the LORD God of Israel: 'I anointed you king over Israel, and I delivered you from the hand of Saul. I gave you your master's house and your master's wives into your keeping, and gave you the house of Israel and Judah. And if that*

had been too little, I also would have given you much more! Why have you despised the commandment of the LORD, to do evil in His sight? You have killed Uriah the Hittite with the sword; you have taken his wife to be your wife, and have killed him with the sword of the people of Ammon.'" (NKJV)

The transformation was nearly tangible. Within a matter of moments, Nathan changed from a gentle storyteller narrating a simple parable into a straight-talking prophet delivering a stern scolding from the Lord, who clearly wasn't happy with David's behavior. It's easy to imagine Nathan's intense gaze and steady voice as he signaled to David the tale he was telling was about to take a sharp turn with the words: "Thus says the LORD God of Israel." Nathan was on a mission from God, and God's message left no room for doubt:

- David was guilty of murdering Uriah.
- David was guilty of stealing Uriah's wife.

what others say

Matthew Henry

Now [Nathan] speaks immediately from God, and in his name. He begins with, *Thus saith the Lord God of Israel*, a name sacred and venerable to David, and which commanded his attention. Nathan now speaks, not as a petitioner for a poor man, but as an ambassador from the great God, with whom is no respect of persons.[7]

John Indermark

In Nathan courage speaks truth to power. Courage afflicts the comfortable. Courage changes the story from third-person objective to second-person accusative: you are the man! And courage relates the consequences of David's treachery (12:10–15).[8]

Always Wanting More

There's the big-screen celebrity who shoplifts even though she has enough clothes, handbags, and shoes to fill the closets of a Pacific Coast mansion and a Manhattan penthouse. There's the Fortune 500 executive who embezzles from his company even though he already has more than enough cash to pay for his expensive toys and his exquisite taste. And then there's the ancient Middle Eastern

go to

Adam and Eve
Genesis 2 and 3

covetousness
Exodus 20:17;
Deuteronomy 5:21;
Romans 2:7

align our thoughts
2 Corinthians 10:5

pray
Philippians 4:6

covetousness
intense desire to
have something

monarch who steals someone else's wife even though he has a harem of beautiful women who call him husband.

Always wanting more is not a new story; in fact, it's as old as human history. For example, Adam and Eve had the entire Garden of Eden to enjoy, yet took the fruit of the one tree they were told they couldn't have.

In His message to David, God spent more words explaining what David had—and could have had, if he had only asked—than He did elaborating on David's crimes. God reminded David that He had anointed him as king, saved him from Saul, and showered him with property and possessions. In going over the list of the ways He had provided for David, God seemed to be underlining important lessons about the greed and **covetousness** that were at the root of his sins of murder and adultery.

When Jesus' half brother James wrote about covetousness and other sins, he must have had someone very much like David in mind:

> Where do wars and fights come from among you? Do they not come from your desires for pleasure that war in your members? You lust and do not have. You murder and covet and cannot obtain. You fight and war. Yet you do not have because you do not ask. You ask and do not receive, because you ask amiss, that you may spend it on your pleasures. Adulterers and adulteresses! Do you not know that friendship with the world is enmity with God? Whoever therefore wants to be a friend of the world makes himself an enemy of God. (James 4:1–4 NKJV)

How do we conquer the innate desire to have what doesn't belong to us?

apply it

- **Learning to be content.** Paul described contentment as something he had learned, implying that it doesn't come naturally. We acquire it by practice. One way is to align our thoughts with God's Word, and another is to pray for contentment.

- **Learning to trust God.** Often we crave more than we have because we refuse to believe that God, the ultimate provider, will make sure we are well cared for in a way that has our best interests in mind. The writer of Hebrews 13:5 encourages believers to "let your conduct be without covetousness; be content with such things as you have. For He Himself has said, 'I will never leave you nor forsake you'" (NKJV).

what others say

Ron Mehl

The truth is, every time we steal something—whether large or small—we are saying, "I will be my own provider in this instance. If I don't take it now, I will be the loser." But the Lord wants us to understand that when we place our trust fully in Him, we are *never* the loser.[9]

God's Judgment

2 SAMUEL 12:10–12 *"Now therefore, the sword shall never depart from your house, because you have despised Me, and have taken the wife of Uriah the Hittite to be your wife." Thus says the LORD: "Behold, I will raise up adversity against you from your own house; and I will take your wives before your eyes and give them to your neighbor, and he shall lie with your wives in the sight of this sun. For you did it secretly, but I will do this thing before all Israel, before the sun."* (NKJV)

God spelled out in no uncertain terms the judgment that would fall upon David. His private sin would bear public—and painful—penalties. Nothing would change concerning God's earlier promises to David and his descendants. However, the king's household would, from that point on, be marked by violence and conflict.

Scholars have noted the sentence David invoked upon the rich man in the parable—a payment of four sheep for the one stolen—was fulfilled in his own family with the deaths of his four sons.

- Bathsheba's newborn child
- **Amnon**
- **Absalom**
- **Adonijah**

what others say

John MacArthur

As long as you are making excuses for your sinfulness, you will never grow spiritually . . . Don't blame your circumstances, your husband, your wife, your boyfriend, your girlfriend, your boss, your employees, or your pastor; blame yourself. Don't even blame the devil. Certainly anything in the world's system contributes to the problem, but sin ultimately occurs as an act of the will—and you are responsible for it.[11]

Amnon
oldest son of David and Ahinoam who raped his half sister, Tamar

Absalom
David's third son by Maacah who conspired to oust his father as king

Adonijah
David's fourth son by Haggith who attempted to succeed David instead of Solomon

something to ponder

How to Spell Relief: C-O-N-F-E-S-S

2 SAMUEL 12:13 *So David said to Nathan, "I have sinned against the LORD." And Nathan said to David, "The LORD also has put away your sin; you shall not die."* (NKJV)

The words Nathan had spoken pierced David's heart. But the pain was only temporary; in fact, the incision had provided instant relief by allowing David to flush the toxic sin from his heart with a simple confession: "I have sinned against the Lord." Those words—and more important, the state of David's heart when he said them—removed the barrier of sin that had blocked his relationship with God, enabling God to show David grace. God showed David grace in forgiving—and forgetting—his sin, and in allowing David to escape the death penalty that would have otherwise been imposed for his crime.

Confession: It's Chicken Soup for the Soul

All Christians sin. The Bible says so: "If we say that we have no sin, we deceive ourselves, and the truth is not in us" (1 John 1:8 NKJV). But God, who is holy, can't tolerate the unholiness of sin. Therefore, sin interferes with a person's relationship with God by any of several ways, including the following:

apply it

1. It disrupts a person's communication with God.

2. It weakens a person's ability to see God's work.

3. It reduces a person's effectiveness in fulfilling God's plans.

So, how is it possible to have a relationship with God when sin is in the way? The answer is simple: "If we confess our sins, He is faithful and just to forgive us our sins and to cleanse us from all unrighteousness" (1 John 1:9 NKJV). It's important to remember, however, that true confession centers on the attitude of the heart instead of the words that are spoken. Here are three key things to keep in mind when confessing sin to God:

1. ***Stop making excuses!*** After hearing such pointed accusations and stern judgment as those just spoken by Nathan, a man like Saul would have tried to talk his way out of trouble by making

excuses. But not David; he understood that excuses aren't the way to begin a conversation with God about sin.

what others say

Robert D. D. Jamieson

It was necessary that God should testify His abhorrence of sin by leaving even His own servant to reap the bitter temporal fruits. David was not himself doomed, according to his own view of what justice demanded; but he had to suffer a quadruple expiation in the successive deaths of four sons, besides a lengthened train of other evils.[10]

2. *Specify the sin.* The Lord doesn't need you to tell Him how you sinned because He already knows! The real value of admitting to God exactly what you did—whether you cheated on your income taxes or you tossed His name around with disrespect during the ball game—comes in showing God that you agree with Him concerning what you did wrong. (David didn't need to specify his sin in this instance because it happened to be the chief topic of conversation.)

what others say

John MacArthur

The word confess in Greek is *homologeo*. The Greek word *logeo* means "to speak." The word logic comes from it and means "a discussion of principles." The other part of *homologeo* is the prefix *homo*. When we say something is homogeneous, we mean it is the same. So *homologeo* means, "to speak the same." Confessing your sin is not begging for forgiveness; it is saying the same thing about your sin that God says—that it is sin and is your fault. Confession is an agreement with God that you have sinned.[12]

3. *Repent.* Repentance goes hand in hand with confession; without repentance, a confession is little more than empty words.

David's sincere sorrow is plain to see in the psalms he is believed to have composed during this time:

something to ponder

• Psalm 32:1–11

go to

execution
Exodus 21:12;
Leviticus 20:10

• Psalm 51:1–19
• Psalm 103:1–22

Nelson's Student Bible Dictionary

True repentance is a "godly sorrow" for sin, an act of turning around and going in the opposite direction. This type of repentance leads to a fundamental change in a person's relationship to God.[13]

The Bible Knowledge Commentary

One may wonder, perhaps, why David was not punished with death as he had so sternly advocated for the guilty man. Adultery and murder both were sufficient cause for the execution of even a king. The answer surely lies in the genuine and contrite repentance which David expressed, not only in the presence of Nathan but more fully in Psalm 51.[14]

Charles Stanley

Ongoing personal purification was one of the chief attributes that made David a man after God's own heart. We all know that he was far from perfect. His record as a murderer and adulterer would eliminate him from any pulpit in America, yet Jesus referred to Himself as the "Offspring of David." How could David commit such gross iniquity and still obtain such divine affirmation? I believe it was because David was zealous to confess and repent whenever God pinpointed David's sin and confronted him with it. Psalm 51 has been the soulful prayer of many a believer who has willfully or blindly offended God, as David's remorse was laid open before God.[15]

Truth and Consequences

2 SAMUEL 12:19–23 When David saw that his servants were whispering, David perceived that the child was dead. Therefore David said to his servants, "Is the child dead?"

And they said, "He is dead."

So David arose from the ground, washed and anointed himself, and changed his clothes; and he went into the house of the LORD and worshiped. Then he went to his own house; and when he requested, they set food before him, and he ate. Then his servants said to him, "What is this that you have done? You fasted and wept for the child while he was alive, but when the child died, you arose and ate food."

And he said, "While the child was alive, I fasted and wept; for I said, 'Who can tell whether the LORD will be gracious to me, that the child may live?' But now he is dead; why should I fast? Can I bring him back again? I shall go to him, but he shall not return to me." (NKJV)

disciplines
Job 5:17;
Proverbs 3:12; 13:24

David's sin, once forgiven, no longer jeopardized his relationship with the Lord or his eternal future. However, God did say He would allow him to endure the consequences of his sin. His infant son became ill and died within a week, despite David's fervent fasting and praying. When the child died, David immediately got up, cleaned up, and began to worship the Lord. Explaining his unexpected and uncustomary behavior to the puzzled servants, he stated that death was final; therefore, it would be useless to continue to plead with God.

How could a loving God allow such a tragedy to happen to David?

1. **To discipline David.** The Lord <u>disciplines</u> those He loves, and David is no exception.

what others say

Alan Redpath

His sin was forgiven, but the consequences he had to take! When God forgives us and restores us to favor, He uses the rod, too, and life is never quite the same again. Oh yes, He restores His repentant child to fellowship, but sometimes a man has to drink the bitter cup; a forgiven man may still have to reap what he has sown.[16]

2. **To preserve His reputation.** God told David his son would die because he had given Israel's enemies reason to show contempt for God. To say that David's actions had given the ungodly good reason to scoff at the Israelites' God is an understatement. The leader of God's people—one who had gained the respect not only of the Israelites but of other nations as well—had committed adultery and murder—crimes even the ungodly nations hated.

Beth Moore

As the chosen king of Israel, the man revered for having the hand of God on him, David was the most well-known, highly-feared figure in the entire world. Through him God was teaching the nation Israel and the heathen nations about Himself. David's heinous, progressive sin did a terrible thing . . . David's actions caused the nations to lose their respect for God.[17]

Blessed at Home and Blessed on the Battlefield

2 Samuel 12:24–31

David went to comfort Bathsheba in her grief. She eventually bore another son, Solomon, which means "peaceful," and whom the Lord called Jedidiah, "loved by the Lord" to indicate His forgiveness. The Lord loved Solomon very much. Meanwhile, Joab was finishing the war against the Ammonites that had begun in 2 Samuel 10. He was leading a successful assault on the Ammonite capital of Rabbah when, in an incredibly honorable act of loyalty to King David, he sent word inviting the king to step in and complete the victory so the king, not Joab, would receive the credit. David did so, in the process securing great wealth—including the Ammonite king's seventy-five-pound gold crown—and making slave laborers of the Ammonite survivors.

Bible scholar Alan Redpath has said, "If we learn about the heinousness of David's sin—and we leave it at that—we have learned little, because we know it; but if we learn about the mercy of God, then we surely have learned something tremendous."[18] Perhaps the biggest lesson in this episode of David's life comes in its conclusion, when God showed mercy in several ways:

- He shaped a strong marriage relationship characterized by love from an illicit liaison based on lust.

- He blessed the marriage with a son.

- He showed great favor to that son.

- He restored David to a position as "victor" over his enemies rather than of one "vanquished" by his sins.

Matthew Henry

God had removed one son from them, but now gave them another instead of him, like Seth instead of Abel. Thus God often balances the griefs of his people with comforts in the same thing wherein he hath afflicted them, setting the one over-against the other.[19]

David Guzik

Joab struggled for more than a year to conquer Rabbah, and the victory only came when David got things right with God. There was an unseen spiritual reason behind the lack of victory at Rabbah.[20]

Chapter Wrap-Up

- David had spent the time since his sins of adultery and murder becoming sick with guilt over his unconfessed sins.

- God sent the prophet Nathan to confront David with his sin; Nathan revealed God's message through a parable that clearly pointed out David's guilt.

- David, failing to see the reflection of himself in the parable, angrily pronounced judgment against the guilty party in the parable; Nathan responded by telling David that *he* was the subject of the story. Then the prophet proceeded to deliver a stern scolding from the Lord for David's sin.

- David immediately confessed his guilt and acknowledged that he had sinned against the Lord.

- His infant son became ill and died, in spite of David's fervent fasting and praying.

- David comforted Bathsheba in her grief over the child and from that point, a solid and loving marriage was knit between the two. They were later blessed with another son, Solomon, whom God greatly favored.

- God granted Israel victory over the Ammonites. Thanks to a selfless move on Joab's part, the conquest was accredited to David.

Study Questions

1. What clues does the Bible provide about the way David spent the months that passed after David committed adultery and murder?

2. How did Nathan present David with God's message concerning his sin?

3. How did David respond to Nathan's story?

4. According to God's rebuke of David, what were the roots of his sins of adultery and murder?

5. What judgment was to befall David as a consequence of his sins?

6. After being confronted with God's rebuke and His judgment, did David attempt to make excuses for his behavior?

7. What evidence does the Bible provide of David's sincere sorrow for his sin?

8. Once David confessed his sin, did God forgive him and remove the consequences of his actions?

9. What blessings from the Lord did David receive at the conclusion of this passage?

2 Samuel 13–18:
Problems in the Palace

Chapter Highlights:
• Rape and Incest
• Sickening Silence
• Absalom's Revenge
• On the Run Again
• Heartbreaking Victory

Let's Get Started

Nathan's chilling prophecy of evil and violence within King David's family had cast a shadow over the palace. The fulfillment of that prediction materialized in a deadly chain of events when the king's son, Amnon, became a rapist; his daughter, Tamar, a victim of rape and incest; and his other son, Absalom, a murderer.

These passages of Scripture can be difficult to digest. By most standards, the material ought to be rated "R" for its mature content. Readers seeking a "happily ever after" for the young shepherd boy certainly won't find a fairy-tale ending in this report of the heinous activities that went on right under the middle-aged king's nose. The events marking this murky segment of David's life in many ways raise more questions than answers, with two troubling questions inevitably bobbing to the surface:

- How could David have been such a sinful man and negligent father, yet still be called a man after God's own heart?

- How could God—the One who made it known that David held a special place in His heart—allow such devastation to rock the lives of both the guilty parties—including His chosen king—and of the innocents, such as Tamar?

While the answers to these questions, at least for now, must be delegated to the "list of things only God knows," it's reassuring to know that God does allow some of His light to penetrate these dark passages. That light comes in the form of lessons—very practical ones—to be learned about things like lust, love, family relationships, and parenting, as well as about God's character, justice, discipline, and sovereignty.

But perhaps the most positive aspect of this episode is that although David probably would have preferred to sweep the whole account—from adultery and murder to cover-ups, confessions, and consequences—under the rug, God certainly didn't edit it out of the Holy Bible.

key point

That's what makes the Bible so special; it gives *real* people with *real* flaws and failures a *realistic* look at how God works in the lives of other *real* people with *real* flaws and failures.

Rape and Incest

the big picture

2 Samuel 13:1–19

David's firstborn son, Amnon, fell madly in love with his beautiful half sister, Tamar. He was consumed with desire for the young woman, to the point of illness. When his friend and cousin, a devious man named Jonadab, discovered why Amnon was so distraught, he cooked up a way for Amnon to lure Tamar into his bedroom so the two could be alone. Amnon played on his illness by asking his father to send Tamar to his room to fix him a meal. When she arrived, he sent away the others in the room and—despite Tamar's protests and her desperate appeal to Amnon's sense of reason—raped her. His "love" instantly turned into hatred, and he sent Tamar away to bear her disgrace alone. Crying bitterly, she tore her royal robe and put ashes on her head as a sign of grief.

Trio of Siblings

Name	Who
Amnon	David's firstborn son with Ahinoam
Absalom	David's son with Maacah
Tamar	David's daughter with Maacah

While it's unlikely that David would have deliberately mistreated or abused his children, that's exactly what he ended up doing.

- *David set a bad example.* Amnon, it seems, had inherited more than his father's eyes. He had received the "I get what I want when it comes to women" attitude David had donned when he took up the practice of accumulating numerous wives long before he had become king. Growing up with a dad who indulged his romantic passions must have made it that much easier for Amnon to allow lust to ignite into violence against his alluring half sister, Tamar, just as lust had opened the doorway for his father's crime of adultery with Bathsheba.

- *David failed to watch over his children.* Providing safety for their children is a fundamental duty of any parent. The sheer size of David's blended family—which included his eight wives named in the Bible, numerous unnamed wives and concubines, twenty sons, and a number of daughters—would have compelled an attentive father to keep a close eye on the comings and goings of his children. He would keep a particularly protective one on his daughters. But apparently, David left the kids largely in the hands of the servants, who, as it turned out, were powerless to discipline them. When Amnon said, "Get out," the servants had no choice but to obey.

- *David failed to instill God's values in his sons.* David probably had taught—or, more likely, commissioned Nathan to teach—his sons the "do's and don'ts" of godly behavior. But apparently he had failed to nurture a relationship with them that would instill the underlying values of those laws. Plus, he had not developed the trust and accountability that would have nudged Amnon toward acting with honor and integrity.

"Train up a child in the way he should go, and when he is old he will not depart from it" (Proverbs 22:6 NKJV). Ironically, that familiar parenting truth is believed to have been written by David's own son, Solomon, some years later. Is it possible that Solomon's recognition of his father's negligence in this area is what compelled him to record that proverb?

what others say

Charles Swindoll

Men, we suffer from this one especially—passive, negligent mistakes. They occur in Scripture rather often, relating to the

home, to the role of a father. Negligent mistakes are a result of laziness or oversight or inconsistency or just a plain lack of discipline . . . David was like many dads. Too busy. Preoccupied. And therefore, negligent. It's a common mistake among successful, high-achieving fathers.[2]

Just as Nathan Had Predicted

David had secured the kingdom in fine fashion; the people of Israel were enjoying peace and safety as never before. How ironic that David could provide safety and protection for the thousands upon thousands of citizens, but he couldn't manage to keep his daughter safe within the walls of his own home! This terribly personal family tragedy was to have public implications, as Nathan had prophesied: the trouble at home ultimately would lead to turmoil in the kingdom.

It Wasn't Really Love at All

It's a common practice to mistake lust for love, and that's exactly what Amnon did when he allowed his desire for Tamar to consume him.

apply it

- *What lust looks like:* Lust is a strong desire, with most uses of the word "lust" in the Bible pointing to a strong, corrupt longing that is either sinful or that opens a door to sinful behavior.

- *What love looks like:* The Bible describes love in much more godly terms, involving both a longing to be with a beloved person, and an interest in his or her welfare.

Lust vs. Love

	Lust	Love
Its focus	"What I want"	"What's best for you"
Its appearance	Impatience, envy, pride, arrogance, rudeness, spiteful, unforgiving (1 Corinthians 13)	Patience, humility, courtesy, kindness, forgiveness, trusting (1 Corinthians 13)
Its source	Sinful human nature (1 John 2:16; Romans 13:13)	God (1 John 4:1, 7)
Its effects	Sin and calamity for all involved (Proverbs 11:6; Matthew 5:28; James 4:2)	Goodness and more love for all involved (1 John 4:20–21)

Given the dramatic difference between "lust" and "love," it's easy to understand how easily Amnon's version of "love"—which really was lust—transformed into hatred!

something to ponder

what others say

Larry and Sue Richards

Rather than take responsibility for his actions, as David had in the case of Bathsheba, Amnon acted as though Tamar had been the responsible party. He transformed the guilt he felt into hatred of Tamar.[3]

The Worst Thing That Could Happen

Women who lived in Israel during this time—around the tenth century BC—were practically powerless in society. They had no significant place in the social, religious, or economic arenas. They completely depended upon the men in their families to provide them with food, shelter, and protection. Even though Tamar was a princess whose powerful father and many brothers might have insulated her against danger of any kind, she was injured in a triple tragedy that stripped her of all honor and hope.

1. She lost her virginity outside of marriage.

2. She became a victim of incest.

3. She lost all hope of marrying since Amnon refused to comply with God's law that stated the <u>rapist</u> of a virgin should marry her.

what others say

The Bible Knowledge Commentary

Such loss of a maiden's virginity was an unbearable curse in Israel (Deut. 22:13–21). Moreover, such relationships between half brothers and sisters were strictly forbidden in the Law. Those guilty of such things were to be cut off from the covenant community (Leviticus 20:17). In this case, of course, Tamar was innocent since she had been assaulted (Deuteronomy 22:25–29).[4]

Robert Alter

If some modern readers may wonder why being banished seems to Tamar worse than being raped, one must say that for

go to

rapist
Deuteronomy 22:29

pariah
outcast

biblical women the social consequence of **pariah** status, when the law offered the remedy of marriage to the rapist, might well seem even more horrible than the physical violation. Rape was a dire fate, but one which could be compensated for by marriage, whereas the violated virgin rejected and abandoned by her violator was an unmarriageable outcast, condemned to a lifetime of "desolation" (v. 20).[5]

Sickening Silence

2 Samuel 13:20–22

When Absalom saw that his sister was upset, he correctly guessed what had taken place, told her to keep quiet for the time being, and sent her to his house. David heard what had happened and was angry, but didn't take any action to console or defend Tamar, or to discipline Amnon. Absalom hated his brother because of his crime against Tamar, but he, too, refused to confront Amnon about the incident.

The silence in this passage is deafening!

- *Tamar was told to be quiet.* Absalom's instructions for Tamar to keep quiet certainly added insult to her injury. Being unable to verbalize what had happened compounded her sense of powerlessness. Her dismal fate was summed up in the Bible's last mention of her: "So Tamar remained desolate in her brother Absalom's house" (2 Samuel 13:20 NKJV). The meanings for the Hebrew word for "desolate" include "grow numb," "devastate," "stupefy," "to be destitute," "to destroy one's self," "to waste," and "to wonder."

Imagine the hours Tamar spent in her brother's home looking on as her sisters and sisters-in-law married and then raised their families while she wasted away in a bleak existence that could only be described by such dismal words.

- *David chose to be quiet.* The list of David's fatal parenting flaws continues to grow longer. Why would a father refuse to do something—anything—to try to make things better for his devastated daughter or to censure his wayward son? Clearly David had not followed parenting principles even remotely resembling Paul's instructions centuries later that parents should raise their children "in the training and admonition of the Lord" (Ephesians 6:4 NKJV).

sheepshearing
Genesis 28:12–13;
1 Samuel 25:2–8

what others say

Robert Alter

That imponderable silence is the key to the mounting avalanche of disaster in the house of David. Where we might expect some after-the-fact defense of his violated daughter, some rebuke or punishment of his rapist son, he hears, is angry, but says nothing and does nothing, leaving the field open for Absalom's murder of his brother.[6]

Ann Spangler

Though David was furious when he heard the news, he did nothing to punish Amnon. Did he favor his son over his daughter, thinking her hurt a small matter? Or was his moral authority so compromised by his own lust for Bathsheba that he simply couldn't bring himself to confront his eldest son?[7]

- *Absalom kept quiet.* Pastor and author Charles R. Swindoll has called anger a "burning fuse of hostility."[8] That perfectly describes anger's role in Absalom's life following his sister's rape. The Bible states that Absalom was furious, but rather than dealing promptly with his anger or dealing with the crime through legal channels, he, as seen in the next passage, let his emotions crackle and spark for two full years before he took action. By that time, his fury had lit the fire of murderous rage.

Amnon's Assassination and Absalom's Absence

the big picture

2 Samuel 13:23–14:24

Absalom loathed his brother for what he had done, but held his peace for two years, when he plotted an opportunity to have his servants kill Amnon during a sheepshearing celebration attended by all of the king's sons. A false report got back to David that Absalom had killed all the king's sons. David and his servants tore their clothes and grieved for the loss. Jonadab set the record straight by telling David that Absalom had been responsible for the murder of Amnon. Absalom fled to stay with his maternal grandfather, the King of Geshur, where he spent the next three years. After recovering from his grief over Amnon's death, David began to want to see Absalom. He missed his son, but didn't know how to restore the relationship. David contrived a way—through a convoluted tale spun by a wise woman from Tekoa—for Absalom to return without fear of punishment for what he had done. He sent Joab to bring back Absalom, but David refused to see him in person or admit him to the palace.

Had the pendulum of parenting tactics swung too far in the opposite direction? First, David had been too lax with Amnon in failing to discipline him for his rape of Tamar; then he had been too strict with Absalom in failing to fully forgive him for his murder of Amnon.

what others say

J. Vernon McGee

It is unfortunate that David did not want to see his son. It actually set the stage for Absalom's rebellion.[9]

Absalom: Israeli Cover Boy

2 SAMUEL 14:25–26 *Now in all Israel there was no one who was praised as much as Absalom for his good looks. From the sole of his foot to the crown of his head there was no blemish in him. And when he cut the hair of his head—at the end of every year he cut it because it was heavy on him—when he cut it, he weighed the hair of his head at two hundred shekels according to the king's standard. (NKJV)*

According to the description of Absalom in this passage, he was a head-turner who might have looked like a model on the cover of a romance novel. Not only was he handsome, but he had a mane of flowing hair that weighed in at about five pounds when, on occasion, he decided to cut it.

If appearances are irrelevant in God's economy, why did the Holy Spirit–inspired writer of this narrative spend two verses on Absalom's appearance?

1. This brings to mind another instance when Israel was taken with a good-looking guy: the tall, dark, and handsome King Saul.

2. This draws attention to the contrast between God's way—not judging by appearance—and the world's way—being influenced by superficial beauty.

something to ponder

3. This alludes to Absalom's later demise after he is <u>caught by his hair</u> in the branches of a tree.

caught by his hair
2 Samuel 18:9

what others say

Robert H. Roe

In the culture of that day a full head of hair signified a strong virile man. It was a symbol of power, virility and masculinity. When you gave yourself to the Lord as a Nazarite and, as long as you were a Nazarite, you were not to shave, cut your hair or touch wine or strong drink. The longer your hair grew the more it indicated you were God's man. It served as a symbol of a virile man of God. When Samson let his head be shaved, he lost his touch with God. He lost his virility, and he got himself blinded. So Absalom, in the eyes of the Jews, looks like a king.[10]

Fighting with Fire

2 SAMUEL 14:27–33 *To Absalom were born three sons, and one daughter whose name was Tamar. She was a woman of beautiful appearance.*

And Absalom dwelt two full years in Jerusalem, but did not see the king's face. Therefore Absalom sent for Joab, to send him to the king, but he would not come to him. And when he sent again the second time, he would not come. So he said to his servants, "See, Joab's field is near mine, and he has barley there; go and set it on fire." And Absalom's servants set the field on fire.

Then Joab arose and came to Absalom's house, and said to him, "Why have your servants set my field on fire?"

And Absalom answered Joab, "Look, I sent to you, saying, 'Come here, so that I may send you to the king, to say, "Why have I come from Geshur? It would be better for me to be there still."' Now therefore, let me see the king's face; but if there is iniquity in me, let him execute me."

So Joab went to the king and told him. And when he had called for Absalom, he came to the king and bowed himself on his face to the ground before the king. Then the king kissed Absalom. (NKJV)

After two more years of separation from David, Absalom asked Joab twice to help him reunite with David. Joab declined both times. Finally, like an attention-starved child finds mischief in order to get his parents to look his way, Absalom set Joab's barley field on fire. "You've got my attention now," Joab seemed to be saying when he finally arranged a meeting between father and son. The tone of the get-together was polite, but it was also a case of "too little, too late." The period of estrangement had made Absalom bitter and vengeful.

Absalom's Revenge

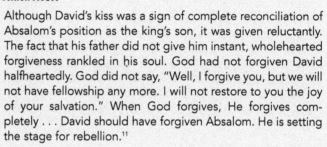

the big picture

2 Samuel 15:1–13

Rumors and speculation about the bad blood between the king and his son must have started creeping into conversations through-out Israel by now. Absalom saw this unrest as the perfect climate in which to begin prying the power from David's hands. With the cunning of a seasoned politician, Absalom:

1. **Garnered public support.** For four years, Absalom made himself available to hear citizens' complaints, hinting that the king was too busy to listen to them. Not only did he glad-hand the people, but he did it with much show. He used a chariot with horses and fifty men, a blatant gesture of his claim to the kingship.
2. **Traveled to Hebron.** Absalom sought—and received—permission from the king to go to Hebron, the heart of David's dynasty, ostensibly to pay a vow he had made to the Lord when he had been living in exile in Geshur.
3. **Orchestrated a coup.** When in Hebron (not coincidentally, the heart of David's dynasty), Absalom announced his intentions to seize power.

Richard D. Phillips

Notice that it is the administration of justice that Absalom especially picks at. David's glaring failure to do right in his own family was apparently mirrored in his failure to establish an effective system for dealing with grievances among the people.[12]

Thomas L. Constable

David was at this time (980–976 B.C.) building his palace in Jerusalem, then constructing a new dwelling place for the ark, and finally making preparations for the temple (5:9–12). This may be the reason David was not meeting the needs of his people as well as he might have done. It probably accounts for David's surprise when Absalom's *coup* began as well.[13]

Robert Roe

The conspiracy increased in strength probably again because of David. I Chronicles tells us David had instituted a centralized kingdom. Instead of the tribes enjoying the old tribal freedom they used to have, they were represented by governors who reported to David in Jerusalem. The tribes, to a large degree, lost all their local tribal rights. They were even required to supply certain things to the king and his staff each month. So the tribes' resentment toward the centralized kingdom added to the strength of the group with Absalom. David is suddenly caught, now, with a real rebellion.[14]

key point

<u>On the Run Again</u>

2 SAMUEL 15:14–18 *So David said to all his servants who were with him at Jerusalem, "Arise, and let us flee, or we shall not escape from Absalom. Make haste to depart, lest he overtake us suddenly and bring disaster upon us, and strike the city with the edge of the sword."*

And the king's servants said to the king, "We are your servants, ready to do whatever my lord the king commands." Then the king went out with all his household after him. But the king left ten women, concubines, to keep the house. And the king went out with all the people after him, and stopped at the outskirts. Then all his servants passed before him; and all the Cherethites, all the Pelethites, and all the Gittites, six hundred men who had followed him from Gath, passed before the king. (NKJV)

go to

began running from Saul
1 Samuel 19:11–12

undying devotion
1 Samuel 18:1–4; 20

loyal followers
1 Samuel 22:1

Ark's entry into Jerusalem
2 Samuel 6:1–19

When David heard his son had staged a takeover, he was convinced his case was hopeless. He wanted to spare the city from destruction, so he and his faithful followers left Jerusalem. Several significant themes mark this passage:

- **Flight.** It wasn't a new experience: As David fled from his familiar and comfortable home in Jerusalem, he must have relived something of the fear and uncertainty he had experienced as he dropped to the ground from his bedroom window and <u>began running from Saul</u> all those years ago. Only this time, he wasn't escaping from a murderous king; he was getting out of town so his vengeful, power-hungry son Absalom wouldn't turn his beloved city, Jerusalem, into a bloody battleground.

- **Unlikely friends.** Earlier in David's life, the son of his pursuer and his rival to the throne, Jonathan, had proclaimed his unlikely yet <u>undying devotion</u> to David. A little later, a small group of indebted, discontented and distressed people formed the core of his <u>loyal followers</u>. Now, it was foreigners—the Cherethites, Pelethites, and Gittites—who remained by David's side. (Remember the Gittites? They were the people from Gath, Goliath's hometown in Philistia. Talk about unlikely friends!)

- **The Ark of the Covenant.** A lively parade of jubilant celebrants had accompanied the <u>Ark's entry into Jerusalem</u>; now, a pathetic stream of joyless refugees attended the Ark's exit from the city. The group included David, his supporters, and the Levites bearing the Ark. David, however, decided the Ark should remain in Jerusalem, so he commissoned the chief priest, Zadok, and his sons to take it back into the city. While there, they would be able to act as spies for David.

David's return of the Ark to Jerusalem made two important statements:

1. He refused to regard the Ark as a good luck charm; and

2. He resolved to keep the center of worship in the nation's capitol, where it belonged—whether or not God intended for him to still be Israel's king.

- **Worship.** David had practically turned cartwheels in worship before; his body language was different now, but he was just as driven to worship. Even though David was literally running for his life, he made an important stop: he trudged up the **Mount of Olives** to worship and pray.

The fact that David was enduring the consequences of his sin didn't prevent him from praying; this shows that he understood the faithfulness of God. God is always there for His followers!

- **Prayer.** While he was on the Mount of Olives, David did what God loves for all of His followers to do: He prayed that God would confound the advice of the usually wise Ahithophel.

go to

Mount of Olives
Zechariah 14:14;
1 Kings 11:7;
2 Kings 23:13;
Nehemiah 8:15;
Ezekiel 11:23;
Matthew 21:1, 24;
26:30, 39

Mount of Olives
mountain east of Jerusalem

what others say

Steven L. McKenzie

David's meekness was apparent as he fled before his son. He was not vengeful or retaliatory but trusted his fate to Yahweh (15:25–26). He went forward in humility with his head and his feet bared, weeping."[15]

David's First Psalm?

The first of fourteen psalms connected to events in David's life is Psalm 3, which is believed to have been composed by David during Absalom's rebellion. The psalm talks about having faith in a God who hears prayer and who protects His children from evil.

something to ponder

Help from Hushai

the big picture

2 Samuel 15:32–37

David, who had been especially distressed to learn that Ahithophel had betrayed him by joining Absalom's conspiracy, recruited his friend Hushai to go to Jeruslem and get into the court as a counselor in order to contradict Ahithophel's advice and serve as a spy.

The appearance of Hushai was a direct answer to David's prayer on the Mount of Olives.

GOD AT WORK

what others say

Steven L. McKenzie

The account in 2 Samuel does not explain why Ahithophel turned against David and went over to Absalom's side. He may have borne a personal grudge against David because of the Bathsheba affair. Bathsheba was the daughter of Eliam (2 Samuel 11:5), and Ahithophel had a son named Eliam, who was among David's best warriors (2 Samuel 15:12; 23:34). If these two Eliams were the same person . . . then Bathsheba was Ahithophel's granddaughter . . . Ahithophel may have acted against David as revenge for Uriah's death and the humiliation of Bathsheba.[16]

A Couple of Old Friends

2 Samuel 16:1–4 When David was a little past the top of the mountain, there was Ziba the servant of Mephibosheth, who met him with a couple of saddled donkeys, and on them two hundred loaves of bread, one hundred clusters of raisins, one hundred summer fruits, and a skin of wine. And the king said to Ziba, "What do you mean to do with these?"

So Ziba said, "The donkeys are for the king's household to ride on, the bread and summer fruit for the young men to eat, and the wine for those who are faint in the wilderness to drink."

Then the king said, "And where is your master's son?"

And Ziba said to the king, "Indeed he is staying in Jerusalem, for he said, 'Today the house of Israel will restore the kingdom of my father to me.'"

So the king said to Ziba, "Here, all that belongs to Mephibosheth is yours."

And Ziba said, "I humbly bow before you, that I may find favor in your sight, my lord, O king!" (NKJV)

While David was on the run, he met Ziba, Mephibosheth's servant, who brought David the news that his master had turned against the king in the hopes of seizing Saul's throne. Ziba, however, appeared faithful to David; he gave him a gift of donkeys in return for the kindness David had shown all those years ago. David took away Mephibosheth's pension and gave it all to Ziba.

Betrayed! And by a man who was practically a member of David's own family! Ziba's report must have thrown a fist into David's already deflating morale when Ziba gave the report of Mephibosheth's disloyalty. David had counted it a privilege to honor the covenant of friendship he and Jonathan had made by not only providing his friend Jonathan's son with a secure future, but by welcoming the young man to his own dinner table each night. It must have been difficult to believe the son of Jonathan now had the audacity to set his sights on the throne. Yet David had no other choice but to believe the report; after all, Mephibosheth's servant was here, giving him valuable and useful gifts, and his master was nowhere to be seen. David's hotheadedness took over as he made an executive decision: He would revoke Mephibosheth's inheritance and give it to Ziba.

Shameful Shimei

the big picture

2 Samuel 16:5–23

Next, David met Shimei, Saul's menacing relative, at Bahurim, just east of the Mount of Olives, with verbal and physical attacks. Although cursing the king was a capital offense, David refused to allow Abishai, his bodyguard and nephew, to behead Shimei. After the encounter with Shimei, David continued to flee eastward toward Manahaim; meanwhile, Absalom went to Jerusalem, where Hushai, David's spy friend, feigned loyalty to Absalom. Ahithophel advised Absalom to sleep with his father's concubines to make a clear statement that he was assuming power.

The restraint David showed in refusing to allow Abishai to kill Shimei is reminiscent of the occasions when David refused to lift a hand against Saul. This is a reminder that the man "after God's own heart" is still very much alive and well; he has just been guilty of nothing more than being human, just as anyone else.

key point

the big picture

2 Samuel 17–18

David's prayer was answered when Absalom took Hushai's advice to "wait awhile" over Ahithophel's counsel to "attack now." The slight mortified Ahithophel, who committed suicide. The delay Hushai recommended gave David and his men a chance to make it to Mahanaim, which was already well fortified after having served as the former capital under Saul's son Ish-bosheth. In Mahanaim, David found refuge and support there, as well as the chance to gather provisions and reorganize his forces. He divided his troops into thirds under the leadership of Joab, Abishai (Joab's brother), and Ittai, and was prepared to lead the maneuver against Absalom's followers himself. His men, however, convinced him it was in Israel's best interest not to lead the attack in person. He reluctantly agreed, issuing clear orders: Absalom was not to be harmed in the battle. However, David's words couldn't protect his son's life. While huge numbers of Absalom's men were falling at the hands of David's heroes in the dense tangle of forest in Ephraim, Absalom tried to escape on his mule. He rode under a large oak tree, snagging his hair in its branches. One of David's soldiers found him struggling to free himself, but refused to harm him because of David's order. Joab, however, didn't have any scruples about disobeying David. He put three javelins in Absalom's heart, then ten of his men hit the king's son to make sure he was dead. When the king received the news, he retreated to his chambers, crying, "O my son Absalom—my son, my son Absalom—if only I had died in your place! O Absalom my son, my son!" (18:33 NKJV).

what others say

Adam Clarke

Joab should have obeyed the king's commandment: and yet the safety of the state required the sacrifice of Absalom. But independently of this, his life was quadruply forfeited to the law:

1. In having murdered his brother Amnon.

2. In having excited an insurrection in the state.

3. In having taken up arms against his own father, (Deuteronomy 21:18, 21).

4. In having lain with his father's concubines (Leviticus 18:29).

Long ago he should have died by the hand of justice; and now all his crimes are visited on him in his last act of rebellion. Yet, in the present circumstances, Joab's act was base and disloyal, and a cowardly murder.[17]

<u>Over-the-Top Grief</u>

Losing a loved one to death is an incomparable sorrow, with grief compounded when a parent loses a child. David had every reason to be heartbroken by his son's demise. Yet the language that expresses

David's sorrow is particularly intense. He wailed the phrase "my son" five times.

Why was David's grief over the top—especially in light of the fact that no love seemed to be lost between the estranged father and son? They hadn't enjoyed a close relationship for many years; theirs had come to be a relationship marked by separation rather than companionship. Further, his son had led a rebellion by attempting to seize control of Israel—a move that David knew to be clearly outside God's plans for the nation. Here are some possible explanations for the king's intense anguish:

1. David may have been keenly aware of his own role in his son's death. Put simply: None of this would have happened if it hadn't been for him.

2. While David was sure of his own eternal security, he may not have been certain of his son's. That may be why he expressed the wish that he could have <u>died in his son's place</u>. This lack of confidence in his older son's eternal destiny is a stark contrast to his certainty that his <u>infant son who died</u> was waiting for him in heaven.

3. David may have spoiled and indulged Absalom above all his other sons.

what others say

Thomas L. Constable

Absalom was never Yahweh's choice to succeed David (cf. 12:24–25; 1 Chronicles 22:9–10). Therefore his attempt to dethrone the Lord's anointed was contrary to God's will and doomed to fail from the beginning. Even though he was personally fertile as a result of God's blessing (14:27), his plan brought God's punishment on himself, even his premature death, rather than further blessing.[18]

Dean William Willimon

I'm glad this story is in the Bible because it lets us know that unhappiness, tragedy, regret are part of loving and living in a family. It was true for King David; it is true at your house and mine . . . If we are hurt by our own families, how much more must God be hurting for the faults and foibles of God's whole human family? What is to become of David's troubled family, or ours? . . . David said that he would have given his life to

died in his son's place
2 Samuel 18:33

infant son who died
2 Samuel 12:18–23

save his son from death. But even kings can't do that. No, it takes a God to do that. At Calvary, on the cross, God's whole, tragic human family was gathered, embraced, saved by a Father who, in grief, loves us yet.[19]

Chapter Wrap-Up

- David's firstborn son, Amnon, raped his beautiful half sister, Tamar. Neither David nor her brother Absalom did anything about it right away, although Absalom was very angry over the matter.

- Absalom allowed his anger to fester for two years, when he plotted a way to have his brother killed to avenge his sister's rape.

- Absalom's murder of Amnon led to a three-year estrangement from his father and, after that, only a cold reconciliation between the two.

- Absalom launched a revolt, sending the king on the run once again—this time, he left Jerusalem to prevent it from being destroyed in any battle that might spring from the conflict.

- David, with the help of his faithful friends and answered prayer, was able to gain some lead time, gather supporters, and regroup from Mahanaim with fresh resolve. He organized a maneuver against Absalom's army, giving orders that his son was not to be harmed in the attack.

- Absalom, fleeing David's soldiers on a mule, became entangled in the branches of a tree. Joab killed him there, and the chapter closed with David's wails of grief over his dead son.

Study Questions

1. What role, if any, did David play in Amnon's crime against Tamar?

2. What did David do when he found out about the rape? What did Absalom do?

3. What happened at a sheepshearing celebration two years after the rape?

4. How did David's parenting tactics seem to change between the time Amnon raped Tamar and the time Absalom murdered Amnon?

5. How did Absalom try to get Joab's attention in order to persuade him to arrange a meeting with his father?

6. What are some things Absalom did to position himself for a takeover?

7. Why did David leave Jerusalem?

8. How did David react to Absalom's death?

Part Seven
DECLINE AND DEATH

2 Samuel 19-20:
Going Home to Jerusalem

Chapter Highlights:
- **Upside-Down Priorities**
- **Famine in the Land**
- **David's Last Words**
- **David's Mighty Men**
- **The Sinful Census**

Let's Get Started

With Absalom dead and his army defeated, nothing stood between David and his throne in Jerusalem. Nothing, that is, except the king's grief and the Israelites' uncertainty. After hearing the news of his son's death, David had retreated to his chambers in Mahanaim, a bereaved father reeling under the weight of unbearable sorrow. For all he cared at that moment, he could have remained in his room crying until his own life ended. His pitiful cries, "O my son Absalom! O Absalom, my son, my son!" echoed through the halls of the palace.

Beyond the courtyards, loyalties remained divided. The Israelites were uncertain about their future. Some had pledged allegiance to a leader who was now dead. Others had remained faithful to David—but where was their king? He certainly wasn't out in the city **gate** congratulating his troops on a job well done. He had closed himself off from his people, so consumed with grief he could hardly be an effective leader.

go to

gate
Deuteronomy 21:19;
22:24;
Joshua 20:14;
Ruth 4:1;
2 Kings 7:1

gate
place where public
affairs were handled

David Gets a Dressing-Down

2 SAMUEL 19:9–14 *Now all the people were in a dispute throughout all the tribes of Israel, saying, "The king saved us from the hand of our enemies, he delivered us from the hand of the Philistines, and now he has fled from the land because of Absalom. But Absalom, whom we anointed over us, has died in battle. Now therefore, why do you say nothing about bringing back the king?"*

So King David sent to Zadok and Abiathar the priests, saying, "Speak to the elders of Judah, saying, 'Why are you the last to bring the king back to his house, since the words of all Israel have come to the king, to his very house? You are my brethren, you are my bone and my flesh. Why then are you the last to bring back the king?' And say to Amasa, 'Are you not my bone and my flesh? God do so to me, and more also, if you are not commander of the army before me continually in place of Joab.'" So he swayed the hearts of all the men of Judah, just as the heart of one man, so that they sent this word to the king: "Return, you and all your servants!" (NKJV)

Joab saw what was going on and knew what needed to be done, so he burst into the king's room to talk some sense into him. Little tact or kindness was couched in the general's threatening words:

2 SAMUEL 19:5–7 *Today you have disgraced all your servants who today have saved your life, the lives of your sons and daughters, the lives of your wives and the lives of your concubines, in that you love your enemies and hate your friends. For you have declared today that you regard neither princes nor servants; for today I perceive that if Absalom had lived and all of us had died today, then it would have pleased you well. Now therefore, arise, go out and speak comfort to your servants. For I swear by the Lord, if you do not go out, not one will stay with you this night. And that will be worse for you than all the evil that has befallen you from your youth until now.* (NKJV)

There's not much to like about Joab, the tough-minded military man with attitude who often had too little regard for David's wishes and too much regard for his own. However, his words made sense: David did need to get back to the business of running the nation; otherwise, Israel would be at risk of suffering even more infighting and rebellion. So the king did as he was advised: He sat in the gate to greet and thank his people as their king and as head of their army.

He also launched a plan for replacing the discord with unity. He would start by appealing to the elders of his own tribe, Judah, for their help in returning him to his rightful place on the throne. After naming Amasa of Judah—Absalom's general and David's own nephew—to replace Joab, David—escorted by the men of Judah—set out on the journey home to Jerusalem.

what others say

Zondervan NIV Bible Commentary

David's army commander begins by upbraiding him for humiliating the very men who are responsible for having saved the king's life as well as the lives of all who are near and dear to him . . . But the heart of Joab's complaint is that David loves those who hate him and hates those who love him.[1]

The Smart Guide to the Bible

Upside-Down Priorities

In the past, even in times of great personal distress or sorrow, David had managed to muster enough self-control to keep moving forward to accomplish God's plans for his life. But now, David seemed to have let his usual order of priorities reverse. In giving in to excessive grief over the death of his traitorous son, he allowed personal pain to divert him from his divine mission of leading God's nation. As difficult as it may be, putting God and His plans above everything else—including family, friends, plans, and passions—is always best. God wants His followers to keep the main things the main things.

apply it

Jerusalem Journey, Rewound

the big picture

2 Samuel 19:15–43

David had taken an emotional beating as he fled Jerusalem. First, he had learned of Mephibosheth's alleged disloyalty. Then he had become the target of the wicked Shimei's curses and stones. Thankfully, the trip back to his beloved city was more promising. After leaving Mahanaim and stopping at the bank of the Jordan River before preparing to cross over toward David's city, he met three men:

1. **Shimei** approached David again. This time, instead of throwing stones, he fell down at the king's feet, confessed his crime, and begged forgiveness. Abishai could barely contain himself, he was still so eager to kill Shimei; David again refused.
2. **Mephibosheth** told David Ziba had lied about his own loyalty and humbly explained that he had remained very devoted to David. David responded to Mephibosheth by offering to divide the land between the two men. Mephibosheth replied that Ziba could have it all.
3. **Barzillai** was an eighty-year-old man from Gilead who had given the king supplies while he was in exile at Mahanaim. David asked his old friend to come home with him so he could return the favor with his hospitality. Barzillai declined, saying his old age would cause him to be a burden to the king, and that he wished to live out his years in his hometown and be buried with the rest of his family. The king understood and, at Barzillai's suggestion, took the servant Chimham as a surrogate.

The chapter closes with David's homecoming, which was marred by more quarreling between the people of Judah and the people of Israel.

something to ponder

The three people who met David on the bank of the Jordan River represented three groups of significant political value: Shimei was from Saul's tribe, a Benjamite, who had with him a thousand of his countrymen; Mephibosheth was Saul's grandson who would presumably have influence over any of Saul's other relatives who might be resistant to David's return; and Barzillai was a man of great wealth and prestige who symbolized the large, Transjordanian area of Israel—key areas in the realm of David's authority.

David's Dealings with Mephibosheth

Theories abound as to why David didn't fully restore Mephibosheth's property. Some scholars say David believed Ziba and thought Mephibosheth was lying, but was obligated by the covenant to provide for the well-being of Jonathan's son. Others assert that David couldn't be certain of the truth so he devised the property split as a reasonable compromise. Still others suggest David believed Mephibosheth, but halved the land in order to keep the loyalty of the influential Ziba. Another particularly interesting theory is that David applied the same kind of wisdom to this situation that Solomon would later use to settle the dispute between the <u>two women</u> claiming the same child. If that was the case, the strategy worked:

Mephibosheth's integrity was revealed in his comment that Ziba could have all the land; it was his relationship to David, not the material possessions, that Mephibosheth valued.

Here Comes Trouble!

go to

two women
1 Kings 3:24–26

violated
2 Samuel 15:16

the big picture

2 Samuel 20

A troublemaker named Sheba, son of Bicri, a Benjamite, stirred up dissension among the people by attempting to incite a rebellion. The people of Israel deserted David to follow Sheba, while the people of Judah remained loyal to David.

After arriving at his home in Jerusalem, David took care of a couple of housekeeping and administrative tasks:

1. **He dealt with his concubines.** When leaving Jerusalem, David had left behind ten concubines, whom Absalom had <u>violated</u> in his absence. Upon his return, he confined

them to the house and no longer slept with them, forcing them to live the rest of their lives as widows.

2. **He replaced Joab with Amasa,** ordering Amasa to rally the troops and report back with the men in three days. Amasa did so, but he didn't return by the deadline David had set, so David told Abishai to take Joab's men, along with the Cherethites, the Pelethites, and all the mighty men, to chase after Sheba. Amasa, figuring it would be better to arrive late than never, joined the party that had gathered in Gibeon. But the new general's tardiness proved deadly. Joab used a sleight-of-hand trick with his sword to fatally wound Amasa and regain command of the army. He and Abishai then launched a pursuit of Sheba that took them across the countryside of Israel. They gained supporters all along the way. Finally, they had Sheba trapped in a walled city. As they prepared to batter the wall down, a wise woman of the city called out to Joab and offered to give Joab the head of Sheba if Joab and his men would spare her city from the attack. They did so and, mission accomplished, returned to Jerusalem, where Joab resumed command of Israel's army.

what others say

Zondervan NIV Bible Commentary

Thus the rebellion of Sheba comes to an inglorious end—all because of the calming advice of the wise woman of Abel. Joab calls off the siege of Abel and returns to Jerusalem. With this, the so-called Court History of David (9:1–20:26) reaches its conclusion for all practical purposes.[2]

Epilogue

The narrative beginning in 1 Samuel 1 and concluding with 2 Samuel 20 is roughly chronological. It tells the story of Samuel, Saul, and David from beginning to end. Second Samuel 21–24, then, serves as an epilogue highlighting the key themes that run through the two books of Samuel.

go to

oath
Joshua 9:15

**expression of God's
judgment or anger**
Leviticus 26:19–29;
Deuteronomy 28:23,
24, 38–42;
1 Kings 17:1;
2 Kings 8:1;
1 Chronicles 21:12;
Psalms 105:16;
107:33–34;
Isaiah 3:1–8; 14:30;
Jeremiah 19:9;
14:15–22; 29:17, 19;
Matthew 24:7;
Luke 21:11;
Revelation 6:5–8

Key Themes

Epilogue Passage	Event	Theme
Chapter 21:1–14	Famine in Israel	God withdraws blessings from the unfaithful.
Chapter 21:15–22	Victory Over Giants	God showers extravagant blessings on the faithful.
Chapter 22	David's Song of Praise	God is due all glory.
Chapter 23:1–7	David's Last Words	God blesses those who obey Him.
Chapter 23:8–39	David's Mighty Men	God's strength, not men's strength, ensures victory.
Chapter 24	David's Sinful Census	God alone is the source of all confidence.

Famine in the Land

2 SAMUEL 21:1 Now there was a famine in the days of David for three years, year after year; and David inquired of the LORD. And the LORD answered, "It is because of Saul and his bloodthirsty house, because he killed the Gibeonites." (NKJV)

At an unspecified time during David's forty-year reign, possibly as early as the year after Saul's death or as late as thirty years after he died, Israel suffered a three-year famine. When David asked God what had brought the disaster upon the land, God cited the injustice committed by Saul and his family when they massacred the Gibeonites during an unrecorded attack, violating an <u>oath</u> Joshua had made many years earlier on behalf of the Israelites.

Because of the climate in the Middle East, the difference between rain and shine often determined whether the Israelites would enjoy feasts or famines. But the famines described in the Bible were no mere coincidence of nature. They were sometimes sent as an <u>expression of God's judgment or anger</u> against His disobedient people.

Just as God occasionally withheld rain or other blessings from the Israelites in response to their disobedience, He sometimes withholds blessings from individuals today when they demonstrate disobedience or rebellion.

what others say

Billy Graham

God sometimes allows Christians to suffer, in order that they might learn the secret of obedience.[3]

However, that doesn't mean that every famine, hurricane, train wreck or terrorist attack is discipline from God.

seven
a number suggesting completion

key point

David R. Reid

Having established the biblical concept that God *can* use tragic events to discipline His people or judge the wicked, let's not jump to the conclusion that *every* tragic event is God's discipline or judgment. Certainly not! In fact, the Lord Jesus *strongly* cautioned against such thinking in Luke 13:1–5, when He rebuked some people who had wrongly concluded that all tragic events are the judgment of God for sin . . . While God can and does use tragic events in sovereign judgment, Luke 13 teaches us that this is not God's normal operating procedure. In fact, unless there is a clear indication of direct judgment, we should assume that the tragic events are *not* the judgment of God for some specific sin.[4]

Another of Saul's Serious Slipups

The heart of God's charge against Saul didn't have anything to do with the fact that he was leading attacks against Israel's enemies; in fact, that's what God wanted Israel's king to do. The bigger issue at hand was Saul's disregard for the oath, or covenant, that Joshua had made with the Gibeonites on behalf of Israel.

what others say

Matthew Henry

That which made this an exceedingly sinful sin was that he not only shed innocent blood, but therein violated the solemn oath by which the nation was bound to protect them. See what brought ruin on Saul's house: it was a bloody house.[5]

the big picture

2 Samuel 21:2–14

David wanted to settle the matter as quickly as possible, so he asked the Gibeonites what he could do to make amends. They answered that they wished for **seven** of Saul's descendants to be publicly executed and their bodies exposed in Saul's hometown of Gibeah in keeping with Numbers 35:33, which states that "you shall not pollute the land where you are; for blood defiles the land" (NKJV). David spared Mephibosheth's life in continued allegiance to his covenant with Jonathan, but he took seven of Saul's other family members and complied with the Gibeonites' wishes.

No Statute of Limitations on Sin!

Given Saul's track record of excuse making, it is difficult to imagine that he would have owned up to his guilt in an incident like this. Whereas David made a habit of asking God to search his heart and expose any wrong He found there, Saul's usual mode of operation had him making excuses for his sin. He would have been more likely to come up with some kind of reason for violating the oath.

Regardless of whether Saul knew he had sinned or not, one thing is certain: God knew. He knew, and He didn't let Saul get away with it—not even after Saul was out of the picture.

what others say

David Guzik

In the context of that culture, the request of the Gibeonites was rather reasonable; they want no monetary compensation or vengeance against Israel at large, only against the family of the man who committed the atrocities against their people.[6]

Thomas C. Constable

Because Saul had been unfaithful to Israel's covenant with the Gibeonites, God punished the nation with famine (lack of fertility). When David, who followed the Mosaic Law, righted this wrong, God restored fertility to the land again. God reduced Saul's line from one of the most powerful-looking men in Israel, Saul, to one of the weakest-looking, Mephibosheth. David's faithfulness to his covenant with Jonathan shows he was a covenant-keeping king like Yahweh. Saul on the other hand broke Israel's covenant with the Gibeonites.[7]

Getting Answers from God

key point

Another clue to David's character emerges in this episode. When things went wrong, he went to God to find out why. Had he not asked God to tell him the cause of the famine, he would not have been able to find out how to restore Israel to God's blessing.

The Overflow of David's Heart

2 Samuel 22

David led a widely observed public life, but his relationship with God was immensely personal. David's song of praise, also recorded as Psalm 18, gives readers a taste of the wonder of that intimate connection. The psalm many scholars suggest may have first been recited shortly after Nathan brought David the news of God's promise that his kingdom would never end puts into action Jesus' words recorded in Matthew 12:34: "Out of the abundance of the heart the mouth speaks" (NKJV). Clearly David spoke these words out of the overflow of a heart that recognized God's lavish blessings: His sovereignty, His provision, His protection, and His love.

David's Last Words

2 SAMUEL 23:1–7 *Now these are the last words of David.*
Thus says David the son of Jesse;
Thus says the man raised up on high,
The anointed of the God of Jacob,
And the sweet psalmist of Israel:
"The Spirit of the LORD spoke by me,
And His word was on my tongue.
The God of Israel said,
The Rock of Israel spoke to me:
'He who rules over men must be just,
Ruling in the fear of God.
And he shall be like the light of the morning when the sun rises,
A morning without clouds,
Like the tender grass springing out of the earth,
By clear shining after rain.'
Although my house is not so with God,
Yet He has made with me an everlasting covenant,
Ordered in all things and secure.
For this is all my salvation and all my desire;
Will He not make it increase?
But the sons of rebellion shall all be as thorns thrust away,
Because they cannot be taken with hands.
But the man who touches them
Must be armed with iron and the shaft of a spear,
And they shall be utterly burned with fire in their place."
(NKJV)

Immediately following David's song of praise is a passage citing his last words. While these were not literally the last words he uttered (his deathbed words to Solomon are recorded in 1 Kings 2), they were most likely his final formal literary composition. What David said of himself in the introduction to this psalm speaks volumes, both about himself and about the coming Messiah:

1. He was of humble beginnings: He called himself the "son of Jesse" (v. 1), highlighting his modest origin and pointing out the coming Messiah's lowly status at birth.

2. He was set apart to be used by God: He said he was "raised up on high" (v. 1) pointing to God's work in exalting the lowly, as He would later do in the life and death of Jesus Christ. He also spoke of being "anointed" (v. 1), which is another word for Messiah.

3. He was divinely inspired: David said, "The Spirit of the LORD spoke by me, and His word was on my tongue," (v. 2 NKJV), also calling to mind Jesus, the Word of God.

4. His kingdom was a flawed model of a coming, perfect kingdom: David acknowledged that while his own reign fell far short of perfection (v. 5), it was his greatest joy to be able to count on God's covenant promise to establish an everlasting kingdom (v. 5).

David's Mighty Men

the big picture

2 Samuel 23:8–39

A list of the men who helped David become king while he was in the cave at Adullam is given here and in 1 Chronicles 11. At first glance, reading these rosters may seem about as appealing as reading a telephone directory. But because nothing in the Bible is there by accident, it's important to stop and consider "What's in it for me?" Here are two possible answers to that question:

1. A reminder of historical authenticity. The Bible was written by a number of authors and historians, many of whom

acted as reporters—divinely inspired ones—who recorded events and stories that they had observed or that they had heard about from other people. Lists providing details such as the one included in David's story make it hard for critics to dismiss the Bible as folklore or myth.

mighty men
1 Samuel 22:1

The roster of David's heroes makes a solid case that David was a real man who drew the support and loyalty of real people during a very real period in Isreal's history.

2. Spiritual lessons. Remembering how these <u>mighty men</u> got their start—as a group of men who were discontent, in debt, and distressed—is an excellent way to remember what God can do with ordinary people with everyday troubles who join His cause and serve Him as their King. God thoroughly equips believers "for every good work" (2 Timothy 3:17 NKJV), just as He equipped these "losers" to become heroes worthy of mention in the greatest Book ever written.

key point

what others say

Robert Alter

This list of military heroes and their exploits is perhaps the strongest candidate of any passage in the Book of Samuel to be considered a text actually written in David's lifetime . . . These fragmentary recollections of particular heroic exploits do not sound like the invention of any later writer but, on the contrary, like memories of remarkable martial acts familiar to the audience (e.g., "he . . . killed the lion in the pit on the day of the snow").[8]

The Sinful Census

the big picture

2 Samuel 24:1–9 and 1 Chronicles 21

The epilogue to the book of Samuel concludes with the account of a time—most likely early in David's reign—when God, for an unnamed reason, had become angry with His people. He allowed Satan to tempt David to count the people of Israel and Judah to determine the strength of his army. Joab couldn't imagine David wanting to do such a thing, and he said so. But David overruled his protests, and Joab was forced to carry out the orders.

go to

census
Exodus 30:11–12;
Numbers 1:1–2

The Bottom Line

Taking a <u>census</u>, in and of itself, was not sinful. But because God judges people by their true motives and intentions, He could see the bottom line: In counting the people, David was taking his eyes off of God's promise to be Israel's protector and provider, and was placing undue confidence in the numbers the census would yield. David knew he had plenty of men; maybe seeing the actual head count in black and white would restore his flagging assurance that Israel was God's blessed nation. Or maybe knowing just how many men he had in his army would give him bragging rights at official state dinners. Either way, counting up his resources amounted to a shortage of trust or an overabundance of pride. Both were clearly outside God's plan for His people and for the leader of His people. He wanted their confidence and their pride to be in Him alone.

apply it

It often seems easier to trust the numbers—or the people, programs, or plans that we can see, feel, and understand—than it is to trust God, whom we can't always see, feel, or understand. Trusting in God involves walking by faith; trusting in numbers involves walking by sight.

A Familiar Routine

the big picture

2 Samuel 24:10–14

No sooner were the numbers in than David began to feel that familiar sinking in his heart: He had done it again; he had sinned against God. The king admitted his guilt and asked forgiveness, and God responded in an unusual way. He allowed David to choose the consequences of his sin. God gave David three choices: seven years of famine to the land; three months of being chased by his enemies; or three days of plague. David chose the latter.

It's a lesson taught over and over throughout David's life: the effects of sin aren't limited to the guilty party. The consequences inevitably spill over to the lives of others, including the lives of innocent people. This was no exception. No matter which judgment David chose, other people were going to suffer. Seven years of famine would cause indescribable hardship and countless casualties.

Three months of subjection to pursuing enemies would leave his nation leaderless, susceptible to inner political turmoil and vulnerable. The three days of plague, while deadly, seemed the least destructive option; its damage would encompass a much smaller time period, and its scope could feasibly include David and his family. (Chances are the king and his family would not have suffered much during either a famine or his exile.)

go to

threshing floor
flat surface prepared for removing the grain from the stalk

The Scoop on Araunah's Threshing Floor

the big picture

2 Samuel 24:15–25

The Lord sent a plague via an angelic envoy, who destroyed seventy thousand men throughout Israel. (Scholars note that these were "fighting men"—the very forces in whom David had placed his trust when he took the census to begin with.) As the angel began to direct the plague over the capital city of Jerusalem, the Lord called an end to the destruction. David, distraught over the supernatural event the Lord had allowed him to witness, confessed his guilt again and begged God to punish himself and his family instead of his "sheep." God responded by telling David to build an altar on Araunah's **threshing floor**, the site that happened to be directly beneath the angel of death. David refused Araunah's gracious offer to give him the site and supplies for the altar and offerings. The king, stressing that a sacrifice that cost him nothing would not be sacrifice at all (Mark 12:43–44), insisted on paying for the land, oxen, and wood. David then built an altar, upon which he presented burnt offerings and fellowship offerings. The Lord accepted the sacrifices and withdrew the plague from Israel.

what others say

Rick Warren

Real worship costs. David knew this and said: "I will not offer to the Lord my God sacrifices that have cost me nothing."[9]

The threshing floor was a common sight in the farmlands of Israel. Usually located at the edge of a village on a large flat segment of rock, it was the place where farmers would beat the stalks of grain or have their animals walk over it in order to separate the kernels of

something to ponder

Abraham had offered Isaac
Genesis 22:2

build the temple
1 Chronicles 22:1

grain from the stalk. Araunah's threshing floor was different from the others in the region, however. What set it apart was its history as well as its future: Located atop Mount Moriah, it was the same hill where <u>Abraham had offered Isaac</u>, and it was the plot of land upon which David's son Solomon eventually would <u>build the temple</u>. Further, it was located near where Jesus would die on the cross. David wouldn't have missed the significance of the occasion; some scholars believe he wrote Psalm 30 in response to this moment.

what others say

Alan Redpath

Have you ever considered the significance of that mountain in the Old Testament? It was always associated with sacrifice; it was always a place where the price was paid. Up Mount Moriah Abraham took Isaac to offer him. Now we find David offering his burnt offerings there, and on that spot Solomon built the temple at such infinite cost. Hundreds of years afterwards, Satan took our blessed Lord to the pinnacle of the temple there and tried to persuade Him to make a public show of His power. Always in Scripture Mount Moriah is a place where the price was paid to the uttermost.[10]

Chapter Wrap-Up

- David, consumed with grief, retreated to his chambers in Mahanaim, but Joab told him sternly that he needed to get back to the business of running the nation; otherwise, Israel would be at risk of suffering even more infighting and rebellion. The king did as he was advised.

- As David headed back home toward Jerusalem, three people met him at the Jordan to help his cross over: Shimei, who asked forgiveness for cursing the king; Mephibosheth, who assured him that he had not been disloyal; and Barzillai, who had helped David earlier.

- David and his entourage returned to Jerusalem, where David soon reestablished his authority and replaced Joab with Amasa; Joab, however, killed him.

- At some point during David's reign, Israel experienced a famine as a consequence of Saul's disregard of an oath with the Gibeonites. When David asked them what he could do, they asked for seven male descendants of Saul. David turned them over for execution, sparing Mephibosheth.

- David spoke some of his last words, expressing that he was of humble beginnings, set apart to be used by God, and divinely inspired.

- David demonstrated distrust of God by conducting a census in Israel; after realizing his sin and confessing to God, God gave him the choice of three calamities. David chose a plague, which took the lives of seventy thousand men.

- David built an altar on the threshing floor he bought from Araunah. The property, located atop Mount Moriah, would eventually be the site of the temple.

Study Questions

1. How did David respond to Absalom's death?

2. How did Joab scold David?

3. Who did David meet on his way back to Jerusalem?

4. What news did Mephibosheth bring to David?

5. Why was there a famine in the land?

6. Why was taking the census sinful?

Chapter Highlights:
- From the Mountaintop
- Last Public Address
- Struggle for Succession
- Solomon: King of Israel
- David's Death

David's Last Days

Let's Get Started

David must have still been trembling after getting the glimpse into the supernatural realm God had just granted. He had seen the mighty angel of the Lord poised atop Mount Moriah on Araunah's threshing floor. And he had watched as the stunning heavenly creature, who at the Lord's command had just killed seventy thousand men of Israel, withdrew his terrible sword and placed it back in its sheath when God said "Stop." Confronted by the power of His Lord and convicted by his sin, David had offered sacrifices to God on an altar he built upon the very property that lay beneath the angel's feet. When David had bought that threshing floor and surrounding land from Araunah, he had taken the first step toward seeing God's promises come to pass. He had secured the real estate for the building project of his deepest dreams, the temple that would stand as the centerpiece of Israel's worship and as a magnificent reminder that God was their king.

atonement
restoring unity with God

From the Mountaintop to the Drawing Board

1 CHRONICLES 22:1 *Then David said, "This is the house of the LORD God, and this is the altar of burnt offering for Israel."* (NKJV)

David recognized that God had not chosen this site merely as a convenient place for him to make personal **atonement** for his sin. The king knew God had selected the spot for a much larger purpose.

It was to be the holiest site in all of Israel, the place where the priests would make atonement for the Israelites' sins. It was to be the site of the temple God had promised him would one day be built.

David understood it to be the will of God that the national place of worship should be fixed there, and he forthwith proceeded to make preparations for the erection of the temple on that spot.

key point

Preparations Begin

the big picture

I Chronicles 22:2–26:8

David understood that he wasn't the man God wanted to build the structure. But he hadn't allowed God's "no" to cause him to become bitter or resentful. He fully submitted himself to God's will and threw his whole heart into any role God would allow him to take in the preparations for the project. As it turned out, the Lord had much more for David to do concerning the Temple than David might have ever imagined. He would have the joy and privilege of laying the groundwork for the splendid structure that would one day be the centerpiece of the nation's worship and a constant reminder that God was really the king of Israel.

what others say

Eerdman's Handbook to the Bible

David never stopped longing to build God a house fit for him. He accepted the set-back of God's refusal and turned all his energy and enthusiasm to the things he could do: selecting the site; amassing materials; deciding the plan.[1]

J. Vernon McGee

The temple speaks of that which is spiritual, of a right relationship with God. From God's viewpoint that was the important thing that went on in David's kingdom—rather than the continual wars, the intrigue, the petty politics such as are considered newsworthy in our day . . . From God's viewpoint, David's preparations for the temple were more important than anything else David did.[2]

David: Recruiter, Supplier, and Logistics Manager

the big picture

I Chronicles 22–26

Exactly *when* David began preparations for the Temple isn't clear, but *what* he did is described in great detail. God gave the king many hats to wear concerning the project closest to his heart!

1. **David the Recruiter.** David selected skilled men who would cut and prepare the stones that would be used in

the construction. He also assigned masons, carpenters, and craftsmen to carry out the work. Further, he used his political clout to encourage Israel's leaders to throw their support into the effort.

2. **David the Supplier.** David had amassed countless treasures as the result of his numerous victories over Israel's enemies, and he had received many generous gifts from neighboring political leaders as well. These treasures included the iron, bronze, and cedar logs that would be used in the structure, as well as about 120 million ounces of gold and about 1.2 ounces of silver (that would be valued at $16–17 billion today!).

3. **David the Logistics Manager.** Worship as the Jews knew it was about to change dramatically. Maintaining a permanent, lavish temple and conducting worship there would require a level of organization previously unnecessary at the portable, relatively modest tabernacle. Inspired by God and careful to stick to the guidelines of the Law of Moses, David mapped out the logistics of maintaining the temple and of carrying out the mechanics of worship.

key point

He also assigned the Levites, who previously had been responsible for carrying the tabernacle and its furnishings from place to place, to maintain the temple. He divided them into groups, giving each group specific duties and setting up rotating shifts of service.

He added a choir to the temple staff. It's not surprising that David added music to the program. After all, music was close to his heart. He was known as "the sweet singer of Israel" whose music had soothed Saul's troubled spirit. He commissioned 228 skilled musicians to incorporate cymbals, lyres, and harps into the worship.

Tim LaHaye

David's administration involved extensive organization and the delegation of leadership and responsibility. Some Christians have supposed that efficient and effective organization is not necessary to carry on God's work. But both in the Old Testament and the New Testament, the principles of organization, planning and dedicated service are very clear.[3]

Thomas L. Constable

The organization of a temple choir is surprising since the Chronicler elsewhere presented Israel's worship as done in compliance with the Mosaic Law, which made no provision for a choir. However the prophets Nathan and Gad had authorized this choir (2 Chronicles 29:25). Furthermore this choir was in harmony with other legislation in the Law directing praise of the Lord (cf. Numbers 10:10; Deuteronomy 10:8; 18:5). Also the general scriptural admonition to rejoice in God's presence encouraged creative expressions of worship in harmony with God's Word.[4]

Other Official Business

the big picture

1 Chronicles 26:29–27:33

- David assigned the people who would carry out various duties, such as tax collection and tithes in areas outside the temple.
- David organized the army, which consisted of 12 divisions of 24,000 men each. He made geographic assignments and set up one-month shifts for each division to fulfill once per year.
- David appointed officials over the tribes and named those who would oversee various aspects of the king's vast administration, including his storehouses and his farming operations. He also named his advisers and counselors.

David Addresses the People

1 CHRONICLES 28:1–7 *Now David assembled at Jerusalem all the leaders of Israel: the officers of the tribes and the captains of the divisions who served the king, the captains over thousands and captains over hundreds, and the stewards over all the substance and possessions of the king and of his sons, with the officials, the valiant men, and all the mighty men of valor. Then King David rose to his feet and said, "Hear me, my brethren and my people: I had it in my heart to build a house of rest for the ark of the covenant of the LORD, and for the footstool of our God, and had made preparations to build it. But God said to me, 'You shall not build a house for My name, because you have been a man of war and have shed blood.' However the LORD God of Israel chose me above all the house of my father to be king over Israel forever, for He has chosen Judah to be the ruler. And of the house of Judah, the house of my father, and among the sons of my father, He was pleased with me to make me king over all Israel. And of all my sons (for the LORD has given me many sons) He has chosen my son Solomon to sit on the throne of the*

kingdom of the LORD over Israel. Now He said to me, 'It is your son Solomon who shall build My house and My courts; for I have chosen him to be My son, and I will be his Father. Moreover I will establish his kingdom forever, if he is steadfast to observe My commandments and My judgments, as it is this day.'" (NKJV)

With the end of his life coming into view, the aging David gathered all the leaders together in order to give them some final instructions. First, he reminded the people of his desire to construct a temple for the Lord. Then, he summed up the Lord's response, and related that just as God had chosen him as king of Israel, He had chosen his son Solomon to succeed David as king and as builder of the temple. Finally, David asked Israel to do their part by following the Lord's commands so they and their descendants could enjoy the blessings God had promised them.

go to

demons
Luke 4:41,
James 2:19

David Addresses Solomon

1 CHRONICLES 28:9–10 *As for you, my son Solomon, know the God of your father, and serve Him with a loyal heart and with a willing mind; for the LORD searches all hearts and understands all the intent of the thoughts. If you seek Him, He will be found by you; but if you forsake Him, He will cast you off forever. Consider now, for the LORD has chosen you to build a house for the sanctuary; be strong, and do it. (NKJV)*

This is the public passing of the torch from a king to his successor. But even more, it's a commission of faith being handed from father to son. These words summed up what David had done with Solomon that he he had failed to do with his other sons: plant seeds of faith into their hearts. David's choice of words is telling:

something to ponder

- *"Know":* The Hebrew word for know, *yada* has many shades of meaning, including the most obvious: "to perceive." But *yada* is wrapped up in another implication as well: "to know by experience." In this case, David couldn't have been speaking more deliberately. He was urging his son not just to *acknowledge* the existence of God, (for even the <u>demons</u> do that!); he was inviting Solomon to *experience* God personally, on a day-to-day basis. "Oh, taste and see that the LORD is good" (Psalm 34:8 NKJV), seems to be his appeal.

- ***"the God of your father"*:** When David said this instead of "the God of Israel," underlined that he was sharing a personal testimony rather than staging a political posture. God had indeed been David's Lord on the most intimate level. David wanted Solomon to understand that.

- ***"serve Him with a loyal heart"*:** For all his sins, David had remained loyal to the Lord. He had never forsaken his God for the gods of other nations, and he had enjoyed the blessings of that loyalty. He very much wanted the same for Solomon.

- ***"the LORD searches all hearts and understands all the intent of the thoughts"*:** This reminder took on added weight coming from the man who, had God not known his heart and understood his intentions, might still be a shepherd.

- ***"the LORD has chosen you"*:** David emphasized that Solomon was set apart for a specific purpose of God in His plan for the nation.

David hadn't seemed to understand his responsibility for guiding future generations with his older sons, but now, with Solomon, it seems he was finally learning how to be an attentive, instructive father. David wanted to make sure he left his son with a clear vision of who he was and how he fit into God's plans.

apply it

There's very little about the future we can accurately predict, except the fact that each of us will one day die. But one thing we can know for certain: All people, whether they're kings or kindergarten teachers, executives or electricians, pastors or parents, will leave a legacy. If that legacy includes any unfinished business, any God-appointed tasks that we may not see to completion, it's our responsibility to pass the vision on to those who will step in after we've stepped aside.

what others say

Dennis and Barbara Rainey

We want to pass on to our children not only the knowledge of who God is and the experience of Him in everyday life, but also what it means to trust Him and obey Him (Psalm 78:5–8). We want each of our children to follow and serve Christ all their lives, so that succeeding generations may know the truth about Him.[5]

Dennis Rainey

A father has the privilege of imprinting young lives that will carry the torch to the next generation.[6]

Blueprints for the Temple

go to

tabernacle
Exodus 25:9, 40;
26:30; 39:32, 42–43;
Numbers 8:4;
Acts 7:44;
Hebrews 8:5

Ark
Genesis 6

the big picture

1 Chronicles 28:11–21

Then David handed Solomon the plans God had given him for the temple and its furnishings, and affirmed that every detail had been provided by inspiration of God. He again encouraged Solomon to be strong and courageous for the task ahead, assuring his son that he would not be alone in the huge task before him. He would have the support of both God and the nation.

Some scholars suggest that the temple plans were given to David in God's own handwriting. Other scholars agree that the directions were revealed by God, but not in a format that was as tangible.

Either way, the instructions God gave David regarding the temple were as direct and specific as the plans He had given Moses for the tabernacle and Noah for the Ark. Details matter to God!

key point

what others say

Zondervan NIV Bible Commentary

David was saying that not only were the temple plans revealed by God (v. 12), But that they were given to him in written form from God, to be handed to Solomon (v. 11), an ultimate testimony to their divine character.[7]

Alan Redpath

The temple of God was to be built in minute detail according to the pattern in the mind and will of God. David received those details from the Lord, who wrote them on his heart by His own hand. In other words, the reward of David's full dedication was a personal revelation from heaven. It wasn't secondhand, but something David received from the Lord Himself, the plan of God's temple which one day He would fill with His glory.[8]

Preliminary Sketches of the Temple

key point

The blueprints for the temple were loosely patterned after the floor plan of the tabernacle. Like the tabernacle, the temple would house two rooms—the holy place and the holiest place. However, beyond that, the temple would feature significant differences. Of course, one of the most significant changes would be the fact that the temple was permanent, not portable.

what others say

Eerdman's Handbook to the Bible

The tabernacle plan was extended by an entry porch, the resulting three rooms forming a scheme similar to some Canaanite temples . . . A series of storage chambers three storeys high ran round the outside of the holiest place and the middle room (the "holy place"). The doorway was flanked by two giant freestanding pillars whose function is uncertain. Comparison with Ezekiel's temple suggests that the whole building stood on a platform above the level of the court-yard.[9]

David's Offerings and Worship

the big picture

2 Chronicles 29:1–22

David again addressed the assembly, stressing his son's youth and experience, and emphasizing that the temple wasn't for a human king but for the Lord God. He told of the materials he had already supplied for the project, and challenged the other leaders to participate in giving to the project. They were eager to do so, and handed over a generous supply of riches. David responded to the people's devotion with great celebration. He praised the Lord, acknowledged God as the source of all gifts, and described himself and his people as undeserving "aliens and pilgrims" with no hope apart from God. He prayed that the dedication and devotion of God's people would endure, and that Solomon would keep His commandments and fulfill His purposes.

Zondervan NIV Bible Commentary

The truth that "everything" we have "comes from God" is the foundation for the doctrine of stewardship. Its basis is this: since our property is his (Psalm 24:1), and since we hold it only temporarily and in trust (1 Chronicles 29:15–16), it should therefore be used for him (Luke 17:10).[10]

Eerdman's Handbook to the Bible

In addition to all he has put by over the years, David makes a last lavish personal gift for the temple building fund (1–5). His example and appeal (5) calls forth a willing, joyful response from the people, and the gifts pour in (6–9). Deeply moved, David thanks God from his heart that such giving is possible from men who apart from God's goodness have nothing. His prayer is one of the greatest in the whole of the Old Testament. It shows, as perhaps no other passage does, just why this man could be described as "a man after God's own heart."[11]

The Rise of Solomon and the Decline of David

1 CHRONICLES 29:22–30 *So they ate and drank before the LORD with great gladness on that day. And they made Solomon the son of David king the second time, and anointed him before the LORD to be the leader, and Zadok to be priest. Then Solomon sat on the throne of the LORD as king instead of David his father, and prospered; and all Israel obeyed him. All the leaders and the mighty men, and also all the sons of King David, submitted themselves to King Solomon. So the LORD exalted Solomon exceedingly in the sight of all Israel, and bestowed on him such royal majesty as had not been on any king before him in Israel.*

Thus David the son of Jesse reigned over all Israel. And the period that he reigned over Israel was forty years; seven years he reigned in Hebron, and thirty-three years he reigned in Jerusalem. So he died in a good old age, full of days and riches and honor; and Solomon his son reigned in his place. Now the acts of King David, first and last, indeed they are written in the book of Samuel the seer, in the book of Nathan the prophet, and in the book of Gad the seer, with all his reign and his might, and the events that happened to him, to Israel, and to all the kingdoms of the lands. (NKJV)

At some point during David's preparations for the temple, the matter of who would succeed him had been disputed and then settled with Solomon's first anointing. The remainder of 2 Chronicles (2 Chronicles 29:22–30) describes the festivities following the celebration, which culminated with Solomon's being anointed a second time. The chapter closes with the writer of Chronicles summing up Solomon's ascension to the throne and David's death—topics more thoroughly detailed in 1 Kings 1 and 2.

Struggle for the Succession

1 KINGS 1:1–4 Now King David was old, advanced in years; and they put covers on him, but he could not get warm. Therefore his servants said to him, "Let a young woman, a virgin, be sought for our lord the king, and let her stand before the king, and let her care for him; and let her lie in your bosom, that our lord the king may be warm." So they sought for a lovely young woman throughout all the territory of Israel, and found Abishag the Shunammite, and brought her to the king. The young woman was very lovely; and she cared for the king, and served him; but the king did not know her. (NKJV)

key point

With Israel's enemies subdued and peace in the nation during David's latter days, the king was able to spend much of his time and energy preparing for his beloved temple project. Nothing could have brought him more joy in his "golden years" than that. However, he wasn't getting any younger. While historians aren't certain of the exact timing of the events marking David's old age, it's likely that sometime after the preparations for the temple were kicked off, when the king was about seventy years old, his health began to deteriorate. He became frail, and felt a constant chill. His servants brought him an attractive young woman from Shunam named Abishag, who cared for him and slept with him (although the relationship was not intimate) in order to keep him warm at night.

Sick and Cold

As difficult as it is to envision the sturdy shepherd boy, the fearless giant-slayer, the resilient refugee, the victorious warrior, and the mighty monarch as a frail, bedridden patient, this passage describes a man who had become just that. The servants who tended to him and undoubtedly loved him wanted to provide every possible comfort for their friend and their king. Their solution may sound a little far-fetched to today's ears, but employing a nurse to also serve as a "bed-warmer" wasn't an uncommon prescription for what ailed the king.

A man of seventy wasn't considered very old compared with the life span of many other ancient Jewish men, but David's years had been extraordinarily full and demanding. Physical hardships plus the mental and emotional traumas David had endured over the past several decades had begun to take their toll.

Adonijah's Power Play

1 KINGS 1:5–6 *Then Adonijah the son of Haggith exalted himself, saying, "I will be king"; and he prepared for himself chariots and horsemen, and fifty men to run before him. (And his father had not rebuked him at any time by saying, "Why have you done so?" He was also very good-looking. His mother had borne him after Absalom.)* (NKJV)

God had ordained Solomon as the son of David who would become the king's successor and the builder of the temple, but the transition wasn't going to be a smooth one. David's spoiled son, Adonijah, viewed his father's deteriorating health as his cue to announce that he would become Israel's next king.

David's sons—that is, all but Solomon—were walking, talking reminders of David's parenting failures. The seeds of indulging passions and acting on impulse David had planted were reaped in Amnon's violent act of rape and incest. David's failure to discipline Amnon and Absalom, and his refusal to fully forgive Absalom, resulted in Absalom's rebellion which, in turn, touched off political

turmoil in the kingdom. Now, Adonijah, born to David's wife Haggith just after the birth of Absalom, appeared to be of the same ilk as his brothers.

His description in this passage seems intended to emphasize that his spoiled nature was the unpleasant by-product of the hands-off policy of discipline David favored.

Adonijah Makes His Move

1 Kings 1:7–10 Then he conferred with Joab the son of Zeruiah and with Abiathar the priest, and they followed and helped Adonijah. But Zadok the priest, Benaiah the son of Jehoiada, Nathan the prophet, Shimei, Rei, and the mighty men who belonged to David were not with Adonijah.

And Adonijah sacrificed sheep and oxen and fattened cattle by the stone of Zoheleth, which is by En Rogel; he also invited all his brothers, the king's sons, and all the men of Judah, the king's servants. But he did not invite Nathan the prophet, Benaiah, the mighty men, or Solomon his brother. (NKJV)

With much fanfare, Adonijah rallied the support of Joab, the commander of David's army, and Abiathar, the priest. However, he failed to win over David's inner circle of friends:

- Zadok, the priest
- Benaiah, one of David's highest-ranking soldiers,
- Nathan, the prophet
- Shimei and Rei, the king's special guards

Making a further display of his intentions, Adonijah held a great feast near En Rogel. Since he made sacrifices a part of the festivities, the event was cloaked in religious overtones that made it appear to be an inauguration approved by God. There were significant omissions from the guest list, however: neither Nathan, Benaiah, Shimei, Rei, nor Solomon was invited.

what others say

Ryrie Study Bible

As a prelude to taking over the throne, Adonijah held a feast but failed to invite Nathan and Solomon. He apparently was planning to kill them, for had they eaten together, he would have been obliged to protect them.[14]

Bathsheba's Plan

the big picture

1 Kings 1:11-19

Nathan saw what Adonijah was doing and went straight to Bathsheba with the news. He urged her to take the matter to the king, and that's exactly what she did. With the confidence of a queen and the tact of a loving wife, she bowed before the king in his chambers and reminded him of his promise to name their son Solomon as his successor.

The marriage of David and Bathsheba may have gotten off to a shaky start, but God had transformed the turbulence into tranquillity. Their relationship was sealed with a deep and abiding love, one that far transcended the momentary passion David had felt upon his first glimpse of the bathing beauty. Evidently, their love had been nourished through the years by the couple's love for God and a shared understanding of how He was working in their lives.

something to ponder

Incidentally, those are two ingredients for a strong marriage today!

They both knew fully well that Solomon was God's choice as Israel's next king. But now Bathsheba could see her husband's oldest son threatening to interfere with that plan. It's safe to assume that worry had begun to crowd into her thoughts and urgent prayers began to fly off her lips as her handmaidens reported to her the arrogant antics of Adonijah. By law, he would become king if David did not name his successor before he died.

If Bathsheba had indeed been worrying and praying, her worries must have been put to rest and her prayers answered when she saw Nathan—the mouthpiece of the Lord—approaching her. His advice to her may have confirmed what had likely been thinking: "We must tell the king."

Living in a Fishbowl

1 KINGS 1:20-21 *And as for you, my lord, O king, the eyes of all Israel are on you, that you should tell them who will sit on the throne of my lord the king after him. Otherwise it will happen, when my lord the king rests with his fathers, that I and my son Solomon will be counted as offenders.* (NKJV)

Heavy bedcovers, thick curtains, and a staff of devoted attendants insulated David from the public's eye in his latter days. But he wasn't dead yet! Bathsheba reminded her husband that he was still very much the anointed king of Israel, and that his sheep—the people of the nation he had fought so hard to secure and protect—were still there. Their eyes were on the palace as they waited for the king's word about their future.

Solomon, King of Israel

the big picture

1 Kings 1:22–40

Bathsheba's words, followed by Nathan's confirmation, injected a burst of energy into David's weakened body. Speaking with all the authority of the God-ordained office he held, he passionately vowed that Solomon would indeed succeed him. And with youthful enthusiasm, he explained precisely how the transition of power was to take place and his orders were followed to a "t."

1. Zadok, Nathan, and Benaiah took Solomon to Gihon on his own mule. The fact that these three were the highest-ranking priest, prophet, and soldier, respectively, and that they accompanied Solomon on the king's mule (a sign of being the appointed successor to the throne), made it clear to anyone watching that they were acting as the king's representatives.

go to

Saul's anointing
1 Samuel 10:1

key point

what others say

Tim LaHaye

Zadok was one of the high priests serving during the reign of King David (2 Samuel 8:17). The ancestors of Zadok will provide the priestly stock that will oversee the Millennial Temple during Christ's one thousand-year reign on earth (Ezekiel 44:15) because of his faithfulness during a time of apostasy as noted in 1 Kings 2:27, 35.[17]

2. While at Gihon, Zadok and Nathan anointed Solomon, blew the trumpet, and shouted, "Long live King Solomon!"

This anointing oil, like David's, was poured from a horn rather than from a fragile flask as with <u>Saul's anointing</u>. The horn signified that Solomon had the strength of God behind him.

It's important to remember that Solomon became king for the same reason his father, David, had become king: The Lord chose them both.

3. Finally, Solomon took his place on David's throne. The Israelites responded to the news with a great celebration. The celebration was so spirited, in fact, that their music and dancing literally shook the ground.

"What's That Racket?"

the big picture

1 Kings 1:41–53

Meanwhile, across the river at Adonijah's so-called inauguration, the guests were wondering what all the racket was about when Abiathar's son, Jonathan, came to deliver a message: Solomon had been anointed king. The message, which provided Adonijah and his supporters more details than they probably cared to hear, was rain on their parade. The partiers became frightened at the thought that they might be condemned as conspirators against the newly anointed king, so they scattered. Adonijah was pretty scared, too. He immediately sought protection by grabbing onto the horns of the altar. When Solomon heard Adonijah was afraid for his life, he assured his trembling brother that he would let him live . . . IF he behaved. If not, Solomon said, he held the right to have him put to death.

Robert Alter

The typical construction of ancient Israelite altars, as archeology has confirmed, featured a curving protuberance at each of the four corners, roughly like the curve of a ram's horn. The association of horn with strength may explain this design. Gripping the horns—actually, probably one horn—of the altar was a plea for sanctuary: at least in principle, though not always in practice, a person in this posture and in this place should be held inviolable by his pursuers.[18]

David's Death

1 Kings 2:1–9

David had previously made some public remarks to his son, but as David sensed the day of his death approaching, he had some important words to say privately to Solomon about his spiritual life:

- He urged Solomon to be strong, to act with integrity, and obey God's law.
- He reminded Solomon that obedience is the only way to prosper.
- He restated God's promise of an unbroken line of rulers.

Zondervan NIV Bible Commentary

David did everything in his power to smooth the way for Solomon to follow him as king, not only in drawing up the plans (cf. 1 Chronicles 28:11–19) for the temple, amassing the necessary materials and funds (cf. 1 Chronicles 22:14–16) and soliciting the help and cooperation of Israel's leadership (cf. 1 Chronicles 22:17–19), but also in admonishing and encouraging Solomon to carry out faithfully the task committed to him (cf. 1 Chronicles 22:6–13; 28:9–20). In Solomon, David found a responsive and humble heart. Amnon, Absalom, and Adonijah, Solomon's three older brothers, were spiritual and morally deficient; but Solomon had a heart prepared by God, and he responded willingly to David's instruction. David's legacy to Solomon was thus much more than a great kingdom with secure borders, tributary nations, and considerable wealth and prestige. Far more important, he instilled in Solomon a love for God and his Word. He gave to Solomon a proper orientation to life and leadership and was himself an out-standing role model, despite his failures, of a man whose heart truly beat for God.[19]

Woodrow Kroll

David wanted to make sure Solomon was a great success. And the advice he gives him at the last breath shows he is a fantastic finisher, this David. He may not have been the kind of father he needed to be all the way through Solomon's life and the other sons' lives, but he's got it together now. To finish well is the great joy of life. And for all of us who are moving into that quarter of life, that are rounding that last turn or getting to the last turn, the concept of finishing well becomes more important every day. Finishing well often means that you provide for the success of your successor. And that's what David's doing here. David is trying to give Solomon the kind of advice that will cause Solomon to be successful. Whether or not Solomon will live by that advice, time will tell.[20]

go to

capture of Jerusalem
1 Chronicles 11:6–8

Unfinished Business

the big picture

1 Kings 2:5–9

Having shared his heart concerning Solomon's relationship to God, David moved to matters concerning Solomon's relationship with people. More specifically, he brought up the names of three people who fell into the category of "unfinished business" on David's "to-do" list: Joab, Barzillai of Gilead, and Shimei.

As a military officer, Joab had served David well, and could boast of a long list of accomplishments—not the least of which was the daring capture of Jerusalem. And as a friend, Joab had been extremely loyal even though he had not always followed David's wishes.

However, Joab had also stirred up plenty of trouble for David:

- He had killed Absalom against David's orders.
- He had killed Abner in an act of treachery.
- He had killed Amasa in an act of treachery.
- He had supported Adonijah in his attempt to seize the throne.

Barzillai
2 Samuel 17:27,
19:31–19

Shimei
2 Samuel 16:5–8

The Bible Knowledge Commentary

In mercy David had not executed the punishment that Joab's actions deserved, probably because Joab had shown David much loyalty and had served him well. But justice had to be done and Solomon had to do it. Joab had been living on borrowed time; soon he had to pay for his crimes.[21]

Blessings for Barzillai

When David had been exiled during Absalom's revolt, Barzillai had provided David with hospitality and provisions. To repay the kindness, David asked Solomon to care for Barzillai's children.

Second Thoughts About Shimei

Shimei, the Benjamite who had cursed David and threatened his life when David was exiled from Jerusalem, received David's pardon when he begged forgiveness upon David's return. Apparently, David was having second thoughts about Shimei's sincerity. He brought his doubts to Solomon's attention and left it to his son to resolve the matter.

David's Death

1 KINGS 2:10–12 *So David rested with his fathers, and was buried in the City of David. The period that David reigned over Israel was forty years; seven years he reigned in Hebron, and in Jerusalem he reigned thirty-three years. Then Solomon sat on the throne of his father David; and his kingdom was firmly established.* (NKJV)

The epic narrative of the man whose life was larger than life concludes with this simple biographical notation. David—the shepherd, the musician, the king, the husband, the father, the grandfather—died, probably in about 970 BC, and was buried in the city that he had established as Israel's religious and political capital.

David "Rested" in Peace After He Got the Job Done

go to

needed him to do
Acts 13:22

Any of dozens of threatening situations could have ended David's life during and before his forty-year reign. Lions could have attacked the young boy who watched over the flocks in the sheepfold. Goliath could have slain the indignant teen who was dying for the chance to take a "sling" at the godless giant. Saul could have speared the young musician who was so sweetly soothing his troubled spirit. The deranged king's men could have murdered the refugee they were chasing across the countryside. And the list goes on: David could have died at the hands of the Philistines, Nabal's men, the Ammonites, his hotheaded commander, or even his sons. But he didn't.

Instead of experiencing an untimely, surprising, and/or violent death, David died without drama, and with many blessings. God blessed His servant with a heart that beat long enough to do what He <u>needed him to do</u>, including establish peace in the land, lay the groundwork for the temple, and carefully pave the way for Solomon's transition to power.

GOD AT WORK

what others say

Woodrow Kroll

David finished well because he began well and he never left the strength he had and that is the fact he was a man after God's own heart. It's hard to finish poorly if you're a man after the heart of God or a woman after the heart of God. That is what God is looking for.[22]

It Wasn't His Permanent Resting Place

The word "rested" was often used by ancient people as a euphemism for death. In David's case, the word couldn't have been more appropriate. After living a life largely characterized by strenuous physical activities such as running and fighting, and by strenuous mental activities such as leading and planning, David became tired. He needed some rest, and that's just what God gave him when He allowed David to draw his last breath.

The Bible Knowledge Commentary

The picturesque phrase *rested with his fathers* beautifully describes David's death and suggests that his activity did not cease forever. Indeed, the bodies of all believers who die simply "rest" until they are resurrected to live with God and serve Him eternally.[23]

It's Not the End of David's Story

There are two ways David's story has no end:

1. *His life didn't end.* Like anyone who chooses to have a relationship with God, David's life did not end with his physical death. He simply shed his aged, worn-out body to enter the glorious eternal presence of the living God. He had yearned to be closer to God's presence all of his life, a longing he had expressed in Psalm 27:4: "One thing I have desired of the LORD, that will I seek: That I may dwell in the house of the LORD all the days of my life, to behold the beauty of the LORD, and to inquire in His temple" (NKJV). When David had done all that God needed him to do on this earth, He fulfilled that longing.

Max Lucado

David doesn't want to chat. He doesn't desire a cup of coffee on the back porch. He doesn't ask for a meal or to spend an evening in God's house. He wants to move in with him . . . forever.[24]

2. *His legacy didn't end.* Everyone leaves a legacy, and fortunately many people leave legacies of faith similar to David's, in that they are characterized by faith in God and a vision for His purpose. But no one else has ever left or ever will leave a legacy as stunning as David's. Not only did he live a life that countless generations behind him could study in order to learn more about God, but he lived a life that was integrally linked to God's plan for sending His Son, Jesus Christ, to the earth to be the Savior of mankind.

- David was physically related to Jesus Christ through many generations of <u>children and grandchildren</u>. That physical relationship established Jesus' claim to David's throne as King of Israel.
- David's earthly kingdom was the forerunner for the eternal kingdom over which Jesus Christ will one day rule.

go to

children and grandchildren
Matthew 1

something to ponder

Thus, the story whose opening page featured a portrait of Hannah, the mother of the prophet who would anoint David as king of Israel, concludes with a page featuring a photograph of another woman, a very young one named Mary, who received an astonishing message from an angelic visitor hundreds of years after David died.

> LUKE 1:30–33 *Then the angel said to her, "Do not be afraid, Mary, for you have found favor with God. And behold, you will conceive in your womb and bring forth a Son, and shall call His name JESUS. He will be great, and will be called the Son of the Highest; and the Lord God will give Him the throne of His father David. And He will reign over the house of Jacob forever, and of His kingdom there will be no end." (NKJV)*

what others say

H. A. Ironside

We need to go remember that David was, after all, a typical character. In very large measure he typified our Lord Jesus Christ. His very name is significant. The word "David" means "The beloved," and God the Father said of our blessed Lord Jesus, "This is My beloved Son [this is My David] in whom I am well pleased" (Matthew 3:17).[25]

Chapter Wrap-Up

- David didn't allow God's "no" to build the temple cause him to become bitter or resentful. He fully submitted himself to God and threw his whole heart into making whatever preparations God would allow him to make.

- David recruited stonecutters, masons, carpenters, and craftsmen; gathered supplies; and organized maintenance of the temple as well as temple worship, adding a choir to the temple staff.

- David presented his last address in order to give the leaders and his son Solomon some final instructions. He related his desire to construct a temple for the Lord, reminded them of God's plan for the nation, and asked them to follow the Lord's commands. He handed over to Solomon the blueprints for the temple, which he said had come directly from God.

- As David began to become weak in his old age, his son Adonijah saw his chance to make a play for power over Israel.

- Nathan reported Adonijah's antics to Bathsheba, who went straight to David to remind him of his promise to make their son, Solomon, his successor.

- The news prompted David to take action. He directed the official appointment—and anointment—of Solomon as the next king of Israel.

- David gave Solomon some final instructions concerning unfinished business concerning Joab, Barzillai, and Shimei; then, having accomplished all on this earth that God had intended, David died.

Study Questions

1. What evidence is there that David didn't resent God's refusal to allow him to build the temple?

2. How had David accumulated the supplies and treasures for the temple?

3. What is one significant difference between temple worship and tabernacle worship?

4. Why did Adonijah feel entitled to his father's throne?

5. What did he do to indicate that he intended to become the next king?

6. How did Bathsheba respond to Nathan's news that Adonijah was planning a coup?

7. What is significant about David's death?

Appendix A - The Answers

1 Samuel 1–3

1. The tabernacle was significant to the ancient Hebrews because it was the center of worship and a symbol of God's presence among His people.

2. During a time when many people had stopped worshipping the way God had prescribed, Elkanah (who was from the priestly tribe of Levi) demonstrated obedience to God by taking his family to worship at the tabernacle at Shiloh.

3. Hannah's heart was heavy both because she was barren and because she had to endure the insults of Elkanah's very fertile other wife, Peninnah.

4. Hannah attempted to remedy her situation first, by pouring out her heart to the Lord in prayer, and second, by pledging her son to the service of the Lord.

5. The Nazirite vow is a dedication of one's self to the service of the Lord. Vow-takers were not to cut their hair, drink wine, or touch dead bodies during their tenure of service, which varies widely in length.

6. Eli saw Hannah's lips moving in silent prayer and sorely misjudged her actions by assuming she was drunk. After she convinced him otherwise, the priest assured her that God would answer her prayer.

7. When God blessed Hannah with a son, she kept her promise to give the boy over to the service of the Lord. She took him to the tabernacle, where she placed him in the care of Eli, and offered a beautiful song of praise and thanksgiving.

8. Eli's sons failed to lead worship with integrity and led the people astray. Their evil practices included taking more of the sacrifice for themselves than the law allowed, taking the meat before the fat had been burned, and despising the offerings of the Lord. Eli failed to rebuke them for their evil behavior.

9. As a young boy, Samuel wore a priestly garment and served alongside Eli, learning from him and taking on responsibilities in the tabernacle.

10. A turning point both in the life of Samuel and in the history of the people of Israel came during the middle of one night when Samuel was a young boy serving alongside Eli in the temple. God spoke to Samuel, giving him a prophecy about Eli and his sons. That distinguished Samuel as a prophet, and it marked the end of the period of the judges and the beginning of the period of prophets.

1 Samuel 4–7

1. The Philistines—fierce people and skilled archers who used iron chariots—controlled the territory in the coastal area of Canaan and almost constantly dominated the Israelites in battles over land. In fact, they had done so for such a long time that the Philistines had come to regard the people of Israel as their slaves.

2. The Israelites suffered great loss: four thousand men died in the battle.

3. Taking the Ark to the battlefront was an attempt to manipulate God. Had they acted with more wisdom, the Israelites would have sought God's will and asked for His protection.

4. Attempting to manipulate God is to focus on the outcome we desire and ignoring God's bigger and better plans. Some people try to manipulate God with their money, their actions, their rituals, and their prayers.

5. The Philistines heard the Israelites' loud celebration of the Ark's arrival and stormed the camp, killing thirty thousand soldiers—including both of Eli's sons—and capturing the Ark of God.

6. When Eli heard the news of the capture of the Ark and the deaths of his sons, he fell off his chair, broke his neck, and died, fulfilling the prophecy young Samuel had given him.

7. The capture of the Ark represented the departure of the glory of God and the removal of His continual provision and protection.

8. The Philistines placed the Ark in the temple of their pagan god, Dagon, which twice fell off its base in front of the Ark. They were then stricken with a painful plague, prompting them to decide to return the ark to the Israelites.

9. Seventy of the men in Beth Shemesh looked inside the Ark of the Covenant, prompting the Lord to put them to death because they had violated His clear instructions stating that no one except the priests would be allowed to touch the holy vessel.

10. When the Israelites finally decided to turn back to God, God gave them victory over their next battle against the Philistines, and Samuel marked the occasion by erecting a monument at Ebenezer.

1 Samuel 8–9

1. Samuel's sons, Joel and Abijah, were corrupt; they took bribes in dispensing justice.

2. The boys' behavior mattered to the Israelites because they needed to know that those who would likely replace Samuel as judge when he died would administer justice with integrity.

3. The Israelites requested a king, so they could be like the other nations.

4. Being ruled by a king would radically change Israel's form of government, and the request demonstrated disdain for Israel's position as God's chosen nation.

5. Seeking a new king demonstrated a lack of faith in God because He had promised Israel that He would do their fighting for them; if they would simply trust Him, He had said, they didn't need to worry about threats from their enemies:

6. The request to remove God from His place of leadership in their nation greatly distressed Samuel, who immediately prayed to the Lord for guidance.

7. Saul was out with his servant looking for his father's donkeys on a search that took longer than planned. When they heard God's prophet was in a nearby town, they decided to ask the prophet for direction. Samuel had been told by God to be expecting a visit from the man who was to become king, so he already had a special dinner prepared upon Saul's arrival.

1 Samuel 10–12

1. Anointing someone with oil was a physical picture of God's spiritual hand of guidance and power "pouring out" on the anointed person's life. Christians are anointed with the Holy Spirit when they put their faith in God.

2. Samuel told Saul he could expect to find men with news of the donkeys; men bearing goats, bread, and wine who were going to worship God; and a group of expressive prophets.

3. Saul's second anointing took place at the Philistine camp, where the Spirit of the Lord came upon Saul and he began to prophesy with the rest of the prophets.

4. Apparently spiritual fervor hadn't up to this point been one of Saul's most notable characteristics, as suggested by the fact that the people from his hometown were surprised to find him in the company of local prophets.

5. When Samuel prepared to introduce the people to their new king, Saul was nowhere to be found—until he was discovered hiding under the baggage.

6. The Israelites accepted Saul as their king after he scored military success against the Ammonites and their evil King Nahash.

7. God sent thunder and rain, as if He were putting His own exclamation mark into Samuel's sermon.

8. They were awestruck by the power over nature demonstrated by God through Samuel and begged for mercy after sinning against God by demanding a king.

1 Samuel 13–15

1. Faith in God and a desire to eliminate intruders from the land motivated Jonathan's desire to drive out the Philistines.

2. God's law forbade anyone but the high priest to present the burnt offering. This act highlighted Saul's disobedience, arrogance, and impatience.

3. Samuel scolded Saul and pointed out his foolishness, pronouncing God's judgment and foretelling of a new king, a better king, to come.

4. Saul used poor judgment in forbidding his men to eat because when the taboo was lifted, they were so famished that they began to slaughter and eat the livestock their enemy had left behind, disobeying God's law about what they could eat.

5. Jonathan nearly lost his life as a consequence of eating honey he found in the forest, an unintentional violation of his father's ban on eating.

6. Following the victory over the Philistines, Saul sinned once again by building an altar for sacrifices.

7. The king had been instructed to completely destroy all the Amalekite men, women, children, and livestock; however, Saul spared the Amalek king Agag and the best livestock.

8. Samuel scolded Saul and informed him that he had been rejected by God.

1 Samuel 16

1. Samuel was grieving because of the tragic rebellion of his friend and king, Saul.

2. The Lord sent Samuel to Bethlehem to anoint the next king of Israel.

3. Samuel questioned the Lord about his assignment because he was afraid that if Saul found out what he was doing, he might have him killed.

4. The Lord alleviated Samuel's fears by giving the prophet a very specific plan of action. Further, God gave Samuel an additional reason to go to Bethlehem: to administer the sacrifice. That would not have been considered suspicious behavior on the part of the priest.

5. Jesse's oldest son, Eliab, would have been the most likely candidate for king not only because he was the firstborn, but also because he had an impressive military record.

6. Samuel used only the Lord's guidance in evaluating Jesse's sons. (And the Lord based *His* choice on the condition of David's heart, not on his appearance.)

7. Samuel poured the oil from a fragile flask (symbolizing impermanence and weakness) when he anointed Saul; he used a durable horn (symbolizing permanence and power) when he anointed David.

8. After David was anointed, he went right back to the sheepfold to wait until God told him what to do next.

9. After David was anointed, the Holy Spirit's presence departed from Saul's life, causing him torment and unrest.

10. David was summoned to King Saul's court to sooth the king's troubled spirit with his music.

1 Samuel 17

1. Goliath was an arrogant, heavily armed giant from Gath.

2. The Philistines and Israelites were preparing to wage a representative battle, meaning the victory would be secured by the winner of a two-person combat.

3. None of the Israelites volunteered to serve as Israel's champion for several possible reasons. Saul was a poor leader and lacked the skills to motivate his men into action; they were intimidated by the giant's size and armament, and they feared losing because the consequences would mean subservience to the Philistines.

4. David went to the Valley of Elah because Jesse sent him there to take a fresh supply of provisions to his brothers, offer a gift of ten cheeses to their commander, find out about his oldest boys' well-being; and return with a token of their safety.

5. David persuaded Saul to let him fight Goliath by stating that he had the skill—after all, he had killed wild animals in the past—and by acknowledging that the Lord would protect him.

6. David refused to take Saul's armor because the older man's garb wouldn't have fit David, who wasn't accustomed to wearing a soldier's gear anyway. Further, he didn't need it because he planned to use a slingshot, which would allow

him to attack the giant from a distance. Most important, he knew he was not fighting a physical battle, so he wouldn't need physical armor.

7. David killed Goliath by striking him between the eyes with the first of five smooth stones he had gathered to use in his sling.

8. Saul wanted to know more about the one who had slain the giant.

1 Samuel 18

1. As a prince, Jonathan was of a higher social standing than David; as heir apparent to Saul's throne—and with a less-than-ideal relationship with his father—Jonathan could have felt threatened by anyone who might attempt to succeed him; and as a warrior, Jonathan could have been jealous of the celebrity of David's success.

2. The two key ingredients of a covenant are commitment to the protection, provision, and well-being of the other party; and permanence, in that the mutual affiliation is everlasting.

3. In a gesture of humility and devotion, Jonathan presented David with his own robe, sword, bow, and belt, expressing a sense of protection and acknowledging that he knew David would become the next king.

4. David achieved great success as a warrior for King Saul's army.

5. The song of praise the women of Israel sang to celebrate David's accomplishments made Saul jealous and angry, and sparked a desire in him to kill the young warrior.

6. First, Saul tried (twice) to kill David with a spear while he played music for the king; second, he tried to have David killed on the battlefield; third, he devised a deceitful plan that would get David killed while securing the bride price Saul set in exchange for allowing David to marry one of his daughters.

7. Each time, the Lord protected David from death.

1 Samuel 19–24

1. Jonathan's friendship with David placed Jonathan in danger because he was deliberately disobeying his father's orders and boldly aligning himself with the person his father saw as his biggest threat. Siding with David against Saul easily could have been a lethal move for the son of such a jealous, hateful, unstable man.

2. When Saul's men ambushed David at his own house, David's wife, Michal, helped David escape through a window, then stuffed a household idol under the covers and placed a thatch of goat's hair on the pillow to make it look like her husband was sleeping. By the time Saul's servants caught on to the ploy, David had made a run for Samuel's hometown, Ramah.

3. Saul's men arrived at Ramah to find Samuel and the prophets in the middle of a session of praise and worship. Paralyzed by the power of the Holy Spirit, they were compelled to join the prophets' chorus of praise.

4. David lied to the chief priest about his reason for being there, and he took sacred bread for his provisions.

5. David sought refuge from Saul in Gath, Goliath's hometown, because, considering Saul's rage against David, his determination to have David killed, and the number of men at Saul's disposal, his homeland wasn't looking to be a very safe place. David must have figured he'd be just as safe—maybe even safer—in a place where Saul and his men were not welcome.

6. The king there turned him away, stating that they had enough crazy people of their own to contend with.

7. The four hundred people who joined David when he sought refuge in the caves of Adullam were family members and people described as being in distress and in debt.

8. Saul ordered the other priests—eighty-six in all, along with their families and all the livestock—to be slain as punishment for what he mistakenly believed, in his paranoia, to be their part in conspiring with David against him.

9. As David fled from Saul and his men, he was practicing and polishing his leadership skills as he took his place at the helm of the band of men who had joined him at Adullam.

10. David spared Saul's life because he honored him as God's anointed king of Israel and because he understood that when to end Saul's reign—and life—was in God's hands, not his.

1 Samuel 25

1. Samuel had ushered in the new form of government, the monarchy, and anointed their first king; established the first school of prophets; organized various procedures for the tabernacle, systems that would later be used in the temple; and collected some of the treasures that would later be placed in the temple of David.

2. After mourning the loss of his mentor and friend, David and his entourage retreated into the wilderness in Maon, where they led a rough and nomadic existence.

3. David was excited to hear of the nearby sheep-shearing because it was a festive time punctuated by merriment, celebration, and feasts, and would give he and his hungry men a welcome opportunity to enjoy some good food.

4. David expected Nabal to offer hospitality as a thanks for the protection he and his men had provided Nabal's family and flocks.

5. David ordered four hundred of his men to take up arms and prepare to kill Nabal as well as every member of his household—an overreaction to the circumstances, to put it mildly.

6. Abigail was known to be wise and gracious; Nabal was known to be a fool.

7. Abigail defused David's anger, persuaded him to call off the attack, shifted his focus back on God, and impressed the king-to-be with her beauty and wisdom.

8. Abigail couldn't tell Nabal the news that night because he was drunk.

9. When David heard that Nabal had died, he praised God for intervening and avenging David. Then he asked Abigail to marry him.

1 Samuel 26–31; 1 Chronicles 10

1. David moved into Philistine territory because he thought he and his men would be safe from Saul and his army there.

2. During his stay in the enemy's land, fear and deceitfulness replaced his usual faith and integrity.

3. Saul was feeling especially desperate because the Philistines were closing in and he felt he had nowhere to turn for guidance since Samuel was dead and God was not speaking to him.

4. The Witch of Endor was surprised by Samuel's appearance.

5. Samuel told Saul that he and his sons would die at the hands of the Philistines the next day.

6. Finding that the Philistines had ransacked his settlement at Ziklag, taken his livestock, and captured his family and friends, causing his followers to consider mutiny, thrust David into despair.

7. David turned to the Lord, who strengthened him and told him what to next.

8. Saul asked his armorbearer to kill him to avoid the possibility of being found alive and being tortured by the Philistines.

9. The Philistines who found Saul cut off his head and stripped off his armor. They put his armor in the temple of the goddess Ashtoreth, fastened his body to the wall of Beth Shan, on the eastern slopes of Mount Gilboa overlooking the Jordan Valley, and put his head in the temple of Dagon.

10. After Saul's death, the people of Jabesh Gilead—whom Saul had rescued from the Ammonites forty years earlier—were so upset by what the Philistines had done to Saul that they traveled by night to retrieve the bodies of Saul and his sons. They burned the bodies, buried the bones, then fasted seven days.

2 Samuel 1–5, 1 Chronicles 11

1. When Saul died, David didn't immediately move to replace him as king of Israel because God told him to go to Judah instead.

2. Saul's son Ishbosheth was a weak and passive ruler; it was Saul's general, Abner, who wielded the power in the leadership of Israel.

3. During his reign as king of Judah, David formalized his break from his ungodly alliance with the Philistines; established friendship with the people of Jabesh Gilead, subsequently earning support from northern Israel; and began to position himself as Saul's replacement.

4. Conflict arose between the two when Abner took Rizpah, one of Saul's concubines, as his own. This indicated he thought he would be king. When Ishbosheth questioned his motives, Abner became angry and switched his loyalty, telling David he would help him secure Saul's kingdom.

5. Joab reacted to the agreement between Abner and David by having Abner killed.

6. Ishbosheth was killed by Benjamite assassins.

7. The people of Israel confirmed David's installation as king with a third anointing.

8. David's first action as king of Israel was to seize control of Jerusalem to establish his capital there.

2 Samuel 6, 1 Chronicles 13–16

1. David wanted to move the Ark of the Covenant to Jerusalem to restore worship as a focal point of the nation's attention.

2. The Ark was to be moved by Koathites, who were to carry it on their shoulders by using the specially designated poles and rods. The Ark was never to be transported on a cart, and, above all, it was never to be touched by human hands. The first attempt at moving the Ark erred on all points: Uzzah and Ahio were not Koathites; they carried the Ark on a cart instead of with the poles, and Uzzah touched it when the oxen stumbled and nearly jarred it off the cart.

3. Uzzah died and the mission to move the Ark was halted.

4. David showed his delight that the Ark was finally brought into Jerusalem by donning the priestly garments and dancing for joy.

5. Michal accused David of being unkingly, undignified, and even immodest; completely missing the fact that he had been expressing all-out praise and worship of God.

6. The men in Michal's life—including her father and David—had not treated her with much respect or consideration. Instead of allowing the disappointments and sorrows to draw her closer to God, she allowed them to drive her far away from Him, making her bitter and miserable.

7. David responded to Michal's rebuke by letting her know in no uncertain terms that the Lord, not Michal, was his audience; that he was acting as the Lord's chosen ruler of Israel, and that he would undergo even more indignities in his service to the Lord.

2 Samuel 7; 1 Chronicles 17

1. David wanted to build a temple for the Lord after comparing his magnificent dwelling with the tabernacle.

2. Nathan initially approved of David's idea to build a temple.

3. The Lord let David know He had different plans for the king by giving His message to Nathan later that night.

4. The Lord told David He did not need him to build a temple because, first of all, He would choose who would build a temple, if there was to be one; second, He did not need a temple; and third, the tabernacle had perfectly suited His plans in the past.

5. The Lord said He would allow a temple to be built—but by David's heir, not by David. He also promised to make David the originator of an everlasting dynasty.

6. The Davidic Covenant was unconditional; it would be fulfilled regardless of the actions of David or anyone else.

7. The Davidic Covenant pointed to the coming Messiah.

8. David responded to the Lord's promise with humility and praise.

2 Samuel 8–10; 1 Chronicles 18–21

1. David and the Israelites defeated and subdued the Philistines, the Moabites, the Edomites, and the Aramaeans.

2. David dedicated the spoils of war to the service of the Lord, and they were later placed in the treasury of the temple by his son Solomon.

3. David asked whether Jonathan still had any living relatives because he wanted to fulfill his covenant promise to show kindness to his family.

4. Mephibosheth's lameness did not concern David in the least.

5. David promised Mephibosheth kindness, restoration of his grandfather, Saul's estate, and a permanent place setting at the royal table.

6. The grace David showed Mephibosheth serves as an example of the grace God shows sinners.

7. The inability of Mephibosheth to do anything to earn David's kindness, or to repay it, illustrates the condition of sinners' inability to earn God's kindness, or to repay it.

8. King Nahash humiliated David's ambassadors by shaving off half of their beards and trimming their robes to an indecent length, touching off war with the hostile act.

9. David responded to the insult first by seeing to the needs of the humiliated messengers, then by fighting and defeating Nahash and the Ammonites.

2 Samuel 11

1. Some possible reasons David may have stayed behind when the rest of his men were off at war include: old age/diminishing stamina, fatigue, or even a spoiled reluctance to endure the hardships of war.

2. David passed up several opportunities to turn away from sin. For example, he could have chosen to be in the right place at the right time—off at battle instead of staying behind; he could have averted his eyes and walked back inside when he saw his neighbor bathing instead of stopping and admiring her beauty; he could have resisted the impulse to ask about her; he could have refused to send his messengers to fetch Bathsheba; and he could have confessed his crime and begged mercy and forgiveness rather than plotting Uriah's death.

3. Bible commentators' assessments of Bathsheba's role in the affair range from casting her as an evil seductress to casting her as an innocent victim. Most likely, she falls somewhere in between the two extremes, possibly closer to the category of "innocent victim" because of her inability to refuse a man as powerful as the king.

4. Jesus taught that sin involves more than the ungodly action itself; it begins with the intent or desire to do wrong: "But I say to you that whoever looks at a woman to lust for her has already committed adultery with her in his heart" (Matthew 5:27–28 NKJV).

5. The news of the coming birth triggered despair rather than celebration because the couple was not married; in fact, each partner was married to another person (or in David's case, persons), and the crime of adultery was to be punished with death, according to the Law.

6. David brought Uriah home hoping he would sleep with Bathsheba and create the impression that he was the baby's father.

7. Uriah's integrity—his refusal to sleep indoors with his wife while his fellow soldiers were enduring the hardships of battle—derailed David's plans.

8. David instructed Joab to put Uriah in the most dangerous zone of combat where he would be certain to be killed.

9. David's eagerness and "fast talking" to set Joab's conscience at ease regarding his part in the mur-

der hints at the possibility that David might have begun to feel some guilt about his crime.

10. David married Bathsheba before the child was born in an effort to make it look as if the child had been conceived in legitimacy.

2 Samuel 12

1. David's prayer during that time—recorded in Psalm 32:3–4—reveals that David was miserable; he may have created the impression that things were fine, but his guilt had made him spiritually, emotionally, and physically ill.

2. Nathan presented God's message to David by means of a parable and by using a subject matter that would have been very familiar to David: sheep.

3. The story Nathan told infuriated David, even though he hadn't yet made the connection that the parable was about him. He was angered by the injustice he saw in the story, and pronounced a severe judgment against the crime and against the condition of the thief's heart.

4. In going over the list of the ways He had provided for David in the past, God seemed to be pointing to greed and covetousness as the roots of David's sins.

5. David's son would die. His private sins would bear public—and painful—penalties. Further, although nothing would change concerning God's earlier promises to David and his descendants, the king's household would, from that point on, be marked by violence and conflict.

6. Rather than trying to make excuses for his sins, Gods words to David pierced the king's heart, compelling him to immediately confess his guilt and acknowledge that he had sinned against the Lord.

7. David's sincere sorrow is plain to see in the psalms he is believed to have composed during this time: Psalms 32:1–11; 51:1–19; and 103:1–22.

8. God immediately and permanently forgave David of his sins; however, He allowed David to experience the consequences, both as a way of disciplining His beloved son, and as a way of preserving His reputation.

9. God blessed David by allowing him to enjoy a loving relationship with Bathsheba; by giving the couple a son, Solomon; by showing favor to that son; and by restoring David as a political victor.

2 Samuel 13–18

1. David had a hand in Amnon's crime against Tamar by setting a bad example concerning women, by neglecting to protect Tamar, and by failing to instill proper values in Amnon.

2. When David discovered what had happened to Tamar, he did nothing. Neither did Absalom, at least for two years.

3. At a sheepshearing celebration, Absalom had Amnon murdered to avenge his sister's rape.

4. David seemed to be too lax with Amnon since he failed to discipline him for his crime against Tamar, and he seemed to be too harsh with Absalom, whom he never fully forgave for the murder of Amnon.

5. Absalom tried to get Joab's attention in order to persuade him to arrange a meeting with his father by setting his barley fields on fire.

6. Absalom positioned himself for a takeover by getting out among the people of Israel and helping them solve their problems and by drumming up support in Hebron, David's homeland.

7. David left Jerusalem to prevent his beloved city from being destroyed in the power struggle.

8. David reacted to Absalom's death by expressing his wish that he could have died in Absalom's place and by lamenting for his son.

2 Samuel 19–20

1. David responded to Absalom's death by secluding himself from the people.

2. Joab scolded David for failing to get back to the business of running the country. If David didn't go out in the city gate to thank the people, Joab said, he would risk even more infighting and rebellion.

3. On his way back to Jerusalem, David met Shimei, Mephibosheth, and Barzillai.

4. Mephibosheth told David his loyalty had never failed.

5. There a famine in the land because Saul had broken a vow with the Gibeonites.

6. The census was sinful because it indicated that David was trusting numbers more than God.

David's Last Days

1. David apparently didn't resent God's refusal to allow him to build the temple because he threw himself into making whatever preparations God did allow him to make.

2. David accumulated the supplies and treasures for the temple as spoils of war and as gifts from leaders of neighboring nations.

3. One significant difference between temple worship and tabernacle worship is the implementation of a permanent choir.

4. Adonijah felt entitled to his father's throne because he was David's oldest living son.

5. Adonijah orchestrated an inaugural celebration to announce his intentions to become the next king.

6. Bathsheba responded to Nathan's news that Adonijah was planning a coup by immediately taking her concerns to David and reminding him of his responsibility to name his successor.

7. The Bible describes David's death as "rest," and suggests that he died only after he had accomplished all that God intended for him to do. David's death wasn't permanent; he would live eternally with his heavenly Father, whom he loved so much. Further, his reign would never end—in accordance with God's promises to make his an everlasting kingdom through his distant offspring, Jesus Christ, the Savior of the world.

Appendix B - The Experts

Alter, Robert—professor of Hebrew and comparative literature and widely respected Bible translator.

Arthur, Kay—founder of Precept Ministries and the author of many books including *Lord, I Need Grace to Make It.*

Brestin, Dee—author of Bible study guides and books on women's issues.

Buchanan, Mark—pastor and writer living in Canada who is a contributor to *Christianity Today* and the author of *Things Unseen: Living in Light of Forever.*

Castleman, Robbie—assistant professor of biblical studies at John Brown University; author of numerous study guides.

Clarke, Adam—a British Methodist theologian most widely known for writing commentaries on the Bible in the early 1800s.

Coffman, James Burton—prolific Bible scholar, author, preacher, and teacher who was considered one of the most influential figures among Churches of Christ until his death in 2006.

Constable, Thomas L.—Bible scholar, professor of Bible exposition at Dallas Theological Seminary, pastor, and speaker who has ministered in nearly three dozen countries and written commentaries on every book of the Bible.

Copenhaver, Martin B.—pastor, Bible scholar, and author whose books include *To Begin at the Beginning: An Introduction to the Christian Faith.*

Deffinbaugh, Robert L.—a graduate of Dallas Theological Seminary; a Bible teacher who has contributed a great many of his Bible study series to the Web site Bible.org.

George, Elizabeth—popular author, teacher, and speaker at women's events.

Gichon, Mordechai—expert in the military history, geology, and archaeology of ancient Israel

Gill, John—biblical scholar and preacher during the early 1700s who pastored a church that later became the Metropolitan Tabernacle, which was led by Charles Spurgeon.

Graham, Billy—best-selling author and evangelist who has led millions of people to Christ through his crusades on every continent and through his radio and television messages.

Guzik, David—the director of Calvary Chapel Bible College Germany, near Siegen, Germany who is widely known for his online study materials and Bible commentaries.

Henry, Matthew—English clergyman who lived from 1662 to 1714, who is most noted for his commentary of the Bible.

Herzog, Chaim—former president of Israel whose illustrious career in Israel's military also included posts as director of military intelligence, military governor of the West Bank, and Israel's ambassador to the United Nations.

Higgs, Liz Curtis—popular author and award-winning speaker who encourages Christian women with her humor and insight.

Hillman, Os—internationally recognized speaker on the subject of faith at work. He is founder and president of Marketplace Leaders, and is the author of eleven books and a daily workplace email devotional.

Indermark, John—pastor and writer whose books include *Neglected Voices* and *Genesis of Grace.*

Ironside, H. A.—pastor of Moody Memorial Church in Chicago, Illinois, for many years.

Jamieson, Robert—co-author of the 1871 Jamieson-Fausset-Brown commentary on the Bible.

Janssen, Al—senior director of resource development at Focus on the Family, who has written, co-written and edited numerous books and articles.

Kaufman, Matt—freelance writer, a contributing editor to *Citizen* magazine, and a former editor of *Boundless* webzine.

Kroll, Woodrow—president and senior Bible teacher for the international media ministry Back to the Bible.

LaHaye, Tim—best-selling author of the *Left Behind* series, founder and president of Family Life Seminars.

Lucado, Max—pastor of Oak Hills Church of Christ in San Antonio, Texas, and the author of several best-selling books.

MacArthur, John—pastor of Grace Community Church, founder of The Masters' Seminary, host of *Grace to You* radio program.

McGee, J. Vernon—popular radio Bible teacher of 1980s–1990s whose commentaries aired on his program, *Thru the Bible Radio*, as well as in print.

McKenzie, Steven L.—professor of Hebrew Bible at Rhodes College and author of many books on Bible studies, including *The Hebrew Bible Today.*

Mehl, Ron—pastor of a large congregation in Beaverton, Oregon, until he died of leukemia in 2003. His books include the Gold Medallion winners *God Works the Night Shift* and *Just in Case I Can't Be There.*

Moore, Beth—writer and teacher of best-selling Bible studies whose public speaking engagements carry her all over the world. Her books include *Things Pondered, A Heart Like His,* and *Praying God's Word.*

Pentecost, J. Dwight—retired professor, Dallas Theological Seminary, and author of several books.

Phillips, Richard D.—retired combat officer for the United States Army who serves as a management consultant and is a frequent speaker on leadership and organization.

Rainey, Barbara—wife, mother of six, and grandmother of seven who has coauthored numerous books with her husband, Dennis, president of FamilyLife.

Rainey, Dennis—president and cofounder of FamilyLife (a division of Campus Crusade for Christ) and a graduate of Dallas Theological Seminary who since 1976 has overseen the rapid growth of FamilyLife Conferences on marriage and parenting. He is the daily host of the nationally syndicated radio program *FamilyLife Today.*

Redpath, Alan—Bible scholar and author who was pastor of several churches in England and senior minister of Moody Memorial Church in Chicago.

Reid, David R.—with an academic background that includes both engineering and theology, Dr. Reid is a former faculty member at Emmaus Bible College in Dubuque, Iowa. He is the author of the bimonthly publication, *Devotions for Growing Christians,* and the producer of the radio program *Talks for Growing Christians.*

Richards, Sue—coauthor of best-selling Zondervan *Teen Study Bible.*

Roe, Robert H.—a pastor at Peninsula Bible Church in Palo Alto, California, who has written numerous articles and Bible commentaries.

Rothschild, Jennifer—popular women's Bible study teacher, author, and speaker/worship leader who is also an accomplished songwriter and recording artist and founder of the online magazine *WomensMinistry.NET.*

Spangler, Ann—author of several best-selling books including, *She Who Laughs, Lasts!* and *Don't Stop Laughing Now!*

Spurgeon, Charles H.—called the "prince of preachers," his sermons held throngs spellbound at the Metropolitan Tabernacle in London in the nineteenth century and now in written form.

Stanley, Charles—senior pastor of the twelve-thousand-member First Baptist Church of Atlanta and a prolific author.

Swindoll, Charles—former pastor of the First Evangelical Free Church in Fullerton, California, and president of the Dallas Theological Seminary in Dallas, Texas. He is the author of many best-selling books.

Vawter, John—pastor who has served as president of Western Seminary and Phoenix Seminary. He is the author of *Uncommon Graces,* nominated for the Gold Medallion Book Award, and founder with his wife, Susan, of the "You're Not Alone" ministry.

Warren, Rick—founding pastor of Saddleback Church in Lake Forest, California, and author of the best-selling books *The Purpose-Driven Church* and *The Purpose-Driven Life.*

Wesley, John—eithteenth-century clergyman and Christian theologian who was an early leader in the Methodist movement.

Wiersbe, Warren—one of the evangelical world's most respected Bible teachers, author of more than one hundred books, and former director of *Back to the Bible,* a radio ministry.

Willimon, William—a bishop in the United Methodist Church in the USA who is best known as a theologian, writer, former Dean of the Chapel at Duke University, and as one of America's best-known preachers. He has written more than fifty books and was named in a 1996 Baylor University survey along with Billy Graham as one of the Twelve Most Effective Preachers in the English-speaking world.

Youngblood, Ronald—professor of Old Testament and Hebrew emeritus, Bethel Seminary San Diego, and author of numerous books.

Endnotes

1 Samuel 1–3

1. Larry Richards, *The Bible: God's Word for the Biblically Inept* (Lancaster, PA: Starburst, 1998), 31.

2. Matthew Henry, *Matthew Henry's Commentary on the Whole Bible* (Peabody, MA: Hendrickson, 1991), 381.

3. J. I. Packer, Merrill C. Tenney, William White Jr., *The Bible Almanac* (Nashville: Nelson, 1980), 441.

4. Robert Alter, *The David Story* (New York: Norton, 1999), 4.

5. Adam Clarke, *Adam Clarke Commentary*, www.studylight.org.

6. Henry, *Matthew Henry's Commentary*, 382.

7. Alter, *David Story*, 9.

8. Clarke, *Adam Clarke Commentary*.

9. Tim LaHaye, *Prophecy Study Bible* (Chattanooga, TN: AMG, 2000), 306.

10. Henry, *Matthew Henry's Commentary*, 386.

1 Samuel 4–7

1. J. Vernon McGee, *Thru the Bible with J. Vernon McGee* (Pasadena, CA: Thru the Bible Radio, 1982), 132.

2. J. I. Packer, Merrill C. Tenney, William White, Jr., *The Bible Almanac* (Nashville: Nelson, 1980), 302.

3. David Guzik, *David Guzik's Commentaries on the Bible*, www.studylight.org.

4. Kay and David Arthur, *Desiring God's Own Heart* (Eugene, OR: Harvest House, 1997), 21.

5. Robert D. D. Jamieson, *Jamieson-Faussett-Brown Commentary*, www.studylight.org.

6. Matthew Henry, *Matthew Henry's Commentary on the Whole Bible* (Peabody, MA: Hendrickson, 1991) 391.

7. John MacArthur, "The Purpose of My Life: Glory," www.biblebb.com.

8. Charles Spurgeon, "Ebenezer!" www.biblebb.com.

1 Samuel 8–9

1. Richard D. Phillips, *The Heart of an Executive* (New York: Galilee/Doubleday, 1999) 16.

2. Ibid.

3. John Wesley, "Wesley's Explanatory Notes," www.studylight.org.

4. *The King James Study Bible for Women* (Nashville: Nelson, 2003), 466.

5. J. Vernon McGee, *Thru the Bible with J. Vernon McGee*, vol. 2 (Pasadena, CA: Thru the Bible Radio, 1982), 139.

6. Robert Alter, *The David Story* (New York: Norton, 1999), 47.

1 Samuel 10–12

1. Matthew Henry, *Matthew Henry's Commentary on the Whole Bible* (Peabody, MA: Hendrickson, 1991), 399.

2. David Guzik, *David Guzik's Commentaries on the Bible*, www.studylight.org.

3. Henry, *Matthew Henry's Commentary*, 400.

4. Richard D. Phillips, *The Heart of an Executive* (New York: Galilee/Doubleday, 1999), 22.

5. *The King James Study Bible for Women* (Nashville: Nelson, 2003), 469.

6. Robert Alter, *The David Story* (New York: Norton, 1999), 59.

1 Samuel 13–15

1. Bob Deffinbaugh, "A Study of 1 Samuel," www.bible.org.

2. Elizabeth George, *A Woman's Walk with God* (Eugene, OR: Harvest House, 2000), 98.

3. *Halley's Bible Handbook* (Grand Rapids, MI: Zondervan, 1965), 135.

4. Adam Clarke, *Adam Clarke Commentary*, www.studylight.org.

5. Henry, *Matthew Henry's Commentary*, 405.

6. Robert Alter, *The David Story* (New York: Norton, 1999), 80.

7. Ibid, 89.

8. Beth Moore, *A Heart Like His* (Nashville: Lifeway, 1996) 17.

9. Clarke, *Adam Clarke Commentary*.

10. Os Hillman, "The Dangers of Overcontrol," www.MarketplaceLeaders.org.

1 Samuel 16

1. Max Lucado, *Come Thirsty* (Nashville: W Publishing, 2004), 120.

2. Matthew Henry, *Matthew Henry's Commentary on the Whole Bible* (Peabody, MA: Hendrickson, 1991), 410.

3. Larry Richards, *The Bible: God's Word for the Biblically Inept* (Lancaster, PA: Starburst, 1998), 35.

4. Adam Clarke, *Adam Clarke Commentary*, www.studylight.org.

5. Charles Swindoll, *David: A Man of Passion & Destiny* (Nashville: W Publishing, 1997), 27.

6. Henry, *Matthew Henry's Commentary*, 411.

7. Beth Moore, *A Heart Like His* (Nashville: Lifeway, 1996), 23.

1 Samuel 17

1. Richard D. Phillips, *The Heart of an Executive* (New York, Galilee/Doubleday, 1999), 49.

2. Charles Swindoll, *David: A Man of Passion & Destiny* (Nashville: W Publishing, 1997), 38.

3. Beth Moore, *A Heart Like His* (Nashville: Lifeway, 1996), 28.

4. Charles Spurgeon, *Spurgeon Collection of Sermons*, www.biblebb.com.

5. Alan Redpath, *The Making of a Man of God* (Grand Rapids, MI: Revell, 1962/1990), 34.

6. David Guzik, *David Guzik's Commentaries on the Bible*, www.studylight.org.

1 Samuel 18

1. Dee Brestin, *The Friendships of Women* (Colorado Springs: Cook, 1997), 115.

2. Charles Swindoll, *David: A Man of Passion & Destiny* (Nashville: W Publishing, 1997), 55.

3. Al Janssen, "The Covenant Marriage," excerpted from *The Marriage Masterpiece*, www.family.org.

4. Liz Curtis Higgs, *Bad Girls of the Bible* (Colorado Springs: Waterbrook, 1999), 200.

5. Sue and Larry Richards, *Every Woman in the Bible* (Nashville: Nelson, 1999), 111.

1 Samuel 19–24

1. Liz Curtis Higgs, *Bad Girls of the Bible* (Colorado Springs: Waterbrook, 1999), 202.

2. Burton Coffman, *Burton Coffman Commentary*, www.studylight.org.

3. Ronald Youngblood, "Jonathan and David," www.Moodymagazine.com.

4. David Guzik, *David Guzik's Commentaries on the Bible*, www.studylight.org.

5. John Gill, *John Gill's Exposition of the Entire Bible*, www.studylight.org.

6. Alan Redpath, *The Making of a Man of God* (Grand Rapids, MI: Revell, 1962/1990), 97.

1 Samuel 25

1. John Indermark, *Neglected Voices* (Nashville: Upper Room, 1999), 23.

2. Jennifer Rothschild, *Walking by Faith: Lessons Learned in the Dark* (Nashville: Lifeway, 2003), 91.

3. Ann Spangler, *Women of the Bible* (Grand Rapids, MI: Zondervan, 2002), 94.

4. Rick Warren, *The Purpose Driven Life* (Grand Rapids, MI: Zondervan, 2002), 135.

5. John Vawter, *Uncommon Graces* (Colorado Springs: NavPress, 1998), 156.

6. Kathy Collard Miller and D. Larry Miller, *What's in the Bible for Couples* (Lancaster, PA: Starburst, 2001), 19.

7. Sue and Larry Richards, *Every Woman in the Bible* (Nashville: Nelson, 1999), 47.

8. Ibid.

1 Samuel 26–31; 1 Chronicles 10

1. Matthew Henry, *Matthew Henry's Commentary on the Whole Bible* (Peabody, MA: Hendrickson, 1991) 429.

2. Alan Redpath, *The Making of a Man of God* (Grand Rapids, MI: Revell, 1962/1990) 139.

3. Ibid., 140.

4. Charles Swindoll, *David: A Man of Passion & Destiny* (Nashville: W Publishing, 1997), 113.

5. Burton Coffman, *Burton Coffman Commentary*, www.Studylight.org.

6. Beth Moore, *A Heart Like His* (Nashville: Lifeway, 1996), 77.

7. David Guzik, *David Guzik's Commentaries on the Bible*, www.studylight.org.

8. Max Lucado, *The Great House of God* (Dallas: Word, 1997), 13.

9. *International Bible Encyclopedia*, www.studylight.org.

2 Samuel 1–5; 1 Chronicles 11

1. Robert Alter, *The David Story* (New York: Norton, 1999), 197.

2. Matthew Henry, *Matthew Henry's Commentary on the Whole Bible* (Peabody, MA: Hendrickson, 1991), 439.

3. John F. Walvoord and Roy B. Zuck, eds., *The Bible Knowledge Commentary*, (Colorado Springs: Victor/Cook, 2004), 458.

4. Richard D. Phillips, *The Heart of an Executive* (New York: Galilee/Doubleday, 1999), 171–72.

5. Burton Coffman, *Burton Coffman Commentary*, www.Studylight.org.

6. Phillips, *Heart of an Executive*, 178.

7. Alfred J. Kolatch, *The Jewish Book of Why* (New York: Penguin/Compass, 2000), 283–284.

8. Chaim Herzog and Mordechai Gichon, *Battles of the Bible* (London: Greenhill Books, 1997), 101.

9. Charles Swindoll, *David: A Man of Passion & Destiny* (Nashville: W Publishing, 1997), 137.

2 Samuel 6; 1 Chronicles 13–16

1. Charles Swindoll, *David: A Man of Passion & Destiny* (Nashville: W Publishing, 1997), 137.

2. Mark Buchanan, "Dance of the God-Struck," www.christianitytoday.com.

3. Kay and David Arthur, *Desiring God's Own Heart* (Eugene, OR: Harvest House, 1997) 80.

4. Max Lucado, *Just Like Jesus* (Nashville: Word, 1998), 82.

5. Rick Warren, *The Purpose Driven Life* (Grand Rapids, MI: Zondervan, 2002), 77.

6. Lucado, *Just Like Jesus*, 81.

7. Liz Curtis Higgs, *Bad Girls of the Bible* (Colorado Springs: Waterbrook, 1999), 209.

8. Ann Spangler, *Women of the Bible* (Grand Rapids, MI: Zondervan, 2002), 91.

9. Mark Buchanan, "Dance of the God-Struck," www.christianitytoday.com.

10. Higgs, *Bad Girls*, 210.

2 Samuel 7; 1 Chronicles 17

1. Matthew Henry, *Matthew Henry's Commentary on the Whole Bible* (Peabody, MA: Hendrickson, 1991), 447.

2. Larry Richards, *The Bible: God's Word for the Biblically Inept* (Lancaster, PA: Starburst, 1998), 65.

3. Tim LaHaye, *Prophecy Study Bible* (Chattanooga, TN: AMG, 2000), 348.

4. J. Dwight Pentecost, *Things to Come* (Grand Rapids, MI: Academie Books/Zondervan, 1958), 104.

5. Charles Swindoll, *David: A Man of Passion & Destiny* (Nashville: W Publishing, 1997), 162.

6. John MacArthur, "The Program of Prayer: The Kingdom Come," www.biblebb.com.

7. Thomas L. Constable, *Bible Study Notes*, www.soniclight.com.

8. Alan Redpath, *The Making of a Man of God* (Grand Rapids, MI: Revell, 1962/1990), 209.

9. John Wesley, "Wesley's Explanatory Notes," www.studylight.org.

10. Charles Stanley, *How to Listen to God* (Nashville: Nelson, 1985), 94.

11. Warren Wiersbe, "The Purpose of Prayer—How to Pray When God Changes Your Plans," www.songtime.com.

12. Ibid.

13. John F. Walvoord and Roy B. Zuck, *The Bible Knowledge Commentary* (Colorado Springs: Victor/Cook, 2004), 464.

14. Robbie Castleman, *King David: Trusting God for a Lifetime* (Colorado Springs: Waterbrook, 1981), 9.

2 Samuel 8–10; 1 Chronicles 18–21

1. Robbie Castleman, *King David: Trusting God for a Lifetime* (Colorado Springs: Waterbrook, 1981), 15.

2. Alan Redpath, *The Making of a Man of God* (Grand Rapids, MI: Revell, 1962/1990), 213.

3. Beth Moore, *A Heart Like His* (Nashville: Lifeway, 1996), 119.

4. John F. Walvoord and Roy B. Zuck, *The Bible Knowledge Commentary* (Colorado Springs: Victor/Cook, 2004), 465.

5. *The Ryrie Study Bible*, New International Version (Chicago: Moody, 1986), 393.

6. John Vawter, *Uncommon Graces* (Colorado Springs: NavPress, 1998), 45.

7. Burton Coffman, "Burton Coffman Commentary," www.studylight.org.

8. Charles Spurgeon, "Spurgeon's Morning and Evening Devotionals," www.studylight.org.

9. Ibid.

10. J. I. Packer, Merrill C. Tenney, William White, Jr., *The Bible Almanac* (Nashville: Nelson, 1980), 312.

11. *Easton's Bible Dictionary*, www.studylight.org.

12. Chaim Herzog and Mordechai Gichon, *Battles of the Bible* (London: Greenhill Books, 1997), 105, 107.

13. Robert Alter, *The David Story* (New York: Norton, 1999), 244.

2 Samuel 11

1. Kay and David Arthur, *Desiring God's Own Heart* (Eugene, OR: Harvest House, 1997), 89.

2. Charles Swindoll, *David: A Man of Passion & Destiny* (Nashville: W Publishing, 1997), 183.

3. David Guzik, *David Guzik's Commentaries on the Bible*, www.studylight.org.

4. Swindoll, *David*, 184.

5. Sue and Larry Richards, *Every Woman in the Bible* (Nashville: Nelson, 1999), 127.

6. Ibid.

7. Ann Spangler, *Women of the Bible* (Grand Rapids, MI: Zondervan, 2002), 106.

8. Matt Kaufman, "Sex in the Real World, Revisited," www.boundless.org, October 17, 2006.

9. Joan Winmill Brown, *Day by Day with Billy Graham*, entry for August 25. (Minneapolis: World Wide Publications, 1976).

10. Ron Mehl, *The Tender Commandments* (Sisters, OR: Multnomah, 1998), 174–75.

11. Kaufman, "Sex in the Real World, Revisited."

12. Ron Mehl, *Tender Commandments*, 185–86.

13. Bob Deffinbaugh, "David and Uriah," www.bible.org.

14. Richard D. Phillips, *The Heart of an Executive* (New York: Galilee/Doubleday, 1999), 203–4.

15. Ibid., 204.

16. Graham, *Day by Day*, August 10.

17. Alan Redpath, *The Making of a Man of God* (Grand Rapids, MI: Revell, 1962/1990), 239–40.

18. Guzik, *David Guzik's Commentaries on the Bible.*

2 Samuel 12

1. *Holman Bible Dictionary*, www.studylight.org.

2. Martin B. Copenhaver, "He Spoke in Parables," *Christian Century*, July 13, 1994, www.findarticles.com.

3. John Indermark, *Neglected Voices* (Nashville: Upper Room, 1999), 83.

4. J. Vernon McGee, *Thru the Bible with J. Vernon McGee* (Pasadena, CA: Thru the Bible Radio, 1982), 214.

5. Robert D. D. Jamieson, *Jamieson-Faussett-Brown Commentary*, www.studylight.org.

6. Adam Clarke, *Adam Clarke Commentary*, www.studylight.org.

7. Matthew Henry, *Matthew Henry's Commentary on the Whole Bible* (Peabody, MA: Hendrickson, 1991), 455.

8. Indermark, *Neglected Voices*, 85.

9. Ron Mehl, *The Tender Commandments* (Sisters, OR: Multnomah, 1998), 196–97.

10. Jamieson, *Jamieson-Faussett-Brown Commentary.*

11. John MacArthur, "The Problem of My Life: Sin," www.biblebb.com.

12. Ibid.

13. Ronald F. Youngblood, F. F. Bruce, and R. K. Harrison, *Nelson's Student Bible Dictionary* (Nashville: Nelson, 2005), 220.

14. John F. Walvoord and Roy B. Zuck, *The Bible Knowledge Commentary* (Colorado Springs: Victor/Cook, 2004), 468.

15. Charles Stanley, *How to Listen to God* (Nashville: Nelson, 1985), 108.

16. Alan Redpath, *The Making of a Man of God* (Grand Rapids, MI: Revell, 1962/1990), 242.

17. Beth Moore, *A Heart Like His* (Nashville: Lifeway, 1996), 142.

18. Redpath, *The Making of a Man of God.*

19. Henry, *Matthew Henry's Commentary*, 456.

20. David Guzik, *David Guzik's Commentaries on the Bible*, www.studylight.org.

2 Samuel 13–18

1. Larry Richards, *The Bible: God's Word for the Biblically Inept* (Lancaster, PA: Starburst, 1998), 65.

2. Charles Swindoll, *Three Steps Forward, Two Steps Back* (New York: Bantam, 1987), 109.

3. Sue and Larry Richards, *Every Woman in the Bible* (Nashville: Nelson, 1999), 133.

4. John F. Walvoord and Roy B. Zuck, *The Bible Knowledge Commentary* (Colorado Springs: Victor/Cook, 2004), 469.

5. Robert Alter, *The David Story* (New York: Norton, 1999), 269–70.

6. Ibid., 271.

7. Ann Spangler, *Women of the Bible* (Grand Rapids, MI: Zondervan, 2002), 109.

8. Swindoll, *Three Steps Forward, Two Steps Back*, 149.

9. J. Vernon McGee, *Thru the Bible with J. Vernon McGee* vol. 2 (Pasadena, CA: Thru the Bible Radio, 1982), 220.

10. Robert H. Roe, "Absalom Revolts, Part 1," December 2, 1979, www.pbc.org.

11. McGee, *Thru the Bible*, 220–21.

12. Richard D. Phillips, *The Heart of an Executive* (New York: Galilee/Doubleday, 1999), 232.

13. Thomas C. Constable, *Bible Study Notes*, www.soniclight.com.

14. Roe, "Absalom Revolts, Part 1."

15. Steven L. McKenzie, *King David: A Biography* (New York: Oxford, 2000), 165.

16. Ibid., 168.

17. Adam Clarke, *Adam Clarke Commentary*, www.studylight.org.

18. Constable, *Bible Study Notes*.

19. William Willimon, "A Tragic Family," www.chapel.duke.edu.

2 Samuel 19–20

1. Kenneth L. Barker and John R. Kohlenberger III, *Zondervan NIV Bible Commentary*, vol. 1 (Grand Rapids, MI: Zondervan, 1994), 472.

2. Ibid., 476.

3. Joan Winmill Brown, *Day By Day with Billy Graham*, entry for October 5. (Minneapolis: World Wide Publications, 1976).

4. David R. Reid, "Devotions for Growing Christians: Tragic Events," www.growingchristians.org.

5. Matthew Henry, *Matthew Henry's Commentary on the Whole Bible* (Peabody, MA: Hendrickson, 1991), 472.

6. David Guzik, *David Guzik's Commentaries on the Bible*, www.studylight.org.

7. Thomas C. Constable, *Bible Study Notes*, www.soniclight.com.

8. Robert Alter, *The David Story* (New York: Norton, 1999), 348.

9. Rick Warren, *The Purpose Driven Life* (Grand Rapids, MI: Zondervan, 2002), 105.

10. Alan Redpath, *The Making of a Man of God* (Grand Rapids, MI: Revell, 1962/1990), 291.

David's Last Days

1. David Alexander and Pat Alexander, *Eerdman's Handbook to the Bible* (Grand Rapids, MI: Eerdmans, 1973), 289.

2. J. Vernon McGee, *Thru the Bible with J. Vernon McGee*, vol. 2 (Pasadena, CA: Thru the Bible Radio, 1982), 395.

3. Tim LaHaye, *Prophecy Study Bible* (Chattanooga, TN: AMG, 2000), 466.

4. Thomas L. Constable, *Bible Study Notes*, www.soniclight.com.

5. Dennis and Barbara Rainey, adapted from *Parenting Today's Adolescent: Helping Your Child Avoid the Traps of Preteen & Teen Years*, www.familylife.com.

6. Dennis Rainey, "Dad University," www.familylife.com.

7. Kenneth L. Barker and John R. Kohlenberger III, *Zondervan NIV Bible Commentary* (Grand Rapids, MI: Zondervan, 1994), 627.

8. Alan Redpath, *The Making of a Man of God* (Grand Rapids, MI: Revell, 1962/1990), 300.

9. Alexander and Alexander, *Eerdman's*, 254.

10. Barker and Kohlenberger III, *Zondervan NIV Bible Commentary*, 627.

11. Alexander and Alexander, *Eerdman's*, 291–92.

12. Robbie Castleman, *King David: Trusting God for a Lifetime* (Colorado Springs: Waterbrook, 1981), 78.

13. Robert D. D. Jamieson, *Jamieson-Faussett-Brown Commentary*, www.studylight.org.

14. *The Ryrie Study Bible*, New International Version (Chicago: Moody, 1986), 393.

15. John Gill, *John Gill's Exposition of the Entire Bible*, www.studylight.org.

16. Richard D. Phillips, *The Heart of an Executive* (New York: Galilee/Doubleday, 1999), 254.

17. Tim LaHaye, *Prophecy Study Bible*, 371.

18. Robert Alter, *The David Story* (New York: Norton, 1999), 372.

19. Barker and Kohlenberger III, *Zondervan NIV Bible Commentary*, 492.

20. Woodrow Kroll, www.backtothebible.org.

21. John F. Walvoord and Roy B. Zuck, *The Bible Knowledge Commentary* (Colorado Springs: Victor/Cook, 2004), 491.

22. Kroll, www.backtothebible.org.

23. Walvoord and Zuck, *Bible Knowledge Commentary*, 491.

24. Max Lucado, *The Great House of God* (Dallas: Word, 1997), 173.

25. H. A. Ironside, *Psalms* (Neptune, NJ: Loizeaux Brothers, 1984), 89–90.

Index

Bathsheba, 253–57,
264–65, 273
dishonored concubines,
306–7
Haggith, 329
harem at Jerusalem, 203
Maacah, 282
Merab, 125–26
Michal, 126–27, 129,
214–18
See also polygamy; psalms
of David
Davidic covenant, 225–30
key points, 227–28
as unconditional, 226
Deffinbaugh, Bob
on Bathsheba's
announcement of
pregnancy, 260
on Jonathan's faith, 69
Deir-Dubban, 141
deities, 176
devil, as liar, 135–37
See also Satan
distressing spirit, 123
See also evil spirit
divination, 176
Doeg, 138, 143
dreams in Scripture, 176

E

Easton's Bible Dictionary
on beards' importance to
ancient Jews, 245
Ebenezer, 34, 35, 139
Edomites, 235–36
*Eerdman's Handbook to the
Bible*
on David's lavish gift to
temple, 327
on David's preparations
for temple, 320
on tabernacle plans, 326
Eglah, 198
Eisenhower, Dwight D.,
104
Ekron, 24
Eli, 50
accuses Hannah of
drunkenness, 11–13
his death, 28
his laxity cursed, 18
his legacy, 29
his sons vs. Samuel's sons,
42
lax with wicked sons, 15,
17, 18

priest at Shiloh, 9
Samuel to succeed him,
18–19
Eliab, 89, 91
assails David, 108–9
worthy soldier, 104–5
Eliam, 253, 294
Elkanah, 3, 8–9, 162
emerods, 31–32
En Dor, 177
En Gedi, 144, 145–46
David's promise to Saul,
239
En Rogel, 330
ephod, 16, 229–30
eternal covenant, 226
Eve, 4, 89, 272
evil spirit, 93–95
See also Lucifer; Satan

F

fasting, 74
fertility, 7
five golden mice, 31–32
five smooth stones, 111–12
Flood, 105
forty days, 105
frankincense, 137

G

Gabriel, 14
Gad (prophet), 141, 322
Galeed, 34
Garden of Eden, as
tabernacle, 4
Gath, 24, 101, 138–39
as city, 170
David in Gath, 168–73
Gaza, 24
Geba, 67
Gentiles, in David's armies,
244
George, Elizabeth
on combating impatience,
70
Geshur, 289
Geshurites, 173
Gezer, 203
giants, 102
Gibeah, 67, 143
Gibeon, 196, 203, 212
Gibeonites, 308–10
Gichon, Mordechai, 203,
246
gigantism, 102
Gihon, 332–33

Gilgal, 55
Saul's sacrifice, 69–72
Gill, John
on David as type of
Christ, 142
on importance of David
naming successor, 332
Girzites, 173
Gittites, 291
glory, of God, 32–33
God, actions
accepts Hannah's
promise, 9–10, 16
allows David's son to die,
276–79
calls Samuel, 18–19
forbids David to build
Temple, 221–24
his silence toward Saul,
175–76
points out Saul to
Samuel, 49–50
prophesies Eli's downfall,
18–19
rebukes David through
Nathan, 267–73
regrets making Saul king,
76
sends sleep on Saul's
soldiers, 166–67
sends thunder while
Samuel speaks, 61
tells David to possess
Hebron, 193–96
tells Samuel to anoint
new king, 83–88
unveils Davidic covenant,
224–25
warns Samuel about
kingship, 44–46
See also God, attributes
God, attributes
communicates by various
means, 20, 176
fights for his people,
47–48
giver and taker of life,
192
glory, 32–33
says no for good reasons,
227
truthful, 136–37
uses young people, 112
See also Christian life;
Holy Spirit, actions;
Jesus, attributes
God's people. *See* Israel;
people of God

Goliath, iii
challenges Israel, 103–4,
105
David offers to fight him,
109–11
killed by David, 111–13
See also Goliath,
characteristics
Goliath, characteristics
armor described, 103
champion of Philistines,
102
compared to devil, 100
description, 101
unbeliever, 100
Goliath's sword, 138–39
Graham, Billy
on Bible's view of sex, 258
on risks of adultery, 261
on why God allows
suffering, 308
Guzik, David
on anointing by Holy
Spirit, 56
on dangers of modern
spiritism, 177
on David's polygamy
leading to adultery,
263
on David's risks in staying
home, 253
on examples inspiring
faith, 114
on Gibeonites' vengeance
on Saul, 310
on meaning of "show-
bread," 138
on spiritual sources of
failure, 279
on trying to manipulate
God, 27–28

H

Hagar, 70, 162
Haggith, 198
Halley's Bible Handbook
on reason for animal
sacrifice, 70–71
Hannah, v, 3, 162, 339
brings her son to temple,
13–14
Eli thinks her drunk,
11–13
Elkanah consoles her, 3,
8–9
her sorrow over
childlessness, 7–8

offers Lord her future son, 9–10

rewarded with more children, 16

Hannah's Song, 14

Hanun, 244–45

harem, 203

harp, 94–95

Hebron, 193, 194–95, 290

as city of refuge, 199

heifer, 86

Heman, 212

Henry, Matthew

on disorder in worship at Shiloh, 12

on doing God's work in God's way, 87

on Elkanah worshiping at Shiloh, 6

on God restoring forgiven sinners, 279

on God's protection as trustworthy, 167

on indulgence of wicked children, 18

on lack of faith causing insecurity, 73

on Nathan as God's ambassador, 271

on power of Ark of Covenant, 30

on rewards of following Christ, 194

on Samuel anointing Saul king, 54

on Satan's rule in faithless hearts, 93

on Saul among the prophets, 57

on Saul's bloody house, 309

on using peacetime for God, 223

Hereth, 141

Herzog, Chaim

on Joab capturing Jerusalem, 203

on the Aramaeans, 246

Higgs, Liz Curtis

on Michal's choice to be miserable, 218

on Michal's idols, 132

on Michal's misunderstanding David, 214

on Saul trapping David via marriage, 126

high places, 6

Hillman, Os

on Saul's fear of losing control, 78

Hiram, 203, 221

Holman Bible Dictionary

on Nathan's use of a parable, 269

holy of holies, 5

See also Ark of the Covenant; tabernacle

holy place, 5

Holy Spirit, actions

anoints Jesus, Christians, 54–56

descends on Saul, 55–57

gives power against sin, 130–31

overcomes Saul's thugs, 129, 133–34

overcomes sin nature, 262

See also God, actions; Jesus, attributes

homosexuality, 118

Hophni, 3, 18, 27, 42

as bad priest, 15

horses, 236

Hushai, 293, 295

I

Ichabod, 29

idols, 171

See also teraphim

impatience, 69–70

Indermark, John

on hypocritical pity, 270

on learning to wait patiently, 151

on Nathan speaking truth to power, 271

infertility, 7

inner court of Tabernacle, 5

International Bible Encyclopedia

on suicide, 183

Ironside, H. A.

on David as "The beloved," 339

Isaac, 194, 316

Ishbosheth, 181, 194, 197, 296

his death, 200–201

Israel

God's chosen nation, 43

government, 20

history, 100

as theocracy, 42–43

See also Ark of the Covenant; covenant; Philistines

Issachar, 244

Ithream, 197, 198

Ittai the Gittite, 244, 296

J

Jabesh Gilead, 60, 182, 192, 194

Jacob, 137, 194

James (apostle), 120

James (brother of Jesus), 272

as Nazirite, 11

Jamieson, Robert D.

on David as exhausted by troubles, 329

on power of Ark of Covenant, 30

on punishment for David's sin, 275

on sinners as severe judges, 270

Janssen, Al

on covenants vs. contracts, 121

Jebusites, 202, 203

Jedidiah, 278

See also Solomon

Jeduthun, 212

Jegar Sahadutha, 34

Jehoshaphat, 237

Jeremiah, 112, 175

Jericho, 25

Jerusalem

as religious center, 207

why David's capital, 202

Jesse, 83, 105

Jesus, attributes

angry without sin, 154

anointed with Holy Spirit, 54

deliverer of Israel, 54

good shepherd, 90–91

Messiah, 54

Messiah of prophecy, 224–26

prefigured by Samuel, 17–18

referenced in tabernacle, 5–6

See also God, actions; Holy Spirit, actions

Joab, 237, 244, 245, 251, 296

assassinates Abner, 198–99

captures Jerusalem, 203

carries out Uriah's murder, 261, 264

David orders his death, 335–36

David's military leader, 196

epilogue and census narrative, 313

fights at Rabbah, 252

kills Absalom against orders, 296

mediates between David, Absalom, 288–89

murders rival Amasa, 307

rebukes David's prolonged mourning, 304

supports Adonijah's attempted coup, 330

Job, 175

Joel (Samuel's son), 41–42

John the Baptist, 11

John the disciple, 120

Jonadab, 282, 287

Jonah, 58

Jonathan

acknowledges David will be king, 122

attacks Philistine post, 67–69

bids farewell to David, 134–35

David's kindness to his son, 238–43, 295

defeats Philistine garrison, 72–73

defends David to Saul, 129, 130

endangered by father's curse, 74–75

his death, 181

last meeting with David, 144

swears friendship with David, 117–21

See also Jonathan, character

Jonathan, character, iii

his friendship for David, 134–35

pure motives, 119

Joseph (Mary's husband), 176

Joshua, 4, 194

Josiah, 112

journal, 109

Judah, 194

Judas, 183
judges, 19, 20
  vs. kings, 46–47

K

Kaufman, Matt
  on Bible's view of sex,
    258
  on God's concern for sex,
    259
Keilah, 144–45
Kerethites, 237
king, in Israel, 42–43
  See also David; Saul
*King James Study Bible for
  Women, The*
  on God permitting
    foolish decisions, 46
  on transition of Israel to
    kingdom, 59
king's mule, 332–33
Kirjath Jearim, 207
Kish, 48–49
Koath, 209
Kolatch, Alfred J.
  on why Jerusalem matters
    to Jews, 202
Kroll, Woodrow
  on David's advice to
    Solomon, 335
  on David's finishing well,
    337

L

LaHaye, Tim
  on importance of plan-
    ning Christian work,
    321
  on Jesus as David's prom-
    ised descendant, 225
  on Samuel as type of
    Christ, 17
  on Zadok's descendants
    in Millennial Temple,
    333
Law, 25
Leah, 162, 194
Levite, Levites, 3, 5, 194,
    208, 209, 321
  David's administrative
    structure, 212
listening to God, 84
Lo Debar, 238, 240, 241
Lot, 235, 245
love vs. lust, 284–85

Lucado, Max
  on David's love for God,
    338
  on God's continuing love
    for David, 180
  on God's view of our
    problems, 85
  on worship changing
    worshiper, 214
  on worship magnifying
    God, 213
Lucifer, 142, 217
  See also Satan
lust, 284–85
lying, 135–37
lyre, 94–95

M

Maacah, 198, 282
MacArthur, John
  on accepting responsibil-
    ity for sins, 273
  on confession of sin, 275
  on glory of God, 33
  on Jesus as David's heir,
    227
Machir, 238
magic, 177
Mahanaim, 194, 196–97,
    295–96, 303
Malchishua, 181
manna, 25
Maon, 151
marriage
  in David's day, 152
  to unbelievers, 158–59
Mary, 112, 339
Mary's song, 14
McGee, J. Vernon
  on David's partial forgive-
    ness of Absalom, 290
  on God's sense of humor,
    49
  on hypocritical judgment,
    270
  on misuse of Ark of
    Covenant, 26
  on temple plans as
    David's legacy, 320
McKenzie, Steven L.
  on Ahithophel joining
    conspiracy, 294
  on David's meekness in
    adversity, 293
meat with blood, 74
mediums, 173–77

Mehl, Ron
  on adultery of the heart,
    259–60
  on God's concern for
    adultery, 259
  on trust in God prevent-
    ing sin, 273
memorials, 34–35
menorah, 5
Mephibosheth, 200,
    238–43, 294–95,
    305–6
  as type of sinner before
    God, 240–41
Merab, 125–26
mercy seat, 25
Merib-baal, 200
  See also Mephibosheth
Messiah, in prophecy,
    224–26
metaphor, 100
Metheg Ammah, 233
Michal
  banished from David's
    presence, 214–18
  David gets her back,
    197
  given to another man,
    160
  marries David, 126–27
  saves David from Saul,
    129, 131–32
  See also Michal, her
    character
Michal, her character,
    131–32
  compared to Abigail,
    215, 216
  daughter of Saul, 217–18
  failings, 215–18
  sorrows, 214–15
Michmash, 67
midwives, 137
mighty men, 137, 172,
    244, 307, 312–13,
    330
militia, in David's day, 244
Miller, Kathy Collard and
    D. Larry
  on risks of marrying
    unbelievers, 159
Miriam, 112
Mizpah, 34, 57, 141
Moabites, 235, 236
monarchy, 20
monuments, in Bible,
    34–35

Moore, Beth
  on David leaving remnant
    among nations, 237
  on David's sin scorned
    among heathen, 278
  on faith as resting in God,
    108
  on rebellion compared to
    witchcraft, 77
  on Saul's lack of true
    repentance, 175
Moses, 24, 58, 105
  and God's glory, 32–33
Moses' mother, 50
most holy place, 5
Mount Gilboa, 234
Mount Moriah, 316
Mount of Olives, 293, 295
murder, 192
music
  role in David's times,
    94–95
  temple music, 321

N

Nabal, 151–52, 153, 158
Nahash, 60, 244–45
Nathan, v, 283, 284, 322,
    330, 332–33
  prophecies of Temple,
    222–24, 228
  pronounces judgment
    against David, 267–73
  secures throne for
    Solomon, 331–33
Nathan's parable, 257
Nazirite, 150
  requirements for Nazirite,
    11
  Samuel as Nazirite, 9–10
Nebuchadnezzar, 176
*Nelson's Student Bible
  Dictionary*
  on true repentance, 276
New Testament, and
  prophecies of Messiah,
    226
Noah, 50
Nob, 135

O

oath, 130
Obed-Edom, 209, 211
obedience, 72
offerings, 70–71

on God's refusal as
redirection, 227
on Holy Spirit in Old
Testament, 92
on Jonathan and David's
friendship, 118
on passive, negligent
mistakes, 283–84
Syrians, 245

T

tabernacle, 4–6
description, 4–5
at Gilgal, 6
meaning of word, 4
plans, 325
symbolism, 5–6
vs. temple, 326
See also Ark of the
Covenant
tablets of stone, 25
Tabor, 55
Tamar (Absalom's
daughter), 289
Tamar (Absalom's sister),
198, 281–87
rape, 282–83
Tanakh, 19
Tell es-Safi, 170
See also Gath
temple, 316, 319
David prepares for
temple, 319–22
man of peace as builder,
227
plans for temple, 319–21,
325
vs. tabernacle, 326
See also Mount Moriah
temptation, 262
Ten Commandments, 24,
25
tent
holy of holies, 6
tent of meeting, 4
teraphim, 129, 176
Testimony, 25
theocracy, 20
Timothy, 112

Tomb of the Patriarchs, 194
tongue, 199
treasury of temple, 236
twelve stone pillars, 34, 35
type, typology, 17, 100
David as type of Jesus,
100, 114–15

U

Uriah, 118, 251, 253, 255,
294
David has him murdered,
261–65
Urim, 174, 176
urim and thummim, 176
Uzzah, 209–10

V

Valley of Elah,100
Vawter, John
on accepting godly advice
gratefully, 158
on ethic of kingdom of
God, 242
veil, of tabernacle, 6
vengeance, 199
virginity, 285
vision vs. blindness, 50

W

Wadlow, Robert Pershing,
102
Warren, Rick
on admonishing,
encouraging fellow
believers, 157
on real worship as costly,
315–16
on worship as
acknowledging God's
love, 213
Wesley, John
on Israel's demand for
king, 43
on prophets not always
divinely inspired, 228

Wiersbe, Warren
on David's humility, 230
on variety of prayer
postures, 229
Wilderness of Paran, 149
Willimon, Dean William
on God's love for
troubled families,
297–98
wise woman of Abel, 307
witchcraft, 177
women in David's day, 152
women as property, 155
Word, Word of God. *See*
Bible
worship, 213–14

Y

Yom Kippur, 5
Youngblood, Ronald
on David and Jonathan's
friendship, 135

Z

Zadok, 212, 237, 292, 303,
327, 330, 332–33
Ziba, 238, 239, 242,
294–95, 305–6
Ziklag, 194
as David's destroyed
stronghold, 178–80
as David's fortress,
170–73
Zimri, 183
Ziph, 144
Ziphites, 165
*Zondervan NIV Bible
Commentary*
on Court History of
David, 307
on David's prolonged
mourning for Absalom,
304
on David's relationship to
Solomon, 334–35
on stewardship, 327
on temple plans as given
by God, 325

www.ingramcontent.com/pod-product-compliance
Ingram Content Group UK Ltd.
Pitfield, Milton Keynes, MK11 3LW, UK
UKHW052243240325
456661UK00008B/88

9 781418 510114